THE SOCIAL PSYCHOLOGY OF EDUCATION

David W. Johnson

University of Minnesota

HOLT, RINEHART AND WINSTON, INC.

New York   Chicago   San Francisco   Atlanta
Dallas   Montreal   Toronto   London   Sydney

To My Parents

Copyright © 1970 by Holt, Rinehart and Winston, Inc.
All rights reserved
Library of Congress Catalog Card Number: 72-118725
ISBN: 0-03-078040-3
Printed in the United States of America
2 3 4 5   038   9 8 7 6 5 4 3 2

Preface

This book is designed to provide an introduction to the social psychology of education by presenting the relevant social psychological theory and research and its implications for education and providing the conceptual framework and cognitive tools needed to diagnose and solve educational problems from a social psychological point of view. The book is aimed at providing insights into how social psychologists think and work as well as providing applications of the social psychological research and theory to education.

The school is approached from the viewpoint that it is an organization, similar in many ways to all other organizations, and unique in many ways. Organizations are characterized by roles, norms, values, climates, and tendencies to grow, develop, and innovate. All these are discussed at length. The primary focus, however, is upon the classroom. The role structure of the classroom is discussed, and specific social psychological variables that influence role performance in the classroom and the interaction between the teacher and the students are examined.

I owe much to many different social psychologists whose work has influenced mine. I cannot thank them all. In writing and rewriting many of the chapters of this book it has become difficult in many cases to know where their ideas and expressions have left off and mine have begun. I have carefully tried to give everyone full credit for the material cited; if I have failed to do so at any point it is through oversight, not intent.

I would like to express appreciation to Matthew B. Miles for his careful editing of the manuscript and helpful suggestions and to Roger T. Johnson for his valuable help in making applications of the material to the classroom. I would also like to thank Bruce Biddle, Philip Jackson, and Roger L. Williams for their helpful readings of the manuscript.

D. W. J.

Minneapolis, Minnesota
February 1970

Contents

CHAPTER 1

THE SOCIAL PSYCHOLOGY OF EDUCATION

What Is Social Psychology?

Social psychology focuses upon the social nature of the individual. It attempts to understand and explain how thought, feeling, and behavior of individuals are influenced by the actual, imagined, or implied presence of other human beings. This definition takes into consideration the fact that even in isolation an individual's behavior may be largely determined by considerations that have their origin in the social environment. A small boy alone in the family kitchen, for example, who looks at the cookie jar and, although he wants a cookie desperately, does not take one because he knows his mother has forbidden him from eating before a meal, is engaged in social behavior. For, early in the establishment of moral behavior, the child in some way invokes or imagines the presence of the mother and behaves accordingly. Correspondingly, people sometimes respond to physical stimuli in the environment as if they were social or directly produced by other people. An individual may kick a stalled car, strike a cabinet door on which he has bumped his head, or curse a leaky faucet. Conversely, an individual sometimes responds to socially produced stimuli as if the stimuli were independent of all human elements. He may read the newspaper, for example, without regard to the characteristics of the social source of the news.

The Relationship between Social Psychology and the Other Behavioral Sciences

Social psychology is only one of the scientific fields concerned with the objective study of human behavior. Psychology, sociology, anthropology, political science, and the other behavioral sciences all study human behavior, but from varying perspectives. Psychology concentrates primarily upon the individual in isolation from other people and deals with such questions as how perception works, how memory works, how thought processes work, and how an organism learns. The other behavioral sciences take as their staring points the political, social, or cultural systems in which an individual lives, and examine their characteristics and how they interact with other similar systems. Political scientists, for instance, examine the characteristics of political systems and how they interact with other political systems. Sociologists examine the characteristics of social systems and how they interact with other social systems. Cultural anthropologists examine the characteristics of cultures and the ways in which cultures interact with one another.

Social psychology attempts to combine and integrate the different behavioral sciences via the study of interpersonal interaction. It studies how a representative from one political system negotiates with a representative from another political system, how a member of a certain social system behaves in relation to members of other social systems (for example, how a lower-class child interacts with middle-class peers), and the problems of a member of one culture suddenly being placed in another culture (for example, the problems a Puerto Rican child has when placed in an American school). In other words, social psychology begins with the individual and looks at political, social, and cultural systems through the eyes of the individual. Political science, sociology, and cultural anthropology begin with the larger systems and look at the individual through the eyes of the systems.

The Development of Social Psychology

Social psychology is a very young behavioral science. The first physical scientific measurement preceded the first social psychological measurement by twenty-one centuries. Around 250 B.C. the Greek astronomer Eratosthenes engaged in one of the first known scientific measurements by calculating the circumference of the earth. He compared the angle of the noon sun in Alexandria with that in Aswan; Aswan being a city that lay directly to the south of Alexandria on the Tropic of Cancer, and where on the day of the summer solstice, the angle of the noon sun is exactly 90 degrees. Eratosthenes' results differ from the present estimates by about 180 miles, or less than 1 percent. The first experimental observation in social psychology, however, was performed in 1897 by Triplett, in an experiment dealing with the effects of competition on human performance. Triplett measured the average time required for his subjects to execute 150 winds on a fishing reel while working alone and while competing in pairs against each other. He found that performance improved when carried out in competition.

Social psychology is almost entirely the product of this century and this generation. More than 90 percent of all social psychological research has been carried out during the last twenty years, and most of it has been conducted during the last few. Although it is not clear why social psychological research was not carried out earlier, it may be hypothesized that before the major changes in the societal control of human behavior, such as the Reformation and the Industrial Revolution, the institutional mechanisms for regulating social behavior, such as law, custom, religion, and etiquette, provided satisfactory explanations of social behavior and enabled individuals to predict human behavior fairly reliably. It was not until such institutional mechanisms broke down that interest in the control and prediction of human behavior became of scientific interest.

Although the first textbooks in social psychology were published in 1908 under the authorship of the psychologist William McDougall

3

and the sociologist E. A. Ross, Kurt Lewin is considered the father of experimental social psychology. A critical feature of Lewin's contribution was his emphasis on the importance of theoretical analysis before conducting research on a problem. His advocacy of the importance of theory and of conceptual analysis and his demonstration that experimental research could be conducted on social psychological problems were extremely important. The classic study conducted by Lewin and two of his graduate students (Lewin, Lippitt, and White, 1939) on autocratic, laissez-faire, and democratic leadership, although it had many deficiencies, had a liberating impact on subsequent researchers and stimulated others to think about the controlled manipulation of complex situational variables.

Lewin's dedication to democracy and his deep interests in social problems have inspired his students and the students of his students to apply the knowledge and technology of social psychology to the solution of applied problems in society. His theories have often proved to be good working models for practitioners. Perhaps the place where Lewin still has his greatest influence is with the applied behavior scientists dealing with organizational change and the solution of current social problems.

The Social Psychology of Education

Education, from a social psychological point of view, is carried on in an organized social environment largely through interpersonal processes. How a student responds in the classroom, for example, will depend upon such factors as the organizational structure and climate of the school, the nature of the classroom norms and procedures, the similarity between the student's goals and the goals of his teacher, and the reactions he thinks his peers, parents, and friends will have to his behavior. It is primarily within the extended teacher-student and student-student interactions in the classroom that education takes place. The nature of the classroom norms, roles, and authority structure are all important social psychological areas of study. Classroom interpersonal processes, however, do not take place within a vacuum; they are affected by the organization within which they take place. Above all the school is an organization subject to all the advantages and disadvantages of current bureaucratic organizations. In addition, schools have unique organizational characteristics that differentiate them from other types of organizations, such as businesses and hospitals, and that have positive and negative consequences for its members.

Social psychology has two contributions to make to education. First, the body of knowledge contained in social psychology provides insights into educational processes which, if applied, will increase the effectiveness of educational organizations. The following chapters of this book present much of the social psychological literature relevant to running an educational program. Second, the methodology of the scientific method as it is used in social psychology provides educators with a problem-solving method which, when combined with social psychological knowledge, will enable them to diagnose problems in educational organizations more accurately and initiate more effective solutions. The methodology of social psychology is presented in the remainder of this chapter and is interspersed in the following chapters where it is appropriate.

The Value of the Scientific Method

Perhaps no body of subject matter is resisted by students in education as much as that dealing with the scientific method and research methodology. Many students state that it is deadly boring. Students often say that they should not be required to study the methodology of science as they are practitioners who apply knowledge and are not interested in becoming researchers who generate knowledge. They state that such areas as teaching and administration involve the basic application of generally known principles and common sense, but *not* controlled experimentation. These students are wrong for several reasons, two of which are discussed below.

First, educational practice seems to be based primarily upon a great deal of common-sense knowledge handed down from one generation of teachers to another. Taking proverbs as being "self-evident" generalizations of common-sense wisdom, we find them notorious for their contradictions: "Birds of a feather flock together" versus "Opposites attract" and "Absence makes the heart grow fonder" versus "Out of sight, out of mind." The common-sense truths about teaching are also filled with contradictions. Some teachers be-

5

lieve that the basic principle of classroom control is keeping one's social distance, "Don't let the students get too close to you, or else they'll think they can get away with anything." Other teachers believe that the basic principle of classroom control is to form close, personal relationships with students, "If the students like you, they'll behave for you."

History is full of examples of the stupidity of common sense. All superstitions are based upon common sense and experience. Countless "self-evident truths" have been proven false after centuries of practice. For thousands of years people have used punishment to raise children because "everyone knows it's effective." Recent research has shown that punishment is effective only under a very limited set of conditions. For hundreds of years it was "self-evident" that all sorts of illnesses could be cured by venesection (that is, bloodletting). "Everyone knew" that a person with a fever was better off with less blood: if he did not get well you took more of his blood until he did. No one knows how many thousands of people were killed by this medical practice. Another "self-evident" medical practice involved giving extra oxygen to premature babies at the time of birth. Everyone knew that premature babies needed oxygen and therefore they were given extra oxygen when they were born. In the late 1930s, however, science proved that the extra oxygen was causing retrolental fibroplasia, a type of blindness found primarily in premature babies. No one knows how many people were blinded by this "self-evident" medical practice.

Education is full of opinions, beliefs, and "self-evident truths" prescribing what constitutes good teaching and administrative practice. Few educational practices have been empirically validated (see Chapter 14).

Since we "know" so little, we have to rely most of the time upon common sense and our experience. We should always keep in mind, however, the tenuousness and fallability of common sense, and that progress in education and the behavioral sciences rests upon our building an empirical base for educational practice through the use of the scientific method. Common-sense, "self-evident truths" are not sufficient to build an effective, efficient method of running a classroom or a school. The empirical validity of educational practice must be established if education is to progress.

Second, since there is very little sound empirical knowledge about how to teach, how to control one's classroom, or how to run a school, teachers, administrators, and other school personnel need a problem-solving technique that generates valid and reliable knowledge about problem situations and how to deal with them. In other words, educators are constantly faced with problems for which there are no "canned" answers. They need, therefore, problem-solving skills that will enable them to diagnose a problem situation and intervene in an effective way. In order to intervene effectively, the diagnosis of the situation must be accurate and valid. Educators need to be able to diagnose problem situations accurately and intervene so that the problem is solved in such a way that it stays solved without deteriorating the problem-solving process. If a child is misbehaving in the classroom, for example, the teacher should intervene on the basis of a diagnosis of the causes of the child's behavior in a way that not only ends the child's misbehavior in the immediate situation, but also prevents it from happening in the future, without seriously damaging the teacher's relationship with the child and ability to influence the child. The scientific method is probably the best problem-solving technique for accurately diagnosing a situation and evaluating the effectiveness of an intervention. Educators, therefore, should be well trained in it.

Methods of Acquiring Knowledge

Since his beginning, man has searched for knowledge that would answer his questions about the world, satisfy his desire to know the truth, and aid him in improving his ways of living. The scientific method has evolved from two basic methods man has used for acquiring knowledge—reasoning (deduction) and observation (induction).

Deductive Reasoning

In the western world, the ancient Greeks, noted for their faith in the power of reason, conviction of a moral order in the universe, and concept of unchangeable fate, founded the belief that the world is an orderly place controlled by rational processes. This belief led to the use of deductive reasoning as a method for acquiring knowledge. In deduction, man reasons that whatever is true of all in-

7

stances of a class must also be true of any single instance that comes within its limits. He endeavors to demonstrate that a particular instance under consideration logically falls within the instances of the entire class, through the use of a syllogism. A syllogism is an argument consisting of three propositions: two premises and a conclusion. In a categorical syllogism two supposedly true statements stand in such a relationship that they logically imply a particular conclusion. If a person accepts the two premises, he must agree to the conclusion that follows. An example of a categorical syllogism is as follows:

All men are mortal.	(Major Premise)
Socrates is a man.	(Minor Premise)
Therefore, Socrates is mortal.	(Conclusion)

Deductive reasoning enables one to organize premises into patterns that provide conclusive evidence for the validity of a particular conclusion. It can only deduce, however, the consequences of pre-existing knowledge, that is, it does not probe beyond that which is already known. The conclusion reached by a deductive argument, furthermore, can be trustworthy only if it is derived from reliable premises that are properly related. The primary weakness of deduction lies in the possibility that one of the premises is not materially true or that the premises are unrelated.

Induction

For centuries the primary method of acquiring knowledge was to deduce it from sources such as the Bible, which were considered "true knowledge." Beginning with Francis Bacon, however, the inductive approach of observing natural events and formulating general laws on the basis of such observation began to be used. For if the conclusions reached through deductive reasoning are true only if derived from true premises, a way of determining whether the basic premises are true is needed. In inductive reasoning an investigator collects evidence that will enable him to establish a generalization as being probably true by observing particular instances (concrete facts), from which a general conclusion about the whole class in which the particular instances belong is made. If one can arrive at general conclusions through induction, he can use them as major premises for deductive inferences.

There are two types of induction, perfect and imperfect. *Perfect induction* involves complete enumeration of all the given instances in a given class. For example, to induce how many residents of a school district are in favor of the schools teaching sex education, one would enumerate every resident, ask his opinion, and count the number of favorable responses. Such complete enumeration, however, cannot be employed as a method of investigation in the solution of most problems. *Imperfect induction* arrives at a generalization by observing only some instances that make up the class and drawing a general conclusion regarding all similar instances. For example, to induce imperfectly how many residents of a school district are in favor of the schools teaching sex education, one would take a random sample of residents, ask their opinions, count the number of favorable responses, and generalize about the opinions of all the residents of the community. It should be emphasized that drawing an inference about a whole class after sampling a few of its members does not necessarily yield absolutely certain knowledge. The size and representativeness of the instances observed largely determine whether one arrives at a sound conclusion. Through imperfect induction the investigator merely arrives at conclusions of varying degrees of probability, for the possibility always exists that the unexamined instances of the class do not agree with his conclusion.

The Scientific Method

Modern scientific research methods are a synthesis of deduction and induction. Induction provides the groundwork for hypotheses, which can be used as major premises for deductive inferences. Deduction explores the logical consequences of each hypothesis by inferring what events would occur or what should be observable under specified conditions *if each hypothesis is true.* After observation of what in fact is the case or does occur under the specified conditions and generalizing from such observations (induction), what each hypothesis predicts can be compared with what in fact occurs. Induction, then, contributes to the refutation (elimination) of hypotheses that are inconsistent with the facts and at least to the partial

9

verification of the hypothesis, if any, that is consistent with the facts. For example, if a child consistently misbehaves in the classroom, all prior observations about the child can be brought together and examined. By induction, several plausible generalizations about the experiences of the child and his behavior can be formed. Using these generalizations as premises, one can deduce after what consequences of his consistent misbehavior the child will likely continue to misbehave and after what consequences he will no longer misbehave, or misbehave less frequently. By careful observation of the child's behavior under each consequence condition, through a process of induction, hypotheses inconsistent with the facts can be eliminated and any hypothesis consistent with the facts as so far observed can be identified. In essence the teacher builds a theory about the child's behavior, deductively derives hypotheses from the theory, and verifies the hypotheses through some objective procedure. The heart of any scientific activity rests on the important relationship between theories and the methods used to obtain appropriate evidence for their verification.

Assumptions of the Scientific Method

The scientific method rests upon the assumption of the uniformity of nature. It assumes that phenomena maintain their essential characteristics under specified conditions over a definite period of time, for without some permanence of natural phenomena, science cannot predict accurately the occurrence of an event. Thus, what has been found to be true in many instances in the past will probably continue to hold true in the future. Since the sun has always come up in the morning, one can predict that it will rise tomorrow morning. Since low-achievement motivation has in the past resulted in probable underachievement, there is a good chance that a future student with low-achievement motivation will underachieve. It is not necessary to assume that nature is absolutely uniform in all respects; but science is possible only to the extent that nature is uniform.

Science assumes that one can group together events, experiences, facts, or objects that are similar; such a classification system provides a tool that helps identify, explain, and evaluate new phenomena. All children whose parents are of a certain income, educational, and occupational level can be classified as middle class. All students who have high IQ's but who are getting low grades are defined as underachievers. Such classification systems are conceptual tools that help organize educational phenomena.

Finally, science assumes that all natural phenomena are determined by a cause or a set of causes; that is, certain essential conditions invariably precede an event. In the behavioral sciences it is agreed that most behavior is caused by a set of causes. Thus, science would assume that there are reasons why one child cooperates with the teacher and another child resists all classroom directives, why one teacher is creative and another teacher conventional, why the teachers under one principal all want to return to his school and the teachers under another principal all want to transfer.

In other words, science assumes that nature is not a chaotic mass of isolated facts, but rather an ordered system. It rejects the possibility that nature is unstable, capricious, temporary, or moody, for the alternative that nature is orderly and relatively permanent. It denies that the occurrence of an event is a matter of chance, an accidental situation, or purely a spontaneous incident, but states that events are determined.

The Goals of Science

The goals of science are the prediction, understanding, and control of the relationship between two or more variables. To understand what a variable is, one must begin with properties. A *property* is something that characterizes some things but not others—red is a property that is characteristic of fire and cardinals but not of water or bluebirds. A *variable* is a set of mutually exclusive properties; blonde and brunette, male and female, old and young, are all properties, but they represent only three variables—hair color, sex, and age. Different properties of the same variable are commonly referred to as values of that variable.

A *relationship* exists between two variables when knowledge of an object's value on one variable enables one to predict its value on another variable more accurately than one could without such knowledge. There is, for example, a relationship between socio-economic class and grades in school, because one can do a better job of predicting an individual's grades when one knows his socio-economic class than when one does not.

A *causal relationship* exists between two variables when a change in one produces a change in the other. Causal relationships are unidirectional; one variable is always the cause, the other always the effect, and the direction of the relationship is never reversed. An increase in IQ, for example, may cause achievement to go up, but an increase in achievement will not cause one's IQ to go up. Three conditions must be met to make the inference that a change in one variable is the cause of a change in another. First, there must be evidence of covariation—changes in one variable must be accompanied by changes in another. Second, there must be evidence that the "cause" variable changes before the "effect" variable. Finally, there must be evidence that the results were not caused by some extraneous variable; that is, alternate explanations for the findings must be excluded.

The three goals of science—prediction, understanding, and control—represent different levels of scientific achievement. Prediction lays the groundwork for understanding and understanding lays the groundwork for control.

Prediction is based upon a correlational relationship between variables; if one knows a student's high-school grade point average, for example, one can predict his college grade point average. Being able to predict an event, however, does not mean that one will understand it. Men were able to predict the effects of eating a poisonous plant long before they were able to understand the precise chemical basis for its effects. When one is interested in prediction, both causal and noncausal relationships are useful.

Understanding is based upon knowing the critical antecedent conditions that cause an event to take place. In order to understand a student's academic performance, for example, one must know about such antecedent conditions as the nature of the student's early environment, the quality of the student's previous schooling, the nature of the family and peer-group pressures, and the student's IQ. The greater the understanding of a relationship between two variables, the more precisely one may predict and the greater the possibility for controlling the relationship. The complexity of the phenomena with which social psychology deals, however, usually results in the understanding of a relationship being based upon a cluster of antecedent conditions, as was illustrated in the above example of understanding academic performance.

Control is present when one can create a particular cause-effect sequence; that is, when one can provide the critical antecedent conditions to cause a desired event to take place. For example, in order to control the academic performance of a certain student of average intelligence, one could provide the critical antecedent conditions such as an enriched early environment, a high quality of schooling, and favorable family and peer-group pressures.

Methods of Science

Scientific methodology is first of all a process of observation; it is the deliberateness and control of the process of observation that is distinctive of science. In scientific observation it is important that different observers should see the same results, that is, a scientific observation should be such that it could have been made by any other observer so situated. This *intersubjectivity* is a mark of objectivity, for it testifies that the observation is uncontaminated by any factors save those common to all observers.

In social psychology there are two common types of research studies, correlational and experimental. The correlation study examines the covariation of two or more variables. If the presence of intensity of one variable tends to match or correspond with the presence or intensity of another variable, there is a correlation between them. For example, if one found that students with positive self-concepts achieved higher grades than do students with negative self-concepts, one could conclude that students' self-concepts and their academic performance are correlated. The fact that there is a correlation between two variables may allow the researcher to make statements about prediction, but not about causation. In a correlational relationship it is not clear which variable "causes" the other; for example, does a positive self-concept "cause" a student to achieve, or does achievement "cause" a positive self-concept? It is also possible that the correlation between two variables is "caused" by a third variable; any correlation between self-concept and academic performance, for example, may be "caused" by other variables such as IQ or early childhood experiences or teacher attitudes toward the student.

In experimental research one distinguishes between the independent and dependent variables. An *experiment* is a situation in which one observes the relationship between two variables by deliberately producing a change in one and looking to see whether this alteration produces a change in the other. The variable that the experimenter changes directly is referred to as the *independent variable,* because its value is independently manipulated by the experimenter. The variable that the experimenter examines to see whether it is affected by changes in the independent variable is called the *dependent variable,* because its value is expected to be dependent on the value of the independent variable. For example, an educator could conduct an experiment in which he deliberately produced a change in several students' academic self-attitudes to see if an increase in positive academic self-attitudes results in an increase in school achievement. The independent variable in this experiment is the students' self-attitudes, the dependent variable is achievement.

Much of scientific methodology deals with the elimination of errors in observation of relationships between variables. In order to *eliminate* observational errors due to individual biasing effects one uses several observers or replicates the observation with a different observer. In setting up an experiment in which a limited number of independent variables are studied one *insulates* the observation from other variables which might confound the results. Even in an experiment one needs to control the possibility of an extraneous variable producing a change in the dependent variable that is attributed to the independent variable by such measures as randomly assigning subjects to the different conditions or carefully matching the subjects who are assigned to different conditions. Finally, in some cases it is possible to measure the direction and extent of error in an observation and make a subsequent *correction* in the analysis and interpretation of the results.

There are many subtle sources of error in the research of the behavioral sciences. For example, one series of studies conducted by Rosenthal (1966) has shown that research assistants familiar with the purpose of the experiment they are conducting are more apt to obtain the desired findings from their subjects than are research assistants who do not know the purpose of the experiment. This was not due to conscious dishonesty, but rather to subtle, not fully identified cues in the experimenter's behavior that conveyed to the subject the experimenter's hypothesis. Not only is the relation between the researcher and the subjects a source of possible bias, but also the subjects' motivation for participating in the research, their conception of the role of a research subject, and even the manner in which they are recruited affect their responses to the research situation. These factors greatly complicate the problems of causal inference and generalization in behavioral science research.

An example of the remarkable compliance of college students in our culture in experimental situations is seen in a study conducted by Orne (1962). As one of a series of experiments he asked a group of acquaintances and strangers to do five pushups as a favor to him. The response was typically, "Why?" or "What are you, some kind of nut?" He next asked several comparable people if they would like to participate in an experiment. The experiment, he stated, was to do five pushups. The typical response was, "Where do I do them?"

Conceptualization and the Language of Science

Some things in the world veritably "leap out" at a person and seemingly demand to be given names. For example, clouds, trees, mountains, houses, people, lakes, dogs, fingers, hair, and the like so stand out to every observer that their word-names form the earliest vocabulary of children just beginning to speak. Names for such obvious things are the words of everyday *ordinary* language; sometimes there are two or more names for the same thing.

Other things in the world are much more subtle and require careful coaxing out of the fabric of reality before they become identifiable. For example, mass, momentum, motivation, IQ, and schizophrenia are much more difficult to discern, and then not directly by eyesight at all. These latter are much more likely to be the terms and concepts that make up the vocabulary of science, and it is the work of the scientist to "cut out" these things, and to give them names. Names for such obscure things are the terms and concepts of *scientific* language, and the general rule is: one thing, one term.

Some times the same term occurs in both ordinary and scientific language; but when it does, it has a different meaning in each language. "Work" to the physicist refers to foot-pounds per second, not to sweat and effort. There is a sense in which the work of the scientist is that of recutting the world into pieces and "things" of new size and shape.

The boundaries of the scientific concepts that are cut out of the "stuff" of reality are often determined by observation of what moves together as one or in a system. Scientific observation consists of taking special notice of coincidence, the occurence of events simultaneous in time, or of systematic change of one variable in relation to one or more others. So then, the language of science also includes relational words and concepts such as greater than, less than, equal to, is, and, if-then, and the like. These are not unique to science; these are the terms of logic that give form to both ordinary and scientific statements.

Actually the language of science is a set of languages. What distinguishes one science from another is the terms and concepts unique to each. The logical-relational terms are common to all, but each scientific discipline has its own separate vocabulary of terms and concepts that are unique to it. Each scientific discipline, then, is a language community that has its own set of agreed-upon conventional terms, its own view of the world, its own way of piecing together or, if you will, cutting up reality into parts, pieces, and segments among which describable and consistent relationships are sought. And whether or not any specific science is of particular value depends upon whether or not through conceptualization with the constructs and terms of that science one can more effectively and efficiently describe, explain, predict, and control portions of the world than can the man-on-the-street who has never heard of that science and its vocabulary and knowledge.

Not surprisingly, then, the most significant advances in science are usually not in terms of identification of previously unknown relationships between already defined concepts, but rather in terms of entirely new groupings or recuttings of the empirical world, establishment of fresh boundaries and configurations that more consistently or understandably account for the observations and measurements of properties and variables that have already been made and recorded.

This book is intended to give the beginning student of social psychology and education a new vocabulary of social psychological concepts (that is where learning a new scientific discipline necessarily begins). Hopefully, what follows will also prepare the student to conceptualize as a particular type of scientist, a social psychologist. If so, he should then be able better to describe, predict, explain, control, and solve classroom problems in education.

SUMMARY

Social psychology is one of the most recently developed scientific fields concerned with the objective study of human behavior. It focuses on the individual and his interpersonal relations with members of his own and other social systems and seeks to understand and explain how an individual's thoughts, feelings, perceptions, and behavior are affected by actual or imagined interaction with other human beings. Significant contributions were made to the development of social psychology by Kurt Lewin, emphasizing the interdependence between theoretical analysis and empirical verification and demonstrating the possibilities of investigating complex social variables under the controlled conditions of an experimental laboratory.

There are two important contributions that social psychology can make to education. First, the application of the scientific method as it is used in social psychology should allow education to build a body of knowledge about teaching and administration based on empirical fact, which can take the place of the contradictory and erroneous "self-evident truths" upon which educational practice is presently based. Second, systematic methods of research, when combined with social psychological knowledge, provide educators with problem-solving techniques, which will enable them to diagnose problems in education more accurately and initiate more effective solutions.

The scientific method is a synthesis of induction and deduction. Induction involves the observation of concrete events in order to formulate general laws about the underlying order of these particular events. Deduction consists of logically deriving a specific conclusion or hypothesis from two general laws, which can then be tested

17

against observable facts. These procedures rest upon the following three assumptions: (1) the fundamental properties of phenomena remain constant under specified conditions over definite periods of time, (2) events, experiences, and objects can be classified according to certain common characteristics, and (3) all phenomena are determined by a cause or set of causes.

The requisites of any successful science are prediction, understanding, and control. If two variables are highly correlated, the scientist is able to make a fairly accurate *prediction* of an object's value on one variable, given his observed value on another variable. From here the researcher hopes to gain an explanation of this observable relationship by discovering the complex of antecedent conditions that account for it. With a complete explanation, along with the capability to manipulate antecedent conditions, one can then *control* events so as to cause a desired event to take place.

Experimental research enables the scientist to go beyond the statements of prediction allowable with correlational data to statements of causation. In an experiment one can directly *observe* whether or not a deliberately produced change in the independent variable *causes* a change in the dependent variable. Also, through procedures such as randomly assigning or matching subjects assigned to different experimental conditions and greatly reducing a subject's stimulus field, extraneous variables producing a change in the dependent variable that are mistakenly attributed to the independent variable are controlled.

2

THE SCHOOL
AS AN
ORGANIZATION

Introduction

Within the school the basic education of the student primarily takes place in the classroom. Most of this book focuses upon the social psychological variables involved in the classroom interactions between the teacher and the students and among the students. Before the nature of the interpersonal processes in the classroom are examined, however, the setting in which they take place, the school, must be analyzed. The school is above all else an organization. It has many of the characteristics common to all organizations. It also has characteristics that are unique to educational organizations.

The Nature of Social Systems

The school is a special type of social organization. A social organization is a special type of social system. A social system is a special type of system. A system is a complex of elements in mutual interaction (Griffiths, 1965). Definite boundaries distinguish the system from its environment; the environment being everything that is outside the system. Systems may be open or closed. An open system is related to and makes exchanges with its environment, while a closed system is not related to and does not make exchanges with its environment. An example of a closed system is a ballistic missile after launching. It will follow its course, carry out its function, no matter what changes take place in the environment. It has a self-contained energy system that is independent from the environment; it needs no input from the environment and it gives no output. An example of an open system is a person. A person is influenced by changes in the environment; if the temperature changes, for example, the body changes. The body takes in resources from the environment, such as oxygen and food, and gives outputs, such as carbon dioxide, which are needed to substain other open systems (such as plants). The school is another example of an open system.

An open system is a recurrent pattern of events, differentiated from but dependent on the larger environment; it is a structuring of events rather than of physical parts and has, therefore, no structure apart from its functioning. A school, for example, is not a building with certain types of rooms; it is a structured interaction between the staff and the students. All open systems involve the flow of energy from the environment through the system itself and back into the environment. While the energy is within the system it is transformed. In other words, the functioning of an open system consists of recurrent cycles of input, transformation, and output (see Figure 1). There are two kinds of inputs to a system, one to be transformed and one that does the transforming. In a school, for example, students are normally the input that is transformed, and teachers, buildings, and materials are the inputs that do the transforming. After the students are transformed from children into socialized, self-actualizing, skilled young adults, they are returned to the environment where they enter other systems, such as economic, occupational organizations.

A social system is a patterned set of activities which are interdependent with respect to some common output (Katz and Kahn, 1966). All social systems have two major concerns: accomplishing their objectives and maintaining themselves over time. A school, for example, must educate its students and maintain itself as a functioning organization in continued operation. Social systems are es-

INPUT————————————➤ TRANSFORMATION PROCESS ——➤OUTPUT
1. That which is trans-   Education   Socialized,
   formed: Children   Self-
2. That which does   Actualizing,
   the transforming: Skilled,
   Personnel, Build-   Young Adults
   ings, Materials

Figure 1.

The school as an open system.

sentially contrived systems made by men (Katz and Kahn, 1966). They can fall apart overnight or last for centuries. They are anchored in the attitudes, perceptions, beliefs, motivations, habits, and expectations of human beings. The functioning of a school, for instance, is anchored in the attitudes, perceptions, and beliefs of the teachers, administrators, students, and other school personnel. There is usually a wide variation among the members of the social system as to what the system objectives are and as to what constitutes appropriate member behavior. The result is variability in member behaviors and system objectives. Yet, in order for the social system to function effectively, member behavior and system objectives need to be relatively stable. Much of the energy of social systems, therefore, is fed into control devices to reduce the variability of human behavior and to produce stable patterns of activity.

The social psychological bases of social systems are comprised of the *role* behaviors of members, the *norms* prescribing and sanctioning these role behaviors, and the *values* in which the norms are embedded (Katz and Kahn, 1966). Roles, norms, and values are discussed in relation to social organizations later in this chapter.

Social Organizations

Our society is an organizational society (Etzioni, 1964). We are born in organizations, educated by organizations, and spend much of our lives working for organizations. Most people spend their leisure time paying, playing, and praying in organizations.

Social organizations are a type of social system with certain de-

---

BOX 2.1 SYSTEMS THEORY AS A MODEL

In Chapter 2 systems theory is used as a model for looking at the functioning of the school. A *model* is a conceptual analogue that is used to suggest empirical research and to provide a frame of reference for understanding the events one observes. The use of models is thinking by analogy. In this case systems theory was borrowed from other branches of the sciences to see if it would be an effective tool for analyzing what happens within organizations. The social psychologist is interested in using systems theory to analyze organizations, but on the basis of such analyses he is not interested in modifying systems theory. Since the flow of conceptualization is entirely from the conceptual to the empirical level, a model is chosen solely on the basis of its heuristic, or tool value (Marx, 1963).

A model organizes a researcher's or practitioner's thought about the phenomena under observation, in this case, schools. Systems theory thereby can guide and organize the research on the school as an organization. It can also be used to guide and organize the action taken by school personnel to improve the functioning of the school.

It should always be remembered that a serious error in the use of models is to forget that at best a model represents only a part of the phenomena being studied. Models are often overgeneralized by social scientists who think that a model, once it is formulated, is more than it is.

---

fining characteristics (Katz and Kahn, 1966). First, an organization must have some formal way of maintaining itself by the selection and training of personnel and through adequate rewarding of the personnel selected. It must also produce some output, whether it be cars or educated adults. Second, an organization has a formal role pattern in which the division of labor results in a functional specificity of roles, that is, the function of each role is clearly specified. Third, there is a clear authority structure that reflects the way in which the control and managerial functions are exercised. Fourth, as part of the managerial structure, there are well-developed regulatory mechanisms and adaptive structures that provide the organization with feedback about its own functioning and the changing character of the environment to guide its activities. Without an awareness of its general effectiveness in accomplishing its objectives and the way in which its outputs have to be adapted to a continually changing environment, an organization will not be able to survive. Finally, there is an explicit formulation of ideology to provide system norms, which buttress the authority structure of the organization.

Modern civilization depends largely upon organizations as the most rational and efficient form of social grouping known. With the development of our highly technical society, organizations have become increasingly more numerous, complex, and efficient. Organizations are essential to society because they function in rational, efficient ways (Etzioni, 1964). The rationality and efficiency of organizations, however, does not come without social and human cost. Many people who work for organizations are deeply frustrated and alienated from their work. Members of many organizations are not committed to their jobs and not involved in their work. They are not experiencing a sense of growth and self-actualization from their work and are, consequently, unhappy with the organization within which they are employed. Not all that enhances rationality, however, reduces happiness and not all that increases happiness reduces efficiency. Human resources are among the major means used by the organization to achieve its goals. Generally, the less the organization alienates its personnel, the more efficient it is. Satisfied workers usually work harder and better than frustrated ones. Within limits, happiness heightens efficiency in organizations, and, conversely, without efficient organizations much of our happiness is unthinkable. Etzioni (1964) notes that without well-run organizations our standard of living, our level of culture, and our democratic life could not be maintained. Thus, to a degree, organizational rationality and human happiness go hand in hand. But the point is reached in any organization where efficiency and happiness cease to support each other. *The problem of modern organizations is thus how to construct human groupings that are as rational as possible, and at the same time produce a minimum of undesirable side effects and a maximum of satisfaction.*

The type of organization designed to accomplish large administrative tasks by systematically coordinating the work of many individuals is called a bureaucracy (Blau, 1956). The bureaucratic organization includes a definite division of labor, a hierarchy of authority with carefully prescribed responsibilities, a system of rules or policy, impersonality in the interaction of its members, employment based upon technical qualifications, and efficiency from a technical standpoint. As dissatisfaction has grown with the effects of a bureaucratic structure upon the happiness and commitment of the members of an organization, there has been a search for alternative ways of structuring complex organizations.

The major alternative to the pyramidal, hierarchical structure for the administration of complex social organizations is the democratic model of administration (Katz and Kahn, 1966). The democratic model involves (1) the separation of legislative and executive power, with the membership as a whole vested with the legislative power, (2) the ability of the membership of the organization to veto administrative decisions, and (3) the ability of the membership to elect the executive officers who hold office for a stipulated term, after which they are either re-elected or replaced by the organization's membership. Thus, in a democratically run school, students, teachers, and other nonadministrative personnel would be able to make school policy, veto decisions made by the administration, and have the power to hire and terminate the employment of the key administrators. Such an involvement in a democratic organization would be, perhaps, the best way to prepare students to live in a democratic society.

Roles, Norms, and Values

Organizations have both an informal and a formal structure. The informal structure will be discussed in the next section. The network of standardized role behaviors in the organization constitutes its formal structure. The roles of various educational personnel (that is, principal, teacher, nurse, counselor, and so forth) and the students, for example, constitute the formal structure of a school. A formalized role system is one in which the rules defining the expected interdependent behavior of individuals in positions in the system are explicitly formulated and sanctions are employed to enforce the rules. Thus, the role requirements of teachers, administrators, students, and other school personnel are explicitly formulated and individuals who conform to their role requirements are rewarded, while those who deviate are punished. Role specification ensures that individuals within the organization engage in the recurring task behaviors that are appropriately interrelated with the repetitive activities of other members of the organization, so as to yield a predictable and desired outcome. For example, the role specification of elementary-school teachers may state that they should organize learning experiences for students in order for students to learn to read. The role specifications of students state that they should take advantage of any learning situations set up by the teacher in order to learn to read. When these two role specifications are appropriately interrelated the desired outcome (that is, students learning to read) results.

The forces that maintain the role system are the task demands, the shared values, and the observance of rules. The formulation of rules and sanctions of rewards and punishments results in an authority system for the organization which, through administering sanctions, ensures that the task demands of the organization are fulfilled and the shared values are conformed with. The accomplishment of the task requirements of an organization depends upon the fulfillment of the organizational role requirements, which depends upon a process of learning the role expectations of other members of the organization, accepting them, and reliably fulfilling them. Unless students reliably fulfill their role requirements, for example, schools would not accomplish their objectives of educating the students. The students' role behaviors depend upon a process of learning what the teachers and other school personnel expect of a student, accepting those expectations as legitimate, and reliably fulfilling them. As roles specify task behaviors within the organization they are, in their purest form, divorced from the personalities of the individuals involved and from any specific motivational ties (such as friendship), which could confuse or burden the role relationship. A more detailed discussion of organizational roles is presented in Chapter 3.

The accomplishment of any systematic activity depends upon the coordination of the behavior and the attitudes of the individual involved. Societies cannot be substained, social organizations cannot achieve their objectives, without the coordination of behavior and attitudes resulting from conformity to group norms. Organizational norms and values have the general function of tying people into the organization so that they remain within it and carry out their role assignments. Norms can be defined as the general expectations of a demand character for all role members of an organization. Values are the more generalized ideological justifications and aspirations of the organization. An example of a school norm is that no one, whether he is a teacher, the principal, or a student, runs down the hall singing at the top of his voice. An example of a value is the belief that education is beneficial and worthwhile. The organizational norms and values are a group product and may not be necessarily identical with the privately held values of a representative sample of the individuals involved in the organization. Students, for example, may have very different values from those of the school, but that does not necessarily change the values of the school.

While roles differentiate one position from another, norms and values integrate the behavior of members of an organization (Katz and Kahn, 1966). Norms make explicit the forms of behavior appropriate for members of an organization and values provide a more elaborate and generalized justification both for appropriate behavior and for the activities and functions of the organization. Norms and values are interrelated and the differences between them are ones of emphasis rather than of uniqueness. Norms refer to the expected behavior sanctioned by the organization and thus have a specific ought or must quality; values furnish the rationale for the normative requirements. Norms and values are discussed in more detail in Chapter 12.

The Informal Structure of the Organization

The role structure and the organizational norms and values make up the formal structure of the organization. In addition, there is often an informal structure, above and beyond the formal structure, formed by the social relations that develop among the members. Many organizational theorists believe that this informal structure is more vital to the understanding of the organization than is the formal structure. In theory, for instance, communications move through ordered channels, the school board informs the superintendent, the superintendent informs the principals, the principals inform the teachers, and the teachers inform the students. Actually, the grapevine in many schools may carry communications so rapidly and effectively that the teachers may know what is coming before the principals do. A secretary who has been in the school for several years may know better than most of her superiors how to get done what she wants done and how to block what she does not want done. The friendliness or hostility of the spouses of the school personnel may exert influences within the school which the formal structure does not show. It is often the informal norms among the teachers or the students that determine what happens in the classroom, not the formal norms of the school. Thus, within any organization, there often develops an informal structure that is different from the formal structure and that determines, to a large extent, what actually happens in the organization.

Managing an Organization

Traditionally, organizations have not focused on the resources of creative human potential that could become available within the organizational setting. McGregor (1960, 1966) has conceptualized the task of management to harness human energy to organizational requirements and proposed two theories of human management, theory X and theory Y. Theory X represents the conventional view of management. McGregor feels that so long as the assumptions of theory X continue to influence managerial strategy, organizations will fail to discover, let alone utilize, the potentialities of the average human being. He proposed, therefore, theory Y, which attempts to integrate the individual's goals and the organization's goals. His formulation of theory Y is based upon the work by Maslow (1954) and others on human motivation and assumes that in today's society, where more basic motivations such as hunger are satisfied for most people, man is primarily motivated by needs for self-actualization. Table 1 contrasts the two theories.

Argyris (1957) objects to those aspects of organization and management that treat individuals as if they were not capable of responsibility, initiative, flexible adaptation, and long-term planning. He states that an organization impedes the development of mature, understanding, adaptable, and self-regulating persons when it treats people as if they are parts in a machine, requires them to perform routine tasks assigned by others and closely checked by supervisors, and expects them to remain loyally obedient to any demands of the

TABLE 1

THEORY X		THEORY Y	
Assumptions about People	Administrative Policies	Assumptions about People	Administrative Policies
1. Naturally inert, lazy, avoids work	1. Drive, "motivate," coerce	1. Naturally active, enterprising	1. Lead
	2. Direct		2. Use self-direction
2. Dependent	3. Routine procedures	2. Independent	3. Open to change
3. Set in ways		3. Growing	
4. Irresponsible	4. Check up	4. Responsible	4. Trust
5. Resistant, hostile	5. Fight, on guard	5. With you	5. Cooperation
6. Unimaginative	6. Prescribe	6. Creative	6. Encourage
7. Short-sighted	7. Plan for them	7. Capable of broad vision, long view	7. Plan with them

FROM Watson, G., SOCIAL PSYCHOLOGY: ISSUES AND INSIGHTS. New York: J. B. Lippincott Company, 1966. By permission of the publisher.

organization. He notes that members of an organization operating on theory X tend to respond by feeling "used," "bored," and vaguely resentful.

Blake and Mouton (1964) recognize two important objectives of management: (1) production and (2) concern for people. They have developed a classification scheme whereby managers can be classified as to the degree to which they emphasize each of the two objectives. Some managers are production oriented, completely ignoring the concerns the organization should have for its members. Others are primarily concerned with the people within the organization and ignore to a large extent the production needs of the organization. The ideal manager is one with whole-hearted concern for both people and production.

Finally, Likert (1961) attempts to incorporate four kinds of motives into management theory: (1) economic, (2) ego satisfaction, (3) security, and (4) new experiences. He states that an ideal manager will use economic incentives of pay and promotion; give recognition, dignity, and a sense of achievement to his subordinates; is careful not to threaten basic security; and stimulates originality, creativity, and the satisfactions of growth.

These and other organizational theorists have promoted what is now known as the "participative" approach to management. The underlying rationale of this approach is that a collaborative, democratic style of leadership, using group decision making, is likely to improve the decisions that are made, increase the commitment of the members of the organization to the decisions, and increase the cohesiveness and morale of the organization. This approach seems to improve problem solving by opening channels of communication. Opening communication channels involves the diagnosis and improvement of interpersonal and intergroup relations under the assumption that mistrust and conflict between persons and groups restricts communication. It is assumed that restrictions on communication, as well as mistrust and conflict, may generate dissatisfaction and inadequate problem solving.

These management theories can be applied to the way in which an administrator manages the school or the way in which a teacher manages a classroom. In Chapter 8 the nature of leadership and supervision is examined in more detail.

Typology of Organizations

Organizations can be classified according to the type of activity in which they are engaged as a subsystem of the larger society. In classifying organizations one is interested in highlighting the sources of variation between organizations while at the same time recognizing the basic similarities among all organizations. One way to solve this paradox is to create a typology. Katz and Kahn (1966) state that for society to endure there must be economically productive activities that meet basic needs and provide basic services. There must also be a central set of values and norms with socializing agencies to inculcate these belief systems and to provide general and specific training for social roles. To insure some viable integration or compromise among the competing groups within society, there must, in addition, be an authoritative decision-making structure for the allocation of resources. Finally, specialized agencies must exist for the creation of knowledge and for the fostering of artistic endeavor.

There are, therefore, four types of generic organizations within our society (Katz and Kahn, 1966). First, there are *productive* or economic organizations that are concerned with providing goods and

29

services; mining, farming, manufacturing, transportation, and communication are included in this category. Second, there are *maintenance* organizations that are concerned with the socialization and training of people for roles in other organizations and in the society at large. Schools and churches are the major examples of maintenance organizations. Third, there are *managerial-political* organizations that coordinate and control people and resources and adjudicate among competing groups. The national, state, and local agencies of government provide the major examples of this category, although pressure groups, labor unions, and other special interest organizations would also be classified as managerial-political. Finally, there are *adaptive* organizations that are intended to create new knowledge, innovative solutions to problems, and the like. The research laboratory is the prototype of such organizations, and universities (as research organizations rather than teaching organizations) also belong in this category.

It should be noted that although most organizations generally specialize in a single function, they make supplementary contributions in other areas. Industrial organizations, for example, though concentrating on the economic function, make contributions to scientific knowledge through research aimed at improving their products and efficiency. Moreover, the various types of organizations are interdependent; without the schools socializing future workers, for example, the industrial organizations could not exist and without the materials made by industrial organizations the schools could not exist.

Educational Organizations: Schools

The school may be viewed as an organization that receives two types of inputs from its environment: (1) students, and (2) teachers, materials, buildings, money, and other resources. The school uses the teachers, materials, and buildings to transform uneducated children into socialized, self-actualizing, skilled young adults, which it then returns to the environment to enter economic, occupational organizations. As an organization, the school is characterized by a role structure and certain norms and values. The role structure consists of the principal, assistant principals, guidance and counseling personnel, curriculum consultants, teachers, students, secretaries, and custodians. These roles specify a division of labor that is thought to be efficient for accomplishing the school's task of educating students and maintaining the school as a functioning organization. The norms and values of the school integrate the different roles by providing an ideological framework to justify and coordinate the task behaviors of the members of the organization.

American schools are typically highly bureaucratic organizations governed by a complex body of law, characterized by a division of labor and formal structure of administrative authority, and staffed by teachers who are certified for their jobs on criteria of technical competence and usually promoted on the basis of seniority (Moeller and Charters, 1966; Brickell, 1964; Wayland, 1964; Miles, 1964a; Corwin, 1965). The rigid authority structure, the red tape involved in getting innovations approved, and the bureaucratic resistance to change of public schools all inhibit the initiation of change within a school (see Chapter 14 for a discussion of innovation in schools). There is some evidence, furthermore, that the larger the school system the less the likelihood that teachers will innovate within a school. Samuels (1967) studied 1887 teachers representing 224 elementary schools located in 13 school systems, ranging in size from an average daily attendance of 2400 to 83,000 students. She hypothesized that the larger the school district, the greater the need for control and coordination among teachers through bureaucratic rules and regulations and the lower the autonomy of the teachers. Her findings support this hypothesis. As the school district size increased, the autonomy of the teacher to make decisions in the professional domain decreased, thereby limiting the teachers' ability to innovate within the classroom.

Schools resemble so-called total institutions, such as prisons and mental hospitals, in that one subgroup of their clientele (the students) are involuntarily committed to the institution, whereas another subgroup (the staff) has greater freedom of movement and, most important, has the ultimate freedom to leave the institution entirely (Jackson, 1968). Under these circumstances it is common for the more privileged group to guard the exits, either figuratively or literally. The reponsibilities of teachers bear some resemblance to the responsibilities of prison guards. That is, in many schools a teacher is expected to patrol the halls, check to see if students have the proper passes, stop any student from leaving the classroom except under a limited set of conditions, stop any student from leaving the school unless he has official permission, check student lockers for stolen items, and check the washrooms for students who might be smoking. It is not uncommon, especially in urban schools, for the school to take on the appearance of a prison, with a high wire fence surrounding the school and policemen guarding the entrances. One of the consequences of the restrictions placed upon students is that often the teachers themselves, in having to guard the students, lose much of their freedom and find that they are also "prisoners" within the school's walls.

Special Organizational Properties of Schools

While the school is an organization and as such shares certain properties with all other organizations, it does have special properties that differentiate it from other types of organizations. For example, the public school is what Carlson (1965) calls a "domesticated" organization; that is, the school is protected and cared for in much the same fashion as a domesticated animal is protected and cared for. Unlike economic organizations, the school is not compelled to attend to all the ordinary and usual needs of an organization, such as recruitment of clients and financial backing. There is no struggle for survival for a domesticated organization; its existence is guaranteed. Funds are not closely tied to the quality of performance. The school does not have to compete on the basis of efficiency with rival organizations; it has a monopoly on education.

There are two consequences of "domestication"; one is that the school has a restricted need for and interest in change, as its organizational survival does not depend upon quality of performance. The second is that, since the efficiency of the school has never really been challenged, few yardsticks have been developed to measure the quality of the school's product or the efficiency of its production. Few controls are present to support consumer demands for high quality, wide distribution, and low cost. The interorganizational principle on which American industrial productivity is presumably based—moderated competition—does not operate at all in the public schools, except in higher education during periods when students make choices of colleges to attend.

Common incentives to motivate members of organizations are

monetary rewards, status rewards, and normative rewards. In most organizations there are economic payoffs for increasing the quality of one's performance. In schools, however, rewards (economic and noneconomic) for the staff are commonly given on the basis of criteria other than actual quality of role performance, such as seniority. Miles (1964a) states that a barrier to change in public education is the lack of economic incentive to adopt innovations. One could hypothesize that if well-educated students resulted in an immediate economic payoff for the teacher, teachers would accept changes more readily and initiate innovations more frequently.

In schools monetary rewards for the students are absent, except in the hazy promise that education will mean more money in the far future through higher salaries. Status rewards, such as grades and special recognition for academic achievement, are the most common type of reward for students, but they are effective only with those students who want and can get status for academic achievement. For some students academic achievement status is a negative incentive; that is, they would be ostracized and teased by their peers for making high grades. The normative rewards of the school, furthermore, are often counterposed against peer-group norms and the students' desire to be accepted by their peers. In the school peergroup loyalty often becomes a powerful and anti-organizational incentive as the school tries to put individuals in competition with one another and as the school fails to direct group loyalties toward academic goals. For a detailed discussion of this issue, see Chapter 12.

Miles (1965, 1966) lists a series of properties of schools that he feels differentiates them from other organizations. The first one is *goal ambiguity*; the goals of educational organizations are ambiguous and, to a large extent, perceived to be immeasurable. Ambiguous goals make for ambiguous role specifications and an inability to measure goal achievement. Since one cannot specify the day-to-day role behaviors of a teacher needed to accomplish the school's objectives, one cannot measure any individual teacher's success in fulfilling his role; it is difficult, therefore, to reward teachers for quality performance or improvement in teaching practices. The wide *variation in input* of students and personnel from the environment is possibly another unique property of schools. Public schools must accept children of a wide range of ability and motivation. Moreover, the range of staff intellectual ability, interpersonal skill, and knowledge of subject matter is probably at least as great as that among pupils. This teacher variability causes considerable stress in educational organizations, and develops the need to provide teaching personnel with methods and curriculum materials which are, in effect, teacher proof.

Miles (1965) notes that, unlike most other organizations, the *role performance of teachers is relatively invisible* to other teachers or superiors. Students can observe the quality of a teacher's execution of his role, but they are usually not allowed to comment and have few sanctions to bring to bear. Since role performance cannot then be evaluated, substitute criteria for teaching effectiveness, such as the teacher's "interest in the students," are used. In comparison with most economic organizations, furthermore, schools have a *low interdependence of parts*. The failure of one teacher to perform his duties does not directly affect the job-relevant behavior of other teachers. One of the consequences of low interdependence is that the behavior of any teacher can become highly routinized in unproductive ways.

Finally, public schools are subject to *control and criticism from the surrounding environment*. They are governed by a school board made up of laymen, most of whom have not been inside a school for twenty years. Nonprofessionals, therefore, often set educational policy. Parents or members of the community, furthermore, can bring pressure on school personnel to a far greater extent than they can bring pressure upon the members of a factory in the local community. The vulnerability of the school to the control and criticism of the local community sharply reduces the school's autonomy. Innovations in school practices can be adopted only in the absence of strong opposition from the community.

The National Educational System

There is a myth about public education in the United States that says it is locally controlled. Actually, there exists a national educational system, which to a large extent controls the functioning of the public schools and, consequently, teacher behavior within the schools (Miles, 1964a; Wayland, 1964). As illustrated in Figure 2, the national educational system consists of formal educational organizations (public schools, universities, and the like), informal educational organizations (military training, Peace Corps, Boy Scouts, summer camps, and the like), governmental agencies (U.S. Office of Education, National Science Foundation, National Institute of Mental Health, and the like), commerical organizations (publishing companies, construction companies, research organizations, and the like), and nonprofit organizations (foundations, testing organizations, accreditation agencies, professional organizations, and the like). (See Miles, 1964b.)

The existence of such a national educational system is necessary in order to integrate and coordinate the functioning of the numerous schools and institutions of higher education that make up the formal educational structure in the United States (Wayland, 1964). The curriculum across public schools must be fairly consistent in order to prepare students for the next educational level; upon entering junior high school, for example, students must be prepared to do the work no matter which elementary school they attended. The selection standards of colleges, graduate schools, and special high schools further influence the curriculum and teaching of the lower levels. Moreover, the leaders of the public schools are products of the colleges and, therefore, tend to act upon the values and orientation of the colleges and graduate schools. Finally, the higher levels of the formal educational structure exert subtle pressures upon the lower levels to build a basic level of competence in their students so that graduate schools, for example, will not have to spend their time and resources teaching English composition to their students.

There are other interrelationships between schools greatly influencing the functioning of any one school (Wayland, 1964). The movement of teachers, administrators, parents, and students from school to school pressures the schools into a standard curriculum; such mobility also serves as a mechanism for diffusion of educational practices. The textbook industry, through its publications and the actions of its salesmen, makes available to local school systems the curriculum patterns in existence in other school systems and pressures different schools to adopt the same curriculum. The results of national examinations serve as a guide for modification of local curricula, modification designed to insure more favorable results on subsequent administration of the same tests. Finally, national organizations such as the National Educational Association,

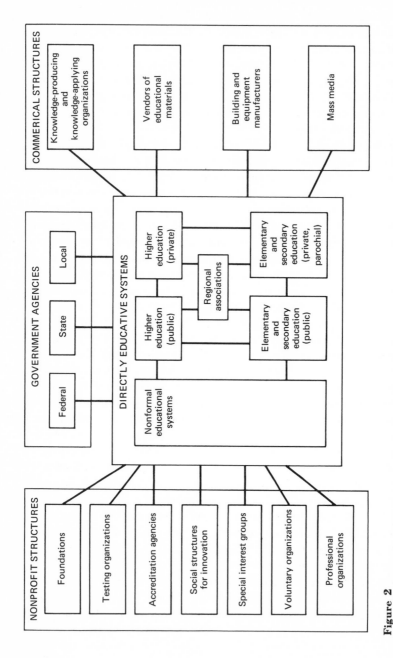

Figure 2
The American educational system. REPRINT WITH THE PERMISSION OF THE PUBLISHER FROM M. B. MILES' *Innovation in Education* (NEW YORK: TEACHERS COLLEGE PRESS), 1964.

teacher-training institutions, and accreditation associations all put pressure upon local schools to adopt standardized materials and procedures that most other schools use and follow.

The Objectives of Educational Organizations

A common definition of the objectives of the school is to prepare students to assume adult roles in society by socializing them into the values and habits of society and teaching them the skills needed to fulfill specific adult roles and to live in a complex, industrial society (Bidwell, 1965; Parsons, 1959). As a result of his educational experience, the student is supposed to have internalized a commitment to the performance of a specific type of adult role, such as teacher, doctor, or factory worker, and to have developed the capacity to competently perform the task behaviors of his choosen adult role.

The school is responsible for ensuring that the students learn the general skills and knowledge necessary to function in a complex, industrial society. This includes being "role responsible"—having the capacity to live up to general expectations of appropriate role behavior, such as promptness, cleanliness, and obedience to organizational authority and having a general "role readiness"—the ability to meet the demands of many organizational settings with the proper cooperation (Parsons, 1959). In addition, the school is responsible for indoctrinating the students into the skills, values, and attitudes necessary to fulfill one's obligations as a citizen in a democracy (Dreeben, 1968).

Parsons (1959) and Miller (1966) note that the school serves as an accrediting agency that allocates manpower to the occupational organizations. To an increasing extent, the amount of education one has determines the type of adult occupational role one will assume. Future occupational status is dependent upon one's level of education, with attendance of college as the most significant dividing line between occupations. Without educational credentials, an individual is barred from a growing list of occupations and, in the case of civil service jobs, individuals must meet educational requirements set by law in order to be eligible for particular jobs. The more ambiguous the criteria by which performance is judged, the more emphasis upon the amount of education of the role occupant. In teaching, for example, it is not clear what makes a competent teacher; teachers, therefore, are rewarded primarily on the basis of their seniority in the system and the amount of education they have. Today those who lack educational credentials are barred from the good, secure jobs; the uncredentialed now serve a life sentence of limited opportunities, no matter what their talent and potential.

There is evidence, furthermore, that the schools allocate manpower in a way that perpetuates the present lower class (Parsons, 1959; Miller, 1966). Entrance into college, for example, is usually dependent upon being placed in a college-preparatory "track" in high school. Being placed in a college-preparatory curriculum in high school is dependent upon achievement in elementary and junior high school, with achievement in elementary school being the most important criterion. In elementary school, achievement is evaluated on the basis of the child's cognitive learning and "responsible citizenship," and in most elementary schools the two factors are not clearly differentiated. The child's preschool experiences influence both his academic performance and his social behavior in the elementary school, with independence training being a major factor in preparing a child for school. Because of their socialization into a different value and behavior structure, lower-class children are much more likely to receive lower grades in elementary school than comparable middle-class children and, consequently, they do not get into a college, and are then limited to a certain level of occupations.

While schools should socialize students into the predominate values of society and teach them the skills needed to fulfill specific adult roles and live in a complex, industrial society, these objectives by themselves seem inadequate. They appear to stress conformity in behavior and values instead of freedom to actualize and grow in individual ways. They imply that it is always the school who changes the students and leave out the possibility that the students sometimes may legitimately change the schools. Certainly other objectives must also be accepted by the school.

Friedenberg (1962), for example, states that schools might better spend their time helping students work out the meaning of their lives under the illumination of discipline study than in trying to build a common pattern of values and responses among adolescents from a diversity of class and ethnic backgrounds. From Friedenberg's point of view, if education is to have any depth, it must start with and be derived from the life experiences of the student. It must cultivate this experience with disciplined and demanding use of the best resources offered by the humanities and the sciences in order to help the individual understand the meaning of his own experience. This approach sharpens the students' perceptions of themselves as individuals rather than asking them to accept membership in a universal cultural heritage. It implies that the school should concentrate on developing the abilities of students to understand, appreciate, learn from, and creatively utilize human differences rather than learn to value conformity and similarity.

An increasing emphasis, at least in elementary schools, is being placed upon teaching students how to learn. Teachers, instead of communicating ready-made conclusions, are teaching students to think for themselves and to use the methods of disciplined inquiry to explore concepts in the various domains of knowledge and to study the world around them. Such an approach is compatible with many dominant values in society, such as being open-minded until direct data are collected on the problem, keeping conclusions tentative, exposing one's conclusions to public review by one's peers, basing decisions upon data rather than subjective feelings, and changing one's attitudes and values as new data are collected. This increasing emphasis upon teaching students inquiry methods rather than content is based upon the rapid change taking place in the sciences in terms of knowledge. Most of the individual facts taught in the elementary school in the sciences, for example, will be untrue, irrelevant, or changed so much as to be of little value by the time the students enter college. Thus many educators are convinced that it is more important to teach the students learning skills rather than content.

It is relatively easy for schools to stifle creative learning and self-direction merely by insisting on systematic learning of so much factual material that there is no time or energy left for anything else. Perhaps the most challenging objective of educational organizations is the development of self-actualizing individuals who are committed to the development of their personal resources and to the experiencing of joy and fulfillment in their lives. There is presently little knowledge about how schools can systematically do so; but even given the lack of systematic programs to develop self-actualizing individuals this objective is for the most part neglected in the public schools.

Finally, perhaps the most significant fact about modern society is that life is changing rapidly. Social change appears to be accelerating at such a rate that within any given person's lifetime, his psychological adjustment has to be continually modified to the radically changing conditions he finds himself within. Yesterday's solutions are often irrelevant to today's problems and no one can know what part of today's wisdom will remain valid tomorrow. The implications are that the school should be preparing students to live in a constantly changing world, perhaps by increasing the students' tolerance for ambiguity and by developing methodological skills for problem solving in students rather than emphasizing bodies of content which might be out of date in a few years.

Appropriate Structure

Once the specific objectives of the school and the classroom have been established, one of the questions needed to be asked about the school as an organization is how appropriate the organizational structure is for meeting the objectives. Taking as a general assumption that yesterday's structures may be inappropriate for meeting today's needs and objectives, a school needs to re-evaluate how well its structure functions in facilitating the accomplishment of the school's objectives. There is probably no greater frustration than the struggles of individuals to meet their needs in an organizational structure that is inappropriate and too rigid to change.

SUMMARY

A school can be viewed as a social organization. A social organization, in turn, is a special type of social system. A social system is any group of people who interact with one another to achieve some common goal. The defining properties that differentiate a social organization from other types of social systems are: (1) the group maintains itself by recruiting and training personnel, (2) group functions performed by each role are well specified, (3) a clearly defined hierarchy of authority, (4) adaptive structures provide information about adequacy of organizational functioning and the changing character of the external environment, and (5) common norms and values that buttress the authority structure.

The network of standardized role behaviors constitutes the formal structure of an organization. The behavior of individuals occupying the different positions of an organization is governed, not by their personal motivations, but by rules defining his role in relation to the incumbents of other organizational positions. The role behavior of members is prescribed so that their actions are coordinated and directed toward achieving organizational goals. Sanctions are also employed to reinforce conformities to the rules specifying appropriate role behavior.

Social organizations are also characterized by a set of norms and values. Norms are defined as the general expectations of a demand character shared by all members of an organization. Values refer to the broad aspirations of the organization and the more generalized ideological justifications of normative requirements. Whereas roles differentiate one position from another, norms and values integrate the behavior of members of an organization.

Schools can be considered a type of social organization concerned with the socialization and training of people for roles in other organizations and in society at large. Like other organizations, a division of labor is prescribed to fulfill this function and the norms and values of the school integrate the different roles of administrator, teacher, and student.

Although sharing the essential defining characteristics with all other organizations, schools do have the following special properties which distinguish them from other types of social organizations: (1) Their existence is guaranteed. (2) Monetary, status, and normative rewards for the staff are commonly given on the basis of criteria other than actual quality of role performance, such as seniority, and rewards for students generally are in the distant future or are ineffectual as an incentive because of peer-group pressures. (3) The goals of educational organizations are ambiguous, making for equivocal role specifications. (4) There is a wide variation in input of students and personnel. (5) The role performance of teachers is generally not observed by other teachers and supervisors. (6) Schools have a low interdependence of parts. (7) Public schools are subject to control and criticism from nonprofessionals outside the organization.

Two significant and rather disconcerting consequences of all of these characteristics are a restricted need for and interest in change and a relative lack of concern for the quality of role performance.

There is a common misconception that public education in the United States is locally controlled. In actuality, there exists a national educational system consisting of a complex of formal and informal educational organizations, government agencies, commercial enterprises, and nonprofit organizations. The interrelationships between these separate groups leads to a great deal of standardization of both curriculum and teaching procedures.

Generally speaking, the objectives of the school are to (1) socialize students into the values and habits of society, (2) teach them the skills needed to fulfill specific adult roles, (3) prepare students for living in a changing world, and (4) develop self-actualizing individuals.

CHAPTER 3

ROLE THEORY, THE ROLE OF THE TEACHER, AND ROLE CONFLICT

Introduction

The following chapters of this book deal with the role structure of the classroom and the social psychological processes that influence (1) the performance of classroom roles and (2) the interaction between the teacher and the students. In order to fully understand the role structure of the classroom, the social psychological theory of roles is presented in this chapter. The role of the teacher is then examined.

Traditional Role Theory

Role theory is basically an analogy. The word role is borrowed from the theater and there is little in its theoretical sense that is not prefigured in its theatrical sense (Brown, 1965). A role in a play exists independently of any particular actor; a social role exists independently of any individual performer. The role of Shakespeare's Hamlet has lasted 350 years, the role of president of the United States has lasted almost 200 years. In both the theater and an organization, a role prescribes certain actions and words unrelated in principle to the person playing the role. There is a theory of acting that holds that the way to play a role well is to live it, to experience the emotions of the character one plays; there is an alternative theory that holds that a role ought to be played with deliberate technique and some emotional detachment. In playing roles in society individuals follow both theories, but in a fixed order: first the conscious technique when one is learning the appropriate role behavior, and later the living of the part when the role behavior becomes automatic and internalized. Finally, a role in a play permits a certain amount of interpretation. Two actors, for example, can give quite different interpretations to the same lines within a play. As with the above, roles in a social system permit a certain amount of creative interpretation.

Traditionally, role theory has evolved around two central concepts, position and role. A *position* is a category of persons occupying a place in a social relation. By exhaustively enumerating all of a person's positions, it is at least theoretically possible to locate him with respect to the social relationships of his society. A man, for example, may concurrently occupy the positions of father, son, church member, teacher, president of a club, and member of an educational association. Such an enumeration of all a given person's concurrent positions is termed his *position set*.

Within a social system each position has associated with it a set of social norms, demands, rules, and expectations that specify the behaviors that an occupant of that position may appropriately initiate toward an occupant of some other position and vice versa. Thus, the term *role* is defined as the set of prescriptions defining the appropriate behavior of an occupant of a position toward other related positions. In actual practice the term role is used to refer to both the position and its associated behavior prescriptions. In a school, for example, with such positions as principal, teacher, and student, there are a set of behavioral prescriptions that specify the behaviors each may appropriately initiate toward the others. When a person refers to a teacher's role, he usually means both the position of teacher and its associated behavioral prescriptions. The role prescriptions prescribe a range of behavior within which all behavior is acceptable. Some positions have a wide range of acceptable behavior, other positions have very narrow ranges.

Related social roles make up a system or structure within which individuals interact. Such interlocking social roles can be defined as a *social system*. Within a social system a particular social role cannot be considered apart from its relation to other social roles. The role of a teacher, for example, cannot be discussed except in terms of other interdependent roles, such as student and principal. The role of husband cannot be discussed except in terms of the interdependent role of wife. Such interdependent roles are said to be *complementary*. An enumeration of all the complementary roles defines the *role set* for a position.

The prescriptions of role behavior within a complementary role relationship define the *rights* (what individuals in complementary roles will do for a person) and *obligations* (what individuals in complementary rules expect from a person). The obligations of a position are the rights of a complementary position; the rights of a position are the obligations of a complementary position. One of the obligations of a teacher, for example, is to present the students with material relevant to learning certain cognitive skills; one of the rights of a student is to have the teacher present material relevant to his learning certain cognitive skills. Another of the rights of a teacher is to have students obey his directives while he is presenting material; one of the obligations of a student is to obey the teacher while the teacher is presenting material. The rights of the teacher, therefore, are the obligations of the student and the obligations of the teacher are the rights of the student. These rights and obligations change with every complementary role relationship; that is, the rights and obligations of a teacher when he is interacting with the principal are different than the teacher's rights and obligations when he is interacting with a student.

Traditional role theory states that some positions are ascribed, others are achieved. *Ascribed positions* are assigned to individuals on the basis of factors over which the individuals do not have any control, such as their sex or age. The positions of boy or girl, old or young, are examples of ascribed positions. *Achieved positions* are accorded largely on the basis of individual achievement. The superintendent of schools or a professor in a university are examples of achieved positions. Achieved and ascribed positions are, however, "ideal types." In practice the positions one encounters consist of some mixture of the two types. The position of superintendent of schools, for example, may be regarded as an achieved position, but (due to unfortunate prejudices in society) such ascribed characteristics as sex (male) and race (white) may be virtual prerequisites for the position.

While it is generally agreed that a social role is defined by a set of behavioral prescriptions, there are three common operational definitions of role used in research on role theory (Deutsch and Krauss, 1965). The first, *prescribed role,* consists of the set of expectations that occupants of complementary positions or individuals who observe and react to a person's position have toward his behavior. The second may be termed the *subjective role* and consists of those specific expectations the occupant of a position perceives as applicable to his own behavior when he interacts with the occupants of complementary positions. The third, *enacted role,* consists of the specific overt behaviors the occupant of a position engages in when he interacts with the occupants of some other position. Under most conditions the correlation between the three operational definitions is quite high; that is, the prescriptions of others are clearly communicated to the occupant of a position, who accepts and internalizes those prescriptions, and behaves in a way that is consistent with the prescriptions. There are times, however, when, due to a lack of communication or the deliberate violation of the prescriptions by the position occupant, there is a discrepancy between the actual and expected behavior.

The concept of social role has been for two decades one of the most central concepts in the behavior sciences. It serves to link sociologists, who focus on analysis of social systems; anthropologists, who study comparative social structures; and psychologists, who examine the effects of social structure upon the personality. As such, it is a uniquely social psychological concept. Its promise, however, has not as yet fully borne fruit. Although the concept of social role has proven to be a very useful frame of reference for examining organized social behavior, it is an ambiguous concept which has never been clearly defined. In addition, there is a great deal of confusing research in the field of role theory. A promising beginning of refining role theory has been begun by Biddle and Thomas (1966), but it is too early to tell what effect their reformulation of role theory will have upon the field.

For the purposes of this book, however, role theory can be used quite fruitfully as a conceptual framework to diagnose what happens within a school and within a classroom. The central question for evaluating role theory is whether it helps one to deal with the world in a way that one was not able to not knowing the theory. That is, do people who know the theory function better than people who do not? If the answer is yes, then the theory, on one level, is good.

Interpersonal Expectations and Role Theory

There are two features of interpersonal expectations that are important for understanding the concept of social role: the anticipatory nature of expectations and their normative quality (Secord and Backman, 1964). A person's behavior is usually contingent upon his anticipation of how others will react toward him. He has, therefore, definite expectations concerning the behavior of the person with whom he interacts. When one tells a joke, he anticipates that the other will have a favorable reaction; when one gives an order, he anticipates that it will be obeyed. This anticipatory quality of interaction is important because it guides the behavior of an individual. He anticipates how the other person might react to his various actions and shapes his behavior accordingly. One's anticipations about the other person's behavior are based upon subtle cues provided by his appearance, by the person's previously known and current behavior, and by the situational context within which interaction takes place.

When interaction is frequent or when the situational context is such that it is highly important for each party to behave in a predictable and interdependent way, well-established expectations arise that have an obligatory, normative quality. The other person is not only expected to behave in a certain way, it is felt that he *should* or *ought* to behave in a certain way.

A person in a position not only anticipates the behavior of individuals in complementary positions, he feels that the others are *obligated* to behave in accordance with his anticipations. This is be-

47

BOX 3.1   THE NATURE OF THEORY

A theory is based upon concepts, facts, and laws (Broad-beck, 1963). To state a fact (for example, an IQ score) is to state that a concept (for example, IQ) has an instance or a number of instances. When a fact is connected with other facts, a generalization or law is formed. Laws, whether quantified or not, have a certain form, expressed either by the verbal "if . . . then . . ." or by an equation. A law states that whenever there is an instance of one kind of fact, there is also an intance of another (for example, if a child has a high IQ, then he will learn to read well, given the motivation, an adequate self-concept, and a supportive classroom setting). A law is always an empirical generalization.

A theory can be defined as a deductively connected set of laws. Certain of the laws are the postulates of the theory. Their truth is assumed so that the truth of other empirical assertions, called theorems, can be determined. For a brief discussion of deduction see Chapter 1.

In the behavioral sciences theory serves two basic functions, a goal function and a tool function (Marx, 1963). The *goal function* of theory is to integrate and order existing empirical laws or facts; theory unifies and systematizes knowledge in ways that summarize and integrate all known facts about the area. A theory is a way of looking at pieces of knowledge in order to make some kind of sense out of them. Individual facts, when looked at one by one, often have little or no value. When the pieces are put together and connected in some pattern or theoretical framework, however, they become understandable and useful. Without a theory, however provisionally or loosely formulated, there is only a miscellany of observations, having no significance. The more ill-defined the theory, the more vague and uncertain is the significance it confers or the data. In every chapter in this book some sort of theory is presented. Some of the theories are very loosely defined, others are quite precise. In reading these theories one should evaluate how well they summarize and integrate the knowledge in the area.

The *tool function* of theory is to generate new predictions or insights into the area that would not otherwise occur. In this way theory suggests, stimulates, and directs new research.

> The more successful the predictions a theory makes in a variety of social contexts, the more powerful the theory. Science makes its greatest advances when it arrives at theories that neatly summarize many observations and predict accurately what can be expected to happen in new situations.

cause the others are assumed to share common role expectations with him. Role expectations, therefore, are normative, and, in varying degrees, a position occupant is disturbed if the other person does not conform as expected.

The Role Structure of the Classroom

Each classroom is a separate subsystem within the school. The classroom traditionally has had two positions—teacher and student. These positions are complementary in that they are interrelated, reinforce each other, and are interdependent. Each cannot function without the other. The teacher is a person who teaches students; students are persons who learn with the aid of a teacher. It is within a series of such relationships that the transformation of the student from an uneducated child to an educated adult takes place.

Successful completion of the school's objectives depends upon the fulfillment of the organizational role requirements. The process of fulfilling the role requirements of teacher or students is the process of learning the expectations of others, accepting, and fulfilling them (Katz and Kahn, 1966). In a classroom the student learns what is expected of him by the teacher, accepts those expectations as legitimate, and fulfills them to the best of his ability. Although the flow of role expectations goes two ways, the greatest degree of influence lies in the downward communication of role expectations in a hierarchy. It is, therefore, the expectations the teacher has toward the role behavior of the students that carries the most weight in the classroom. In order for the students to function effectively in their roles, the teacher's expectations must be clearly communicated, the students must be motivated to accept the expectations as legitimate and as something they wish to conform to, and the students must

49

understand what they have to do to fulfill the role expectations. It is not always the case that students do understand what is expected of them. For example, in many classrooms teachers act as if they expect all students to be striving for an "A" in the class. There are students who would be satisfied with a "C" but do not understand just exactly what they have to do in order to obtain it.

The reliability of role behavior is an intrinsic requirement of any organization. Every organization faces the task of somehow reducing the variability, instability, and spontaneity of individual acts. In a classroom, therefore, both the teacher and the students must fulfill their role requirements reliably. A classroom where the teacher and the students engage in individual, spontaneous acts that differ from day to day and from hour to hour would be complete chaos. In order to coordinate the behavior of the teacher and the students in ways that accomplish the school's objectives there must be reliability in student and teacher behavior. This does not mean, however, that there is no room for spontaneity and divergent behavior in the classroom.

In discussing the structure of the classroom it should be noted that within the classroom there are numerous activities which must take place in a limited amount of time. Jackson (1968), for example, states that the elementary school teacher engages in as many as 1000 interpersonal interchanges each day. There are, in addition, a number of activities that have to take place with numerous students in a limited amount of time in the elementary classroom. It is the crowded condition of the classroom and the press of time that keeps the teacher so busy. In such a situation reliability of role behavior (that is, the conformity of students to the role expectations of the teacher) serves as the major source of control to avoid chaos and to accomplish the school's goals. In addition, the time pressures, the crowded conditions, and the fast pace of classroom life all interfere with the teacher's freedom to analyze, evaluate, and modify what is happening within the classroom.

Finally, most classrooms are fairly isolated from one another, which, among other things, limits the amount of communication possible between teachers. It is a unique school in which teachers discuss their classroom problems, techniques, and progress with one another and their principal (Chesler, Schmuck, and Lippitt, 1963). In most schools teachers practice their own methods, rarely hearing, or even caring, if one of their colleagues is experimenting with some new teaching device or technique.

The Teacher as a Bureaucrat

Since the school is a bureaucratic organization it follows that the teacher is a bureaucratic functionary (Brickell, 1964; Wayland, 1964; Miles, 1964b). The record-keeping, the supervision of the use of standardized instructional materials, the presentation of cognitive information in highly ritualized ways, the official time-keeping, and the control over classroom supplies all represent bureaucratic teacher role expectations. Since the teacher is a low-level bureaucratic functionary his ability to influence school policy or initiate change within the school as a whole is usually very small. His ability to resist change, however, is quite large. Most teachers perceive themselves to be professionals, and they resent and resist having an administrator tell them how to conduct themselves in their classrooms. Given this resistance to directives on how to teach, and the low visibility of the teacher's classroom behavior (i.e., teachers are rarely observed by anyone except their students), teachers are not only unreceptive to directives to change but often do not carry out directed changes within their classrooms.

It is a myth, however, that the teacher is an autonomous being in his classroom. The bureaucratic requirements, the control over instructional materials by the national educational system, the evaluation of performance by state and national achievement examinations, all influence and restrict the teacher's behavior within his classroom. Perhaps the only two areas in which teachers can readily innovate are the mode of presentation of materials and the way in which the teacher relates to the students. Even at this level, however, studies show that teachers usually are not innovators (Pellegrin, 1966).

The Teacher's Classroom Role

There have been several discussions of the role of the teacher in the classroom. Beck and his associates (1968) state that in the classroom the teacher has three major role behaviors that relate to the four major types of decisions teachers are called upon to make. The three teacher role behaviors are: (1) putting students in contact with subject matter, which may be accomplished through lectures, assigned readings, programmed learning, films, educational TV; (2) mediating between curriculum plans and the students in order to stimulate the best involvement of each individual student in the materials presented; and (3) creating specific classroom conditions, that is, the classroom environment and the normative structure. These three role behaviors relate to the major decisions teachers are called upon to make. First, the teacher must be able to select from broad school purposes and subject-matter goals a set of specific instructional objectives that he will pursue with a given class. Second, once goals are clarified, the teacher must be able to select learning experiences that will maximize the possibility of achieving those objectives. Third, the teacher must decide on the organization of learning experiences over time and the relationship of activities in subject areas at any given time. Finally, the teacher must decide on how to evaluate pupil performance, when to evaluate, and how to use the evaluation data to improve learning and teaching.

In an earlier discussion, Amidon and Hunter (1966) define teaching as an interactive process, primarily involving classroom talk, which takes place between the teacher and the students and occurs during certain definable activities. The teaching activities that they recognize and that are, therefore, the role behaviors of the teacher, are: motivating the students, planning for classroom activities, informing students, leading discussions with students, disciplining students, counseling students, and evaluating students. These are classroom activities that directly involve the teacher with the students. Teachers also participate, however, in a wide variety of professional acts that do not directly involve them with pupils, such as planning outside the classroom for teaching, meeting with parents, joining in staff meetings, and engaging in community affairs.

The work of Amidon and Hunter (1966) is based upon the research on Flander's Interaction Analysis for observing the direct and indirect use of teacher influence in the classroom (Amidon and Flanders, 1966; Amidon and Hough, 1967). Direct influence consists of stating the teacher's own opinion or ideas, directing the pupil's action, criticizing his behavior, or justifying the teacher's authority or use of that authority. Indirect influence consists of soliciting the opinions or ideas of the pupils, applying or enlarging on those opinions or ideas, praising or encouraging the participation of pupils, or clarifying and accepting their feelings. The results of the research basically support the notion that teacher flexibility in the use of direct methods of influence in the classroom is highly predictive of teacher success in terms of student achievement. The teachers of classes in which achievement is above average differ from the teachers of below-average classes in their ability to shift their behavior, as it is necessary, from direct to indirect use of influence. The relatively ineffective teachers do not use the social skills of communication that are involved in accepting, clarifying, and making use of the ideas and feelings of students. The effective teachers have these skills, even though they are not in use a major portion of the time. Although they are used sparingly, they are effective when needed.

Jackson (1968) states that in the elementary classroom, the pressure of numbers and time force the teacher to fulfill the role of traffic cop, judge, supply sergeant, and timekeeper, or to delegate these responsibilities to the students. That is, as teaching commonly involves talking, the teacher acts as a gatekeeper or traffic cop who manages the flow of the classroom dialogue. It is the teacher who decides who will speak and in what order: in a class or group discussion the teacher calls upon certain students to answer questions and recite in class and ignores other students. Second, the teacher serves as a supply sergeant by deciding how the material resources and the classroom space are going to be used and by whom. If Johnny and Beth both want the pair of big scissors, or to look through the microscope, or to use the pencil sharpener, the teacher must decide who will use what in what order. Closely related to the job of distributing material resources is the third role of the elementary teacher, that of judge, or the person who grants special privileges to deserving students. There are many small jobs that have to be done in the classroom, such as handing out materials, cleaning the blackboards, or serving on the safety patrol. The teacher is usually the one who decides who will have these special privileges. Finally, the teacher serves as an official timekeeper by deciding when the various classroom activities begin and end. In many schools the teacher is assisted in time-keeping by an elaborate system of bells and buzzers. The teacher, however, is still responsible for watching the clock in his classroom.

When one looks at the role of college professor much of the above discussion holds. There are, however, a few additional comments that might be made. As teaching machines are used to communicate facts, and educational television brings the best lectures to more students, college professors may have to become good discussion leaders and tutors rather than lecturers. In addition, it may be their responsibility to facilitate the students' development of an inquiry process, a thinking process, which can be used to deal with problems they will face after being graduated. Finally, the college professor must be proficient in his academic area and in the inquiry process to adequately evaluate the work of his students.

Much of the above discussion of the teacher's role is based upon a combination of logical analysis and direct observation of what teachers actually do in the classroom. Smith and Geoffrey (1968) have formalized the process of combining educational theory and observations of educational practice to build theories about the educational process. The diagram in Figure 3 illustrates their point of view. The approach taken by Smith and Geoffrey, which they call microethnography, consists of direct observation of the classroom by a social scientist who uses educational theory to shape his observations into conceptual order. He then builds a model or a theory about what actually happens in the classroom. This theory can then be tested by verificational research, revised on the basis of the findings, and used to train teachers and other educators. In terms of this framework, the discussions of the teacher's role presented in this chapter have moved only to step three, constructing a model from combining educational theory and observations of what actually takes place in the classroom. The point of view represented by Smith and Geoffrey would state that such models should be subjected to a program of research to establish their validity. Hopefully, future research will clarify what teachers *are* and *should be* doing in the classroom. The point of view of this book is that the research should focus upon discovering the conditions under which different approaches to teaching are effective with different types of students. A teacher should have several alternative definitions of the teacher's role that can be applied under the appropriate conditions with the appropriate type of students. At the very least, a teacher should have at least one explicit model of teaching which he can discuss, evaluate, and modify as his experience dictates. Many of the later chapters in this book hopefully will provide some cognitive tools for building such a model.

The Teacher's Nonclassroom Role

In most schools teachers have a variety of nonclassroom role requirements, such as patrolling the halls, supervising the students in the cafeteria, and policing the playground. In addition, the role ex-

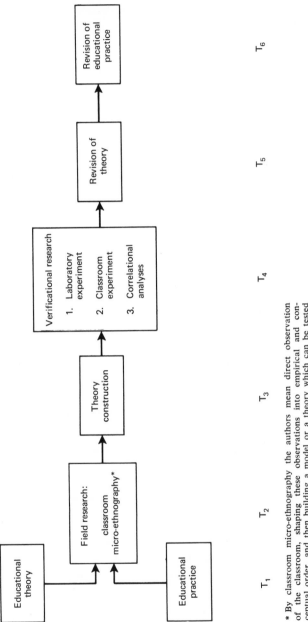

Figure 3.
A process model integrating educational research styles, M. SMITH AND WILLIAM GEOFFREY, P. 249. COPYRIGHT educational practice, and educational theory. FROM © 1968 BY HOLT, RINEHART AND WINSTON, INC. REPRINT-*The Complexities of an Urban Classroom* BY LOUIS ED BY PERMISSION OF HOLT, RINEHART AND WINSTON, INC.

* By classroom micro-ethnography the authors mean direct observation of the classroom, shaping these observations into empirical and conceptual order, and then building a model or a theory which can be tested by verificational research.

pectations of the teacher often do not end with the school day. The teacher's role is one that demands conformity and conventionality, not only in the classroom but even in the teacher's private life (Backman and Secord, 1968). Although the situation may be changing in the urban areas, parents, principals, superintendents, and school board members traditionally are especially sensitive to any suggestion that a teacher's behavior does not conform closely to society's mores, and are apt to make their disapproval known when they encounter deviant actions. Such pressures for conformity and conventionality serve to inhibit the creativity and innovation of the teacher. Any innovation that might appear to call for unconventional or unusual behavior will be resisted. Perhaps the freedom of the teacher to experiment with new behavior is especially limited, furthermore, when he is required to enforce school codes for dress, haircuts, and behavior that curtail individual expression among his students.

The Role and Personality of the Teacher

Role theory, up to this point, has treated the individual as fulfilling the role expectations of serveral different positions in different social systems. Such a characterization is incomplete, for a person is an integrated and coherent whole rather than merely the sum of a set of compartmentalized roles (Deutsch and Krauss, 1965), as illustrated by the fact that the behavior of a given individual will show a certain degree of consistency across different roles. The global term *personality* refers to such uniformities within the behavior of one individual. The personality one brings to a role determines the manner of its interpretation: the manic personality of one individual makes him an active, easily excitable teacher while the depressive personality of another individual makes him a passive, rarely excitable transmittor of information.

The relationship between role and personality is reciprocal. On the one hand, a person is apt to select roles that allow him to behave in a manner compatible with his personality. On the other hand, aspects of a role may be incorporated into a person's personality. There is evidence to support both positions. With regard to the selection of roles compatible with one's personality, there is some evidence to suggest that the personalities of American public-school teachers are compatible with the traditional role requirements of the position of a teacher. Davis (1964), for example, in a survey of over 33,000 seniors shortly before their graduation in June, 1961, found that 70 percent of the seniors choosing education as a career preferred to "work with people rather than things." Only the fields of nursing, social work, and clinical psychology surpassed this proportion. In such fields as physics, chemistry, and engineering, however, less than 20 percent preferred to "work with people rather than things." Rosenberg (1957) found similar results in a previous study. Teachers also score higher than the norms on personality traits such as sociability, friendliness, and personal relations(MacLean, Gowan, and Gowan, 1955). Lee (1963) found that college seniors shifting to science teaching score higher on social interests, sociability, and personal relations than those seniors continuing in science.

Not only is there evidence that teachers tend to be "people oriented," but they are conventional and conservative also. Davis (1964) found that education seniors described themselves as "conventional in opinions and values" to a greater extent than any other group in his study except nursing seniors. Strong (1943), on the basis of the responses of 238 female elementary-school teachers to the Vocational Interest Blank, reported that compared with adult women in general the teachers liked religious people, fashionably dressed people, teetotalers, and thrifty people. They disliked irreligious people, unconventional people, women who smoke, carelessly dressed people, foreigners, independents in politics, and people who take chances. Gowan (1955) in a summary of the research on teachers on the Minnesota Multiphasic Personality Inventory concluded that to a greater extent than the average individual, teachers (1) are responsible, conscientious, conforming, and friendly and (2) emphasize control of self and adaptation to the needs and demands of others.

From the above evidence it may be concluded that individuals with personality needs compatible with the teacher's role requirements (warm, valuing human relations and somewhat conventional and conforming in life style), opt for the vocation of teaching. It should be noted, however, that most of the evidence is correlational and, therefore, a causal relationship has not been established. The same findings could be explained as representing evidence that socialization into the teaching role results in personality changes that are compatible with the teaching role.

The values and attitudes associated with particular positions may themselves be incorporated into the structure of an individual's personality and thus exert a pervasive influence across the totality of his social interaction (Deutsch and Krauss, 1965). Kretch, Crutchfield, and Ballachey (1962), for example, in a discussion of a study by Waller (1932) on "What Teaching Does to Teachers," quote the following passage:

> There is first that certain inflexibility or unbendingness of person-ality which is thought to mark the person who has taught. That stiff and formal manner into which the young teacher compresses himself every morning when he puts on his collar becomes, they say, a plaster case which at length he cannot loosen. One has noticed, too, that in his personal relationships the teacher is marked by reserve. . . . As if this reserve were not in itself enough to dis-courage ill-considered advances, it is supplemented, when one has become very much the teacher, by certain outward barriers. . . . Along with this goes dignity . . . that consists of an abnormal con-cern over a restricted role and the restricted but well-defined status that goes with it. One who has taught long enough may wax un-enthusiastic on any subject under the sun. . . . The didactic manner, the authoritative manner, the flat, assured tones of voice that go with them, are bred in the teacher by his dealings in the classroom, . . . and it is said that these traits are carried over by the teacher into his personal relations. It is said, and it would be difficult to deny, that the teacher mind is not creative. . . . If these traits . . . are found among the generality of teachers, it is because these traits have survival value in the schools of today. If one does not have them when he joins the faculty, he must develop them or die the academic death. (pp. 501, 502)

Merton (1940) has noted, similarly, the effects of the bureau-cratic role upon the personality of the bureaucrat and McGregor (1960) and Argyris (1957) have noted that occupying a lower-level industrial position effects one's personality.

The interrelationship between personality and role was demon-strated rather dramatically by Abravanel (1962, in Brown, 1965), who showed that the personality perceived in behavior depends upon the role that is presumed to apply. Subjects listened to a recording of one end of a telephone conversation. Some were told that the speaker was a college student and some were told that he was the chairman of an academic department. The listener, who was never heard, was sup-posed to be a college instructor, either the teacher of the student or a member of the chairman's department. From the talk on the telephone one gathered that the talker was about to see the dean and expected to be asked about the instructor's teaching. "I'm afraid your teaching hasn't been . . ." said the talker. Afterwards subjects were asked to characterize the presumed student or the presumed chairman. The subjects characterized the student as being "aggressive, ambitious, and egotistical"; they characterized the chairman as "hesitant, compassionate, and indecisive."

Given the people orientation and conservatism of teachers' personalities, it may be hypothesized that teachers will accept innovations in educational practice that increase (1) the interpersonal rewards of working with people and (2) the contact with others, or that (3) are congruent with conservative values. The conservative values characteristic of many teachers are likely to contribute, moreover, to a general resistance to change and to a low motivation to modernize their teaching practices.

Role Conflicts

What happens when the principal of a school expects a teacher to be strict and domineering in the classroom and the students expect him to be understanding and democractic? What happens when some students want the teacher to allow quiet discussions during study periods and other students expect the teacher to enforce strict rules of silence? What happens when a quiet, meek teacher is expected to act like a lion? What happens when a teacher sees his own son misbehaving on the playground? The above instances are examples of role conflicts. Role conflicts can be divided into four major types: intrarole conflict, role ambiguity, personality-role conflict, and interrole conflict.

Intrarole Conflict

Intrarole conflict exists when the occupant of a position has incompatible or competing role expectations placed upon him by occupants of complementary positions. The teacher, for example, may be expected to handle student tardiness one way by the students and another way by the principal. Conflicting role expectations may be incompatible or competing. When expectations are incompatible, the behavior required by one is mutually exclusive of the behavior required by the other, as when the students expect the teacher to ignore student tardiness and the principal expects the teacher to report absolutely every instance of tardiness. When expectations are competing, the expected behaviors are not mutually exclusive but time limitations force the teacher to choose one over the other. That is, role expectations are competing when the teacher cannot adequately honor all the role expectations because of limitations of time, such as when the principal expects the teacher to take the tardy subject aside for counseling and the students expect the teacher to present a full period of lecture material.

Role Ambiguity

Role ambiguity refers to the situation where, within a set of complementary positions, there is a wide variation from person to person within each position regarding the role expectations of one of the positions. That is, expectations regarding the role of teacher held by complementary roles, student, principal, parent, and so forth may show considerable variation from person to person within each type of position. Snyder (1964), for example, reports from a study of teacher expectations held by a sample of midwestern parents that almost one fourth thought that the teacher absolutely must or probably should give specific attention to poor students even when it slows the progress of the rest of the class; at the same time, slightly over one half of the parents thought that the teacher should not do so.

Personality-Role Conflict

Getzels and Guba (1954) pointed out that one's personality can become a source of role conflict when a person is unable to fulfill the requirements of a role because the demands are incompatible with personal needs. For example, teachers who have little patience or are generally hostile toward others may be unhappy in their instructional role, or may be assessed as inadequate for teaching. The strong orientation of teachers toward people, furthermore, especially the need to be liked, may well be a source of role conflict when the teacher meets hostility and antagonism from students and parents (Backman and Secord, 1968). Jenkins and Lippitt (1951), for example, found that teachers strongly desire friendly relations with parents and pupils, but the parents and pupils appeared to be unaware of the teacher's need to be liked.

Interrole Conflict

An individual living in a complex society is a member of many different social systems within which he occupies a position with certain role expectations. Within a single day a man may perform the roles of husband, father, employee, customer, and club member. Interrole conflict occurs when the same individual occupies two competing or incompatible positions simultaneously.

Despite this multiplicity of roles, conflicts as to what is the appropriate role behavior to perform at any given moment in any one situation are infrequent. There are two reasons for this. First, individuals usually occupy positions successively rather than simultaneously. That is, the roles of husband and employee usually do not conflict because the individual occupies the positions at different times of the day. Second, easily discernable situational cues are usually available which will trigger the appropriate role behavior. That is, when one's wife walks into one's office, one assumes the role behaviors of husband; when the principal walks into one's office, one assumes the role behaviors of teacher. Charters and Newcomb (1952) conducted a study demonstrating that when confronted by a situation in which one could respond with one role equally as well as another, the situational cues that make one's membership in one social system more salient than one's membership in other social systems will determine which role one will assume. They identified students from a large psychology class who were members of the Roman Catholic Church. The Catholic students were divided into two groups, one experimental and one control. The members of the experimental group were informed that they had been selected to help construct an attitude scale relevant for members of the Roman Catholic Church. Membership in the Catholic Church was further emphasized by a discussion of the "basic assumptions which underly the opinions of all Catholics." The subjects in the control group had no knowledge that they had been especially selected for the study and in introducing the study no mention was made of its religious bearing. Both groups were then given a series of attitude statements of which only a small number were relevant to membership in the

Catholic Church. These statements were so worded that the students could respond to them as members of the Catholic Church or as members of a psychology class, or as members of other groups. The results indicate that subjects in the experimental group for whom saliency of membership in the Catholic Church had been experimentally enhanced responded to the "Catholic" items in a significantly more orthodox Catholic manner than did the control subjects.

In most instances individuals remain unaware of the "cross pressures" of various roles since they do not severely overlap. Under such conditions as catastrophes, however, the individual may find himself in the inevitable position of having to make a choice among his many group loyalties. Killian (1952) conducted a study of the reactions of persons in four southwestern communities to physical disasters like explosions and tornadoes, and found that conflicting group loyalties and contradictory roles were significant factors affecting individual behavior in critical situations. Workers, for instance, were faced with the conflicting demands of helping a friend or rushing home to help one's family, or working to save the plant. Such conflicts tended to be resolved in favor of one's primary groups, such as family and friends. There were, however, some exceptional cases in which the reverse was true, as where a state policeman ignored calls for help from his friends and neighbors in order to drive out of the community and summon help from surrounding towns. Killian concludes that such factors as feelings of responsibility or special training may predispose the individual to adhere to secondary-group demands even in a disaster. He states, furthermore, that an individual's actions in disasters involve the resolution of conflicts deriving from the prescriptions of roles that, under ordinary circumstances, have not been realized as potentially incompatible.

A classic example of where an ascribed role conflicts with an achieved role is seen in a study by Komarovsky (1946) of female students at Barnard College in New York City. She found that the cultural definitions of the ascribed female role and the college definition of the student role were incompatible. The female students interested in a professional career were "expected" to excel academically by their intellectually oriented peers and the faculty. Socially oriented peers and their families, on the other hand, expected the girls to concentrate on the "social graces" and pursuing a husband. Approximately 40 percent of the students in Komarovsky's study reported that on occasions they tried to resolve the conflict by concealing their intellectual abilities, which threatened their popularity with men. A follow-up study by Wallin (1950) concluded that the conflict between preparing for a career and pursuing a husband occurs primarily in women who face strong pressures to seek a career and who are also exposed to a strong tradition of male dominance.

Finally, another type of interrole conflict deals with conflicts between two ascribed roles, that of marginal men. A marginal man is a man who lives in two antagonistic cultures simultaneously. Members of the various minority ethnic groups in American society are examples of marginal men. Child (1943) studied the responses of second-generation Italian-American males to the conflicts between their Italian heritage and their American heritage. He noted three major types of response to the situation: those who reject the Italian background and emphasize "American" values and behavioral patterns, those who identify closely with the Italian community and reject Americans and American values and behaviors, and those who become apathetic or withdrawn in an attempt to deny the conflict.

Consequences of Role Conflict

There is little research on the consequences of role conflict. It is usually assumed, however, that role conflict reduces the teacher's satisfaction with his work and interferes with his effectiveness. Charters (1963) states that role conflict is probably disruptive, tension inducing, and, over a period of prolonged exposure, produces anxiety. He also feels that disagreement or conflict in role definitions is a form of occupational disadvantage, driving the more competent persons out of the ranks of teaching and leaving behind those who are the most compliant and submissive or those who are most able to tolerate ambiguity and cope with conflict. Katz and Kahn (1966) state that emotionally, a person who experiences a high degree of role conflict has a sense of futility about his role and attempts to withdraw from his co-workers. They also feel that when role conflict is intense job satisfaction will be low.

Resolving Role Conflicts

Each member of a social system is presented with a variety of role conflicts which interfere with his role performance. There are a number of both social systems strategies and individual strategies for dealing with role conflicts.

Social System Strategies

Organizations have various ways of reducing role conflicts among their employees, primarily through *structural arrangements* and by building mechanisms for reduction of role conflicts within the organization (Secord and Backman, 1964). One structural arrangement to reduce role conflict is the ranking of role obligations in a hierarchy of priorities so that the teacher has little difficulty in making a choice. Attending an inservice training program, for example, may be considered more important than conducting a class. Other structural arrangements for minimizing role conflicts are the differences in the power of various other roles to exert *sanctions*, restrictions on multiple-position occupancy, and spacial and temporal separation of situations in which role conflicts might occur. Teachers, for example, will usually fulfill their principal's role expectations before fulfilling their student's role expectations because the principal has greater power to exert sanctions than do the students. Most schools do not allow a teacher to have his own children as students in order to minimize the chance of a conflict between the teacher and the parent roles. Finally, through the physical and temporal separation of roles (that is, an individual is required to take the roles of parents and teacher in two different physical settings at different times of the day) role conflict is minimized. In small towns, however, teachers may still be expected to be in their roles twenty-four hours a day.

Organizations have various mechanisms for reducing role ambiguity and other types of role conflicts, such as formal channels of communication, liaison or coordinating committees, manuals of operation, training and indoctrination of new members, and rituals or ceremonies that reaffirm the rights and obligations of the organization's members (Secord and Backman, 1964). There are in addition several mechanisms to protect members particularly vulnerable to conflicting expectations from sanctions. In the school, for example, there are several norms and values which serve to protect the teacher. One is the norm of the privacy of the classroom; this insures that occupants of complementary positions other than students will not enter the classroom and place conflicting expectations upon or sanction the teacher. The organizational norm that one always supports the actions of one's subordinates in the authority structure is also a protective norm. A manager, for example, will never criticize a foreman in front of a group of workers. Similarly, fellow teachers and the principal are not supposed to criticize a teacher in front of his students, parents, or other community members. The tenure regulations in many schools protect the teacher in the exercise of her role against the sanction of dismissal. The values of academic freedom and the professionalism of teachers also provide teachers with greater leeway in the performance of their roles. One cannot force a teacher to behave in a way that violates his academic freedom, and the more one sees a teacher as a professional the more latitude one gives him to define his role. All of these norms and values serve to protect the teacher from role conflicts.

Individual Strategies

An individual may reduce role conflicts through holding certain orientations toward role conflict situations or through psychological defense mechanisms. In one of the classic studies in the social psychology of education Gross, Mason, and McEachern (1958) developed a systematic theory of intrarole conflict resolution, where an individual is subject to conflicting expectations concerning a single position. They interviewed 105 school superintendents who represented a 48 percent stratified random sample of all school superintendents in Massachusetts in 1952–1953. Four situations were presented to each superintendent, all representing problems with which all superintendents must deal and which were judged likely to arouse incompatible expectations from complementary positions on the basis of pretest data. The situations concerned: (1) the hiring and promotion of teachers, (2) the superintendent's allocation of his after-office hours, (3) priority the superintendent gives financial or educational needs in drawing up the school budget, and (4) salary increases for teachers. To take one situation as an example, in the case of teacher's salaries the following expectations were presented to the superintendents:

1. Expect me to recommend the highest possible salary increases for teachers so that their incomes are commensurate with their professional responsibilities.

2. Expect me to recommend the lowest possible salary increases for teachers.
3. Have no expectations one way or another.

The superintendents were asked to indicate which of the three statements most nearly represented what each of eighteen different groups, including local politicians, parents, teachers, taxpayers, school board members, and the superintendent's family, expected the superintendent to do in regard to teacher's salaries. They were then asked whether or not they felt that the expectations the others held were "legitimate." If different groups held incompatible expectations, they were asked what sanctions the groups could bring on the superintendent if he picked one of the other alternatives for dealing with teachers' salaries.

An individual who is faced with conflicting expectations A and B may choose one of four alternatives, he may conform to A, he may conform to B, he may choose to compromise by partially meeting both expectations, or he may attempt to avoid conforming to either expectation. Gross and his associates posited that the choice an individual makes in an intrarole conflict situation will be a function of three variables: the perceived legitimacy of the expectations, the perceived strength of the sanctions applied for nonconformity, and the orientation of the individual relative to legitimacy and sanctions.

First, Gross and his associates assumed that individuals are predisposed to conform to expectations that they perceive as legitimate and to avoid confirming to expectations that they perceive as illegitimate. An expectation is perceived as a legitimate obligation by an individual if he believes that the occupants of complementary positions "have a right" to hold such an expectation. Second, Gross and his associates assumed that individuals are predisposed to accept the expectations that they believe will result in the strongest negative sanctions if they fail to comply. Third, they assumed that individuals are different according to their primacy of orientation to the legitimacy or to the sanction aspect of the expectations. They posited three types of orientation to role expectations: (1) a person who gives primacy to the legitimacy dimension of role expectations is categorized as one who has a *moral* orientation to expectations; (2) a person who gives primacy to the sanction dimension of role expectations is said to have an *expedient* orientation; and (3) an individual who is predisposed to compromise and adopt a course of behavior that emerges from a balancing of the two would have a *moral-expedient* orientation. On the basis of their responses to a questionnaire the superintendents were classified into one of the three types. The interview data was then used to see how the superintendents did in fact act when faced with an intrarole conflict. The theory predicted the actual behavior (based upon the interview response) of the superintendents in 91 percent of the cases, which was taken as strong evidence to confirm the validity of the theory.

There are a number of psychological mechanisms that individuals can use to resolve role conflicts. Burchard (1954), for example, interviewed a number of military chaplains to find how they resolved the conflict between the warrior role of military officer and the nonviolent role of minister. He found four types of defense mechanisms being used: (1) rationalization, that is, "Someone has to carry the gospel to these boys"; (2) compartmentalization, that is, "Render therefore unto Caesar the things which are Caesar's and unto God the things that are God's"; (3) repression, that is, "I don't see any conflict"; and (4) withdrawal, that is, "I'd rather not talk about it." In an earlier study Cousins (1951) presented subjects with a role conflict in a contrived situation. The subjects were asked to assume the role of a student monitor pledged to enforce an unpopular curfew rule. They were then asked whether they would report or not report two student violators to the school authorities. The conflict in this situation is between the role of monitor and the role of student. After making their decision, the subjects were asked to select three reasons for their decision from a list of six. Persons who chose not to perform the prescribed role of monitor selected self-defensive mechanisms as reasons more frequently than did subjects who chose to enact the prescribed role of monitor. The self-defensive mechanisms chosen were rationalization, displacement, and wish-fulfilling fantasy. The subjects who chose to report the student violators, furthermore, accepted their own responsibility for the decision; those who chose not to report the students attributed responsibility away from the self.

Finally, Burchard (1954) and Getzels and Guba (1954) have suggested that where individuals are faced with conflicting expectations arising from occupying several positions, they are likely to resolve conflict by choosing certain roles over others. This suggests that the individuals have an established set of role hierarchies or priorities. Getzels and Guba have suggested two determinants of the relative position of a role in such an individual hierarchy, (1) the need structure of the individual and (2) the legitimacy of the role expectations.

Intuition versus Verified Knowledge: Performing the Teacher Role

Perhaps the most important aspect of how a teacher performs his role within the classroom is the basis upon which he makes the long-range and moment-to-moment decisions about what to do. Two bases for such decisions are the teacher's (1) intuition and common sense and (2) verified knowledge. These bases are often seen as contradictory while in actuality they are probably complementary. To discuss them it is necessary to review the basic deterministic assumptions of science. The basic assumption of the behavioral sciences is that behavior is a function of its antecedents. These antecedents can be discovered by the observation and analysis of empirical events. All the laws of human behavior are in principle susceptible of discovery. Once enough of them are known, human behavior can be predicted. And if enough of the determinants are manipulable, human behavior can be controlled. Much of human behavior is now unpredictable because its laws, though discoverable, are as yet unknown; but at some point in the future most (if not all) human behavior will be predictable and controllable.

In predicting and understanding human behavior, there are two somewhat independent but complementary problems. One has to do with the ways in which knowledge is acquired or discovered and the other has to do with the ways of verifying knowledge once it is discovered. Knowledge is most often acquired through intuitive processes. When operating intuitively within the classroom, for example, the teacher arrives at an answer to a classroom problem with little, if any, awareness of the process by which he reached it. By definition, when a person operates on an intuitive level he can rarely provide an adequate account of how he obtained his answer, and he may be unaware of just what aspects of the situation he was responding to.

Many teachers have deep insights into human behavior and operate quite creatively and effectively within the classroom using only their intuition. The complexities of the classroom situation and the crudeness of behavioral science knowledge make it essential that teachers develop their intuitive skills as highly as possible. The teacher should always keep upmost in his mind, however, that for every intuitive hunch that is correct there are hundreds that are false. But the deficiencies of speculative wisdom usually do not lie in their inaccuracy. They may be quite accurate. Their fault is that they give no adequate basis for knowing whether or not they are accurate. In order to advance knowledge one must verify his hunches to find out which ones receive empirical support.

To verify his intuitions the teacher must attempt to understand explicitly the relationships between the variables in the classroom situation (that is, apply the scientific method). He must bring together all the related bits of information which are available, place them within a conceptual scheme, and systematically analyze the determinants or causes of behavior under examination. Once he understands the causes of behavior, he can intervene to predict and modify student behavior within the situation. From such an explicit conceptualization, hunches can be either confirmed or disconfirmed on the basis of how useful they are in increasing the productiveness of both the teacher and the student within the situation.

The focus of this book is to provide the reader with a systematic knowledge of the social psychological theory and research that may be helpful in dealing with educational situations. Many of the following chapters deal specifically with variables such as self-attitudes, role expectations, and classroom climate which influence the behavior of teachers and students within the classroom. Hopefully such a presentation will provide the readers with a basis for conceptualizing educational situations in ways that can lead to the improvement of their functioning within educational organizations.

Applications to the Classroom

There are many ways in which knowledge of role theory makes it possible to function better in an educational organization. Awareness that role expectations are normative and that the process of role behavior involves learning the expectations of others, accepting them, and fulfilling them could reduce role conflict for educators. This is applicable to all roles within the educational organization, but this discussion will focus on teachers. A worthwhile activity for a teacher would be to consider his role in terms of his rights and obligations, realizing that his obligations are the rights of others and

BOX 3.2   THEORY, RESEARCH, AND GENERALIZATION
OF RESULTS TO APPLIED SITUATIONS

All the methods and techniques of social psychology are
designed to provide data to evaluate theories. The essence
of the dialogue between theories and findings is to broaden
one's understanding of "reality" and increase the range of
applicability of one's conclusions. That is, the purpose of
building and testing theories is to improve the generalization
of verified knowledge to practical situations. This is only
possible to the extent that one employs methods that provide
a good test of one's theories and good theories for guiding
one's pursuit of new data.

For the practitioner reading behavioral science theory and
research it should be kept in mind that research results are
never absolutely certain and, therefore, theories are never
forever fixed. No finding is sacrosanct and any theory is potentially subject to alterations when new data are available.
When theories and research findings are generalized to applied
situations, furthermore, the practitioner must remember that
it is not an absolute truth being generalized, it is a probability statement that given certain conditions, a relationship
between two variables may hold.

There are two major problems in generalizing research
findings to practical situations. First, since applied situations
are usually much more complex than research situations,
there is no way to tell for certain whether the necessary conditions for the desired relationship between two variables
are present or whether or not they are confounded by other
variables present in the complex applied situation that were
absent or controlled in the experimental situation. The second
problem comes from the characteristics of the subjects used
in the research. The important question here is how similar
they are to the persons to whom one wants to generalize the
findings. What is found to be highly probable behavior under
certain conditions for white, middle-class sophomores may or
may not be highly probable under the same conditions for
lower-class, nonwhite elementary-school students; only further
research can tell.

It is very difficult, therefore, to make specific generalizations
from social psychological research and theory to applied
situations, such as classrooms. The implications of social
psychological research for the classroom are hypotheses for

action that increases the educator's ability to deal with the interpersonal aspects of education.

In all of the chapters in this book there are inferences made about how the material presented can be applied to the classroom or school. At the end of many of the chapters there are specific sections dealing with classroom applications, which are included to make the book of value for practical use. One of the objectives of this book is to apply the research and theories of social psychology to the classroom, to make the tools of the social psychologist available to teachers. These tools are very powerful if the reader is able to build bridges between their present use in social psychology and their possible use in his own unique situation. Although many suggestions are made concerning the use of the tools, the creative and personal match of tool to situation is the responsibility of the reader. May your thinking be fruitful and productive.

that his rights are someone else's obligations. In the school, the teacher is in the important hierarchical position between students and the administration, with parents also involved, sometimes directly, sometimes through students, and sometimes through administration. When a teacher lists his rights and obligations, he does so in terms of students, administrators, and parents. It is very possible that when this is done there will be role conflicts that must be resolved for productive interaction within the organization. Under most conditions, such role conflicts cannot be effectively dealt with unless they are made overt. Once they are out in the open, strategies for dealing with them can be planned and implemented. This chapter discusses many of the possible strategies. Perhaps the most fruitful one, however, is to sit down with the administrators and students and negotiate a list of rights and obligations that are acceptable to both. Certainly it would improve the functioning of many classrooms if the rights and obligations of the students and the teacher were clear to every member.

SUMMARY

A useful conceptual framework for systematizing the myriad of events taking place within the school and within the classroom is role theory. The two central concepts of this theory are position and role. A position is a category of persons occupying a place in a given social relationship. The complement of concurrent positions of a given person is termed his position set. By role is meant the set of prescriptions defining what the behavior of the occupant of a position should be toward other related positions. The complement of role relationships a person has by virtue of occupying a particular position is termed his role set. Role prescriptions with a complementary role relationship specify the obligations and rights of a given position with respect to the complementary position; the obligation of one position being the rights of the other and vice versa. Three operational definitions of role can be designated: (1) prescribed role—the behavior expected of position occupants when interacting with other position occupants which is prescribed by the social system as a whole, (2) subjective role—specific expectations the occupant of a position perceives as applicable to his own behavior when he interacts with other position occupants, (3) enacted role—the specific overt behaviors of the occupant of a position when interacting with other position occupants. In most cases the correlation between these operational definitions is high, in that the prescriptions of others are clearly communicated to the occupant of a position, who accepts and internalizes those prescriptions, and behaves in a way which is consistent with the prescriptions.

Each classroom in a school can be considered a separate subsystem, the two basic complementary positions of which are teacher and student. The school's educational objectives are most effectively reached if the expectations the classroom teacher has toward the role behavior of the students are clearly communicated to the students, the students are motivated to accept the expectations and wish to conform to them, and the students have a good understanding of what they must do to fulfill these role expectations.

A general characteristic of the role of a teacher is its bureaucratic nature. Record-keeping, standardized instructional materials and evaluation procedures, and supply sergeant duties restrict a teacher's behavior and discourage much innovating. A number of authors have described the more specific activities which make up the teacher's role. Among these are putting students in contact with subject matter, motivating students, planning for classroom activities, disciplining students, evaluating students, and managing the general flow of classroom dialogue. Other researchers have investigated teacher influence in the classroom and have concluded that teacher flexibility in the use of direct and indirect methods of influence is highly related to student achievement.

An individual's behavior, however, is not completely determined by role expectations; each individual has a distinct personality that lends to a certain style and consistency of response across different roles. The relationship between role and personality in many cases is reciprocal. On the one hand, a person is apt to select roles that serve to gratify important personal needs. There is some evidence that individuals with personality needs compatible with the teacher's role expectations that require teachers to establish friendly relationships with others and to live conventional private as well as public lives, choose teaching as a career.

Implicit in the fact that one occupies a number of positions is the possibility that he will face conflicting role demands. Four types of role conflicts can be designated: (1) *intrarole conflict* occurs when the occupant of a position has incompatible and competing role expectations placed upon him by members of his role set. (2) *Role ambiguity* refers to the situation where, within a set of complementary positions, there is a wide variation from person to person within each position regarding the role expectations of one of the positions. (3) *Personality-role conflict* exists when a person is unable to fulfill the requirements of a role because the demands are incompatible with personal needs. (4) *Interrole conflict* occurs when the same individual occupies positions in two different groups which make contradictory demands upon him.

Social system strategies and individual strategies exist to resolve role conflicts. Structural arrangements that function to reduce role conflict are: ranking of role obligations in a hierarchy of priorities, differences in power of various other roles to exert sanctions, restrictions on multiple position occupancy, and spatial temporal separation of situations or roles. Individuals may decrease conflicting role demands by (1) holding certain orientations toward role conflict situations, such as giving primacy to either the legitimacy of expectations or the strength of sanctions applied for nonconformity, or (2) by utilizing psychological defense mechanisms such as rationalization, compartmentalization, repression, or withdrawal.

73

THE ROLE
OF THE STUDENT

The Student Role

Public elementary and secondary schools resemble so-called total institutions, such as prisons and mental hospitals, in that one subgroup of their clientele (the students) are involuntarily committed to the institution (Jackson, 1968). For the student, the school situation is one of forced membership, imposed goals and norms, an imposed task, and an imposed authority structure with a teacher playing a supervisory and administrative role. In order for the school to function effectively the students must take on the appropriate role behavior. Without student role compliance there is chaos and confusion. When, for example, a classroom is composed of a number of students who do not pay attention to the teacher, who threaten the teacher's control of the class, who refuse to do assigned work or even to follow directions, very little teaching or learning can take place.

In general, the role of the student is to adhere to the organizational norms of the school and to apply himself to the accomplishment of the objectives defined for him by the school. A student must defer to the teacher as the initiator of activity and as the source of authority in the classroom. He must often delay the satisfaction of immediate interests for the sake of long range goals. He is expected to be attentive, to follow directions, to work hard, and to follow the rules of social interaction prescribed by the teacher. The degree of the student's internalization of these role requirements affects their successful fulfillment and the consequent success of the student within the school. In discussing the students' role definition, however, it should be remembered that the schools do not always (and perhaps seldom) have the students' best interests at heart. There seems to be a growing suspicion by many behavioral scientists (including educators) that many schools operate in ways that are destructive of the students' individuality, self-esteem, creativeness, happiness, and mental health. When schools miseducate instead of educate, when schools operate against the self-interests of the students as individual human beings, then perhaps the most healthy response is for the students to refuse to meet their role requirements until the school makes some basic changes.

The school child performs a significant range of other roles in addition to the role of the student. The ascribed roles for boys and girls, for example, define different patterns of behavior for each at various age levels. Although there are no significant differences in intelligence between boys and girls, most studies show that boys represent about 75 percent of the stutterers, 70 to 80 percent of the slow readers, and a large majority of the dropouts in later school years (Beck et al., 1968). Other roles students may play are son, daughter, brother, sister, boyfriend, girlfriend, peer-group leader, and so on. These roles may or may not conflict with the role of the student at certain times.

In a recent book, Jackson (1968) developed a provocative discussion of the students' role in an elementary school after he observed individual classrooms in several different schools. The rest of this section is based upon his book. Briefly, he states that crowded conditions coupled with the necessity to accomplish many different activities in a short amount of time result in the development of capacities in students for ignoring interruptions and distractions, for delay in the fulfillment of their impulses, and for disengagement of their feelings. An additional pressure is the teacher's constant evaluation of the students' behavior and the differences in power between the students and the teacher.

Due to the lack of sufficient time to complete many different activities, students must learn to adhere to a strict time schedule. The result is often that activities begin before the arousal of interest and terminate before its dissipation. When the bell rings, for example, students must either come in from recess or take out their spelling books or stop working on drawings and begin reading depending upon established norms or specific instructions from the teacher.

Students are required to *ignore distractions and interruptions*, and be able to return to their work quickly after their attention has been drawn elsewhere momentarily. In addition, they are required to ignore those who are around them. For example, the teacher may take a small group of students off into a corner and have them read aloud while the other students work at their desks; the ability to "tune out" the reading group and work independently of direct teacher supervision is a prerequisite for working productively at one's desk. Students, then, must behave as if they were alone, when in fact they are not.

One of the inevitable outcomes of being in a classroom is the experiencing of *delay*. Students are forced to take turns, forced to work in groups whose progress toward goals may be the speed of the slowest member, and forced to prepare for a future that is several years away. Much of students' time is spent in waiting— waiting in line for lunch, recess, dismissal, water, and the like. They also wait for the teacher to give them permission to talk, recite, get a library book, receive a grade for their work, and so forth. The denial of desire is the ultimate outcome of many of the delays occurring in the classroom. When considered by themselves, most of these denials are psychologically trivial, but when considered cumulatively their significance increases. Part of learning how to function successfully in school involves learning how to give up desire as well as how to wait for its fulfillment.

If students are to face the demands of classroom life with equanimity they must learn to be *patient*. This means that they must be able, at least temporarily, to disengage their feelings from their actions. It also means that when conditions are appropriate they must be able to re-engage feelings and actions. They must wait patiently for their turn to come, but when it does come they must still be capable of zestful participation.

When the student enters the classroom his achievements, or lack of them, become official and a semi-public record of his progress gradually accumulates. A student must learn to adapt to the continued and pervasive *spirit of evaluation* that will dominate his school years. Evaluation is an important fact of life in the classroom; tests are as much a part of the school environment as are pencils, paper, and textbooks. Learning how to function successfully in a classroom, furthermore, (that is, the successful adoption of the student role) involves learning how to witness and occasionally participate in the evaluation of others as well as learning how to handle situations in which one's own work or behavior are evaluated.

Jackson states that, in regard to evaluation, the student has three jobs. First, he is to behave in such a way as to enhance the likelihood of praise and reduce the probability of punishment, he must learn how the reward system works in the classroom and use that knowledge to increase the flow of rewards to himself. Second he learns to try to publicize positive evaluations and conceal negative ones. Third, he must learn to win the approval of two audiences at the same time, the teacher and his peers; that is, how to become a good student while remaining a good guy. Most students learn that rewards are granted to those who conform to the expectations of the teacher.

Another feature of classroom life to which the students must become accustomed is the difference in *power and authority* between himself and the teacher. Among other things, this involves paying attention to the teacher. At the heart of the teacher's authority is his command over the student's attention. Students are supposed to attend to certain matters while they are in the classroom and much of the teacher's energies are spent in making sure this happens. At school the child must learn how to look and listen. The teacher, in other words, is the student's first "boss." It is expected that children will adapt to the teacher's authority by becoming "good workers" and "model students." The ability to comply with educational authority if transferred to many out-of-school settings, such as employment organizations, is important.

The crowds, the praise, and the power that combine to give a distinctive flavor to classroom life collectively form a hidden curriculum that each student (and teacher) must master if he is to make his way satisfactorily through the school. These demands make up the organizational role requirements that must be learned. The reward system of the school is linked to success in both the organizational and the academic curricula, indeed, many of the rewards dispensed are really more closely related to the mastery of the organizational curriculum than to the academic curriculum. For example, in many schools students are given credit (rewards) for "trying"; by "trying" is not meant academic achievement, but rather conformity to the organizational requirements that define the "model student." In schools, as in prisons, good behavior pays off.

A student, therefore, becomes "school-wise" or "teacher-wise" when he has discovered how to respond with a minimum amount of pain and discomfort to the demands, both official and unofficial, of classroom life. Often this is focused on the organizational curriculum; teachers express more anger about violations of role regulations and routines than about signs of intellectual deficiencies. Factors that affect the child's being able to adapt successfully to the role requirements of the school include general intelligence, personality, and cultural background—children able to conform to the attitudes and values necessary for success in school make out better than those who cannot.

Psychological Success and Failure

Several theorists (Lewin et al., 1944; Argyris, 1964a, for example) have stated that the experiencing of psychological success or psychological failure is a major factor in determining one's self-esteem, involvement in learning, commitment to role performance, and level of aspiration. Psychological success is defined as being dependent upon the following (Lewin et al., 1944):

1. The person is able to define his own goals.
2. The goals are related to his central needs and values.
3. The achievement of the goals represents a realistic level of aspiration for the person.

As the student is forced to attend school, forced to work on imposed tasks toward imposed goals one could hypothesize that there is little opportunity within a school to experience psychological success and a great deal of opportunity to experience psychological failure. Within most classrooms students are able to define their own goals only within very narrow limits and the goals are by and large not related to the students' central needs and values but are future-oriented toward preparing the students to function adequately in adult roles. Middle-class children seem to be able to make the best of a bad situation and function reasonably well within the school, buying the idea that being a good student will mean one will have a better life in the distant future. As lower-class children often do not see education leading to future rewards (Coleman et al., 1966), their behavior is frequently a completely different matter.

An individual seeking psychological success will need a situation in which he can experience a significant degree of (1) self-responsibility and self-control—in order to define his goals, (2) commitment—to persevere to achieve his goals, (3) productiveness and work—to achieve his goals, and (4) the utilization of his more important resources—in order that the accomplishment of his goals seems like a challenging but realistic level of aspiration (Argyris, 1964a). When the situation does not meet these standards, the probability is that the person will be experiencing psychological failure.

Little work has been done on the consequences of experiencing psychological failure on the behavior of students. Argyris, however, has conducted some research on the consequences of psychological failure in economic organizations. His primary finding is that when workers are experiencing psychological failure they engage in a variety of antagonistic adaptive activities against the organization. Examples of such activities are (1) psychological withdrawal, characterized by a lack of involvement in or commitment to what they are doing; (2) absenteeism and turnover; (3) aggression against those responsible—in a school this can take the form of refusing to learn, refusing to cooperate with the school, destruction of property, cheating, discipline problems, absenteeism, tardiness, discourteousness, and so on; (4) lowered level of aspiration; (5) alienation; and (6) asking for increased compensation for the degree of dissatisfaction, tension, and stress experienced—the greater the dissatisfaction, the greater the rewards demanded. Argyris provides evidence, furthermore, that the more the rigidity, specialization, tight control, and directive leadership the worker experiences, the more he will tend to engage in the above antagonistic, adaptive activities.

Thus one could predict from Argyris' work that the more rigid the structure of the school, the tighter the controls placed upon students, the more directive the leadership of the school personnel and the more the psychological failure the student experiences, the greater will be his tendency to develop adaptive activities which are antagonistic toward the school.

Variables Affecting Student Role Performance

There are several variables that affect the way in which students perform their roles. Two of these variables—achievement motivation and self-attitudes—will be examined in depth in the next two chapters.

Implications for the Classroom

Every teacher wants a successful, quiet, democratic, busy, controlled classroom, but there are difficulties in achieving this image. The classroom is often democratic only in that the teacher has thirty-one votes and each of the thirty students has one vote. Whenever the students want a majority, all they have to do is sway one of the teacher's votes. It is also true that teachers expend more energy and anxiety over classroom management and discipline than they do over the cognitive and affective growth of their students. Related to Chapter 3, the student's obligations are often reviewed, but their rights (the other side of the coin) are not considered.

One of the most useful "bridges" to the classroom from this chapter is the concept of the "psychological success or failure" of the student. Psychological success is more likely when the student can define his own self-related goals with realistic aspiration levels. One of the primary goals of the school has to be independence in terms of self-reliance, self-control, and self-esteem. Any student who continues to rely on teachers and the school to define his learning goals and any teacher who does not allow students to define their learning goals is in trouble. Many are.

It is not practical in terms of the system to give students complete freedom to choose their own goals from kindergarten on, but it is possible to continually and carefully widen the parameters so that more and more possibilities are available for choice. Giving the student a stake in his learning and entertaining an environment which encourages student initiative will go far toward encouraging psychological success. In a classroom where a student can experience only psychological failure the teacher will have to continually increase the student's rewards to obtain his cooperation and conformity. Many teachers are breaking their backs creating rewards great enough to do so. According to Lewin's theory, increasing the students' chances for psychological success lessens the necessity for large rewards, thereby making teaching an easier life.

SUMMARY

The role of a student in American schools today consists of many facets. Not only is he expected to perform well academically, but he must conform to certain implicit organizational role requirements if he is to make his way satisfactorily. He must obey the commands of teachers for his attention and shift his involvement from one activity to the next according to a strict time schedule. A student is forced to deny immediate desires for later rewards in a number of situations. And he must be constantly concerned with behaving in such a way as to obtain the favorable evaluation of both teachers and peers. Under the conditions of imposed tasks and goals in the schools, students are likely to experience psychological failure. In addition, the general inability to define their own goals, and thus the high probability that these goals are not related to their central needs and values, could lead to students becoming alienated, lowering their levels of aspiration, and refusing to cooperate with school authorities.

CHAPTER 5

SELF-ATTITUDES AND ACADEMIC ACHIEVEMENT

Symbolic-Interactionist Theory of the Self

When a child is born he has no sense of self. It is during the first two or three years of his life that he develops a kind of crude self-aware-ness, such as being able to make distinctions between what is part of his body and what is part of something else, and it takes many more years before full adult self-awareness comes into being. Self-attitudes develop through social interaction and as the child interacts with objects and persons he comes to perceive himself as an object sep-arate and distinct from other objects and other persons (Lindesmith and Strauss, 1968). In the process of interaction with other people the child begins to recognize that others react to him in certain ways and he begins to react to his own actions and personal qualities as he expects others to react. He learns to think of himself as having characteristics that are perceived by others. To give an oversimplified example, a child who is perceived by those he has contacts with as "bright" will begin to expect new acquaintances to react similarly, and will consider himself bright. This emerging capacity to take the point of view of others and to see oneself as an object, gives rise to beliefs and attitudes about oneself, in short, a self-concept. George Herbert Mead (1934) states:

> The self arises in conduct, when the individual becomes a social object in experience to himself. This takes place when the individual assumes that attitude or uses the gesture which another individual would use and responds to it himself or tends to so respond. . . . The child gradually becomes a social being in his own experience, and he acts toward himself in a manner analogous to that in which he acts toward others.

In noting that a person's evaluation of himself is determined by the way he thinks other people judge him Cooley (1902) developed the concept of "the looking-glass self."

> As we see our face, figure, and dress in the glass, and are interested in them because they are ours, and pleased or otherwise with them . . . as in imagination we perceive in another's mind some thought of our appearance, manners, aims, deeds, character, friends, and so on, and are variously affected by it. (p. 184)

The "looking-glass" or "reflected" self is a person's self-image, which is formed on the basis of perceiving how others react toward him.

To the extent that a person is able to take the role of others, he can respond to himself from their perspective and, hence, become an object to himself. In doing so the person can either take the role of specific people toward himself or take the generalized role of the community, group, or society toward himself. In this way, the attitudes of significant people and of the group become incorporated into the structure of the self.

The symbolic-interactionist theory of the self has been formalized by Kinch (1963) and is a good example of the way in which deductive reasoning can extend a theory. He defines the self-concept as the organization of qualities (traits that the individual might express in terms of adjectives—ambitious, intelligent; and roles in which he places himself—father, professor, and the like) that the individual attributes to himself. He defines three basic postulates of the formalized theory:

1. The individual's self-concept is based on his perception of the way others are responding to him.
2. The individual's self-concept functions to direct his behavior.
3. The individual's perception of the responses of others toward him reflects the actual responses of others toward him.

He notes that these postulates are not expected to hold under all conditions and defines four basic concepts or variables within these propositions:

1. The individual's self-concept (S). (Defined above.)
2. His perception of the response of others toward him (P). (The response of the individual to those behaviors of others that he perceives as directed toward him.)
3. The actual responses of others toward him (A). (The actual behavior of the others, that is, in response to the individual.)
4. His behavior (B). (The activity of the individual relevant to the social situation.)

By the use of simple logic it is possible to take the three basic propositions and deduce from them three more. For example, from postulates 1 and 2 we can conclude that the way an individual perceives the response of others toward him will influence his behavior, for if his perception determines his self-concept and his self-concept guides his behavior, then his perception will determine his behavior. In symbolic form:

$$\text{if } P \rightarrow S \qquad \text{postulate 1}$$
$$\text{and } S \rightarrow B \qquad \text{postulate 2}$$
$$\text{then } P \rightarrow B \qquad \text{postulate 4}$$

Therefore, the fourth proposition of the theory is:

4. The way the individual perceives the responses of others toward him will influence his behavior.

Similarly, from postulates 1 and 3 it is possible to deduce a fifth proposition and from propositions 3 and 4 it is possible to get a sixth proposition:

5. The actual responses of others to the individual will determine the way he sees himself (his self-concept).
6. The actual response of others toward the individual will affect the behavior of the individual.

The theory can then be summarized in the following statement: "The actual responses of others to the individual will be important in determining how the individual will perceive himself; this perception will influence his self-conception which, in turn, will guide his behavior."

The above theory is an excellent example of a formal theory. A formal theory consists of a set of well-defined variables and a series of logically (deductively) interrelated statements about the predicted relationships among the variables. The theory of the self presented above fulfills such a definition by having four basic variables and a series of six propositions about the relationships between them.

These propositions are not, however, the complete theory. For instance, while it is true that the individual's perception of the responses of others toward him form the basis of his self-concept the responses of some people will be more important than the responses of others in influencing the individual's self-concept. Thus, those people who are especially "significant" for the person (that is, his "significant others") will have a great deal of influence upon his self-concept, while the responses of others who are relatively insignificant for the person will have little influence.

The way in which the responses of others affect an individual's self-concept needs some further elaboration. The responses of one's associates do not automatically form one's self-concept. One must (1) accurately perceive how he is being responded to by others around him and (2) compare this reflection of self against a standard, a set of expectations that he and his "significant others" hold as to how he should behave and what characteristics he should have (Backman and Secord, 1968).

Complexity and Consistency of Self-Attitudes

Much of the research on the self-concept assumes that the self-concept is unidimensional; that is, the person has one major self-

---

BOX 5.1   DEFINING A CONCEPT

For many years the research and theory dealing with the self-concept was in a state of confusion due to different definitions given to the concept by different theorists. Many theorists, furthermore, did not point to any clear empirical reference in defining the self-concept. Although most of the conflicting and ambiguous definitions of the self-concept are not discussed in this chapter, a brief note concerning how one defines a concept is appropriate here. A concept is a definition of relatively overt aspects of experience (see Chapter 1). It names what is the same in different individuals or situations, a character which they all exemplify. There are two criteria for an adequate definition of a concept. First, it must be identifiable; that is, it must be defined so that we know when we do or do not have an instance of it and, therefore, it must be defined in terms of observable characteristics. Second, it must have significance, usefulness, meaningfulness. A concept is significant only when it enters into laws; that is, when it is correlated with other concepts, events, facts, and the like. When many other concepts and facts are related to or associated with a concept, it has significance. The more laws into which a concept enters, the more significant it is.

From this discussion it is evident that many of the social psychological concepts discussed in this book are not adequately defined. As social psychology develops as a field this situation will change, perhaps by refining many of the concepts now in use or perhaps by finding new concepts that "cut up" reality in more adequate ways.

---

concept that influences his behavior. This assumption is very questionable. Most theorists now agree that the self-concept is not a unitary conception, but consists of the symbolic representations a person has made to himself of his various characteristics, such as his physical, biological, psychological, ethical, and social characteristics (Deutsch and Krauss, 1965). The symbolic representations the individual has made, furthermore, usually include representations of things with which he has identified or is identified with, such as his actions, productions, memberships, and possessions (Deutsch and Solomon, 1959). In other words, a person has many different self-attitudes connected with such things as his physical and psychological characteristics and his possessions and actions. The implication of this for the school is that an individual's self-attitudes relating to achievement will be complex; instead of, or in addition to, a general conception of his academic ability he will have self-attitudes regarding the various subjects and requirements of the school. For instance, a student might think of himself as being very capable in math but poor in English, fairly good in social studies but inadequate in science, and so on.

The self-concept, therefore, consists of a complex set of elements which are organized into a systematic relationship. One way of characterizing this organization is in terms of self-consistency; the elements of the individual's self-concept are organized into a structure which is internally consistent (Deutsch and Krauss). In general, a consistent structure has the properties of a "good Gestalt"; it is made up of elements that are perceived as "belonging together." For example, if a child perceives himself as a highly motivated student and as being bright, he would also tend to see himself as a high achiever.

From cognitive balance theory (Heider, 1959) it is possible to predict somewhat what will happen when an inconsistent element is introduced into the structure. In general, inconsistent information will produce a change in a person's self-attitudes to the extent that it cannot be denied, repressed, or distorted in a way that makes it consistent. The change will then take place in the element that will result in the smallest change in the overall structure of the attitude. For example, if a child perceives himself as a highly motivated student and as being bright and is informed by the teacher that he has failed a major examination, he will change his self-attitudes in a way which will make them consistent with the test results (given that he cannot rationalize or deny his performance). He may decide that he is bright but unmotivated, or that he is motivated but not so bright. The way in which he restores consistency in his attitude structure will depend upon the minimal change necessary in order to do so.

The striving for consistency in the person's self-attitudes implies that he will strive to behave in ways that are consistent with his self-attitudes. If the child perceives himself as bright and motivated, he will strive to perform well academically; if, however, the child perceives himself as being stupid and unmotivated he will strive to perform poorly academically. In other words, events which coincide with self-expectancy are consonant and sought out; events which are contrary to self-expectancy are dissonant and are avoided or minimized.

Self-Attitudes and Academic Achievement

When one applies the self-concept theory of the symbolic interactionists to academic achievement, it is postulated that a child's self-attitudes concerning achievement in general and in specific subjects are acquired during interaction with significant others who hold expectations of the child as a learner. This postulate is supported by a variety of studies (Rosen, Levinger, and Lippett, 1960; Clarke, 1960; Staines, 1956; Davidson and Lang, 1960; Videbeck, 1960; Helper, 1960). Brookover (1962), for instance, in a study of seventh grade children, found that a student's self-concept of ability is positively related to the image he perceives parents, teachers, and peers hold of him.

The second postulate is that one's self-attitudes concerning achievement function to direct his academic performance. There is considerable correlational evidence that self-attitudes and academic achievement are related. Bodwin (1957) found the correlations between immature self-concepts and reading disabilities to be 0.72 for third-grade students and 0.62 for sixth-grade students. Shaw (1961) and Shaw and Alves (1963) report that bright underachieving males have more negative self-concepts than do students who are equally bright but achieving. Bledsoe (1964) found that fouth- and sixth-grade boys' self-esteem and academic achievement are positively correlated to a significant degree. Correlations for girls, however, were much lower and generally not statistically significant. Combs (1964) in a study exploring the way in which achievers and underachievers perceive themselves and their relations to the world around them, concluded that the underachiever fails to achieve because he lacks a feeling of personal adequacy and has a feeling of being rejected by his peers and adults. Passow and Goldberg (1962) conducted personal interviews with intellectually gifted achievers

BOX 5.2 REPLICATION OF RESEARCH

In this section the reader is confronted with brief yet detailed reports of dozens of researches that may appear to be unnecessarily repetitious, but in actuality are not. A very important aspect of scientific endeavor called *replication* is involved.

Complete induction is generally, if not always, a practical impossibility. At best only partial induction is possible in the testing (vertification or refutation) of hypotheses or the drawing of descriptive generalizations. The problem of induction is simply that complete verification of any hypothesis is impossible because even though all past observations may have been identical, the next instance may still be the exception to the rule. The fact that all elephants so far observed have been some color other than orange does not assure that the next elephant seen will not be orange.

Good research, then, is performed so carefully and described so completely by those reporting it that others can repeat or *replicate* the same investigation with different subjects under nearly identical conditions. Replication of specific research with the same results (or the "same" within the expectations of chance variations) is generally taken by the scientific community as further verification or *justification* of the matter under investigation. Replication with different results demands further explanation, or if there are contradictory results over several replications, the scientific community may interpret the whole lot as refutation of the matter under investigation.

Furthermore, near replications may be performed with only slight variations in order to demonstrate the precise conditions under which correlations vary or statistical laws hold with differing probabilities. Complex relationships among many contingent variables rarely come to be understood except after a long series of replications and near replications of intertwined researches. For this reason research should be both performed *and read* not in isolation but in maximum relation to as many other pertinent researches as possible. In fact, only in relation to other pertinent studies is the significance of any single research report likely to be apparent.

and nonachievers in the Evanston (Illinois) Township High School. The attitude toward the self was established and compared with achievement (measured by intelligence and academic grades). A "general" relationship was reported between underachievement and low self-concept.

Rosenberg (1965) conducted a study of self-attitudes among eleventh- and twelfth-grade students in ten New York public high schools. Subjects were randomly selected from categories that were stratified as to school size. The major aim of the study was to specify the bearing of certain social factors on the self-esteem of the student and to specify the bearing of certain social factors on significant attitudes and behaviors of which school achievement was one. He found a positive correlation between high school achievement and self-esteem. Hummel and Sprinthall (1965) did a study of bright adolescent boys from a suburban high school in which they held mental ability and certain social variables constant. Significant differences were found between underachievers and superior achievers on scales postulated to measure aspects of ego functioning. Mc-Kenzie (1964) in a study comparing over- and under-achievement with normal achievement on the clinical and validity scales of the Minnesota Multiphasic Personality Inventory found that underachievers tended to internalize their conflicts and were characterized as being impulsive, lacking long-range goals, and having low self-esteem.

Wattenberg and Clifford (1964) studied kindergarten children to see if there was any relationship between self-concept and reading progress. Mental ability and self-concept were tested, and two and one-half years later reading progress was measured and self-concept measures were repeated. To measure self-concept, tape recordings were made of remarks by the children while drawing pictures of their families and responding to an incomplete sentence test. Self-references were looked for among these remarks. Teachers and clinically trained observers rated the children as to feelings of competence and worth. The researchers found that kindergarten self-concept is significantly predictive of progress in reading, but that it was not significantly related to mental ability. Campbell (1966) in a study of self-esteem and achievement found a relationship between the two for the total group of fourth, fifth, and sixth grades in a suburban school. There was a more pronounced relationship for boys than for girls. The author concludes, however, that there was not a high enough correlation to predict achievement from self-esteem and intelligence.

Quimby (1967) tested the self-concept by a Q-sort method of achievers and underachievers who had been selected on the basis of grade point average. She found a relationship between low self-ideal and underachievement. She assumes that a student with the adequate self-concept, feeling that he can succeed, will put forth the necessary academic effort; the student with the inadequate self-concept, feeling that he cannot succeed, will not put forth the necessary academic effort. Williams and Cole (1968) found significantly positive correlations between self-concept measures and conception of school, social status at school, emotional adjustment, mental ability, reading ability, and mathematical achievement.

Finally, a study by Brookover and Thomas (1964) dealt with the correlation between the self-concept of academic achievement in general and in specific academic subjects. The children studied were 1050 white seventh-grade students, 513 males and 537 females, in an urban school system. An eight-item multiple-choice questionnaire was administered in two separate forms: (1) to measure the self-concept of ability in general and (2) to measure the self-concept of ability in four specific subjects—arithmetic, English, social studies, and science. Grade point averages in the four school subjects were used as an index of academic achievement. The intelligence factor, as measured by the California Test of Mental Maturity, was controlled. They found that there was a significant positive relationship between self-concept of ability and grade point average and that this relationship persisted even when measured intelligence was controlled. The correlation was 0.42 for boys and 0.39 for girls. High-achieving groups also had a significantly higher mean concept of ability than did the low-achieving groups with comparable measured intelligence scores. While findings indicated that specific self-concept of ability is a significantly better predictor of grade point average in math, social studies, and science for males, the same did not hold for females except in social studies.

There is, therefore, support for the postulated relationship between self-attitudes and academic achievement. As noted before, however, a correlational relationship does not indicate causation; academic achievement could cause positive self-attitudes just as positive self-attitudes could cause academic achievement, or they both could be caused by a third variable such as social class or the quality of past school experiences. Until a study clearly proves that the self-attitudes concerning achievement held by an individual significantly influence the level of his future performance, the question of causation will not be answered.

It should be emphasized that although the consistency of the relationship between self-attitudes and academic achievement found in different age levels and with different types of students provides reasonably solid evidence of a relationship between the two, the interpretation of such a relationship is always relative to the situation under which it was found and its size does not represent any absolute fact. Although it has been done above to summarize the existing research, it is absurd to speak of a general relationship between self-attitudes and achievement. One has to stipulate what type of self-attitudes, measured by what instruments, in what population, and to consider what kind of achievement, measured by what instruments, or judged by what standards. Always the correlation or size of the relationship between two variables is purely relative to the circumstances under which it was obtained and should be interpreted in the light of those circumstances. The implication of this is, while Brookover found a correlation of 0.42 for boys (controlling for ability) in the population he studied between self-attitudes and achievement, the correlation could be much higher or lower in other populations and under different conditions. What the studies reviewed have not demonstrated are the conditions under which the relationship between self-attitudes and achievement will be high and the conditions under which it will be low. In some instances it is clear. If the teacher, for example, knows that a student is an underachiever or if the student comes from a background that places him at a disadvantage in the school, the teacher can find out whether or not self-attitudes concerning achievement are contributing to the low performance through talking with the student or observing him. In other situations it might be much more difficult to determine whether raising a child's self-attitudes concerning his ability to achieve will appreciably raise his actual performance. *What is important for the teacher is to be able to diagnose when self-attitudes concerning achievement are affecting actual achievement in order to intervene in ways that will raise the self-attitudes of the student in question and, consequently, raise his actual achievement.*

Self-Fulfilling Prophecy and Self-Attitudes

A child believes that he cannot comprehend arithmetic. During arithmetic period, therefore, the child daydreams, worries anxiously about what will happen to him due to his inability to understand multiplication, and generally ignores the lesson and the assigned work. Because of his lack of study he fails the arithmetic examination. The child has just engaged in a self-fulfilling prophecy. The self-fulfilling prophecy is, in the beginning, a false definition of the situation that evokes a new behavior, which enables the originally false conception to come true (Merton, 1957).

Consider the case of two children coming to a new school at the beginning of the year. One child expects his new classmates to dislike and reject him and, therefore, he is very guarded and suspicious of his classmates, which, in turn, makes his classmates withdraw and look elsewhere for a friendly companion. "See," he might say, "I was right. I knew they'd reject me." The other student, however, comes to school expecting that almost everyone will be congenial, friendly, and good-natured; he initiates warmth and friendliness and, consequently, he finds his classmates to be all that he expected. Each of these children has engaged in a self-fulfilling prophecy.

A student's self-attitudes can readily lead to a self-fulfilling prophecy. A student who thinks he cannot learn to read may fulfill his own prophecy, a student who thinks he is unlikeable may find his subsequent behavior causing his expectations to be confirmed. For the teacher the problem is to be able to break the cycle of negative self-fulfilling prophecies and create positive self-fulfilling prophecies to increase the level of achievement of the students in the classroom. The way in which the vicious circle of the negative self-fulfilling prophecy is broken is by abandoning the initial definition of the situation that has set the circle in motion (Merton, 1957). When the original assumption is questioned and a new definition of the situation is achieved the circle is broken. When the student who thinks he is too stupid to learn to read changes his self-conception of his reading ability the self-fulfilling aspects of his self-attitude end.

Changing Self-Attitudes

There is, therefore, strong evidence that self-attitudes concerning achievement are related to academic achievement. There is not, however, evidence that having a positive self-concept "causes" the student to achieve well. But there is evidence (see below) that one may raise academic achievement by changing a student's self-attitudes.

Symbolic-interaction theory implies that, since self-attitudes are acquired during interaction with significant others who hold expectations of the student as a learner, self-attitudes may be changed by changing the expectations of the student as a learner of his significant others. There is, for example, strong experimental evidence that a person's self-attitudes in an experimental situation may be manipulated by information given to him by an experimenter. Deutsch and Solomon (1959) created self-attitudes concerning ability on an experimental task by telling some subjects that they performed exceptionally well on the task and telling other subjects they performed exceedingly poorly. Glass (1964) manipulated self-attitudes by giving subjects a battery of personality and achievement tests and feeding back information that they had performed at either a high level of personality maturity or at a low level. From these and many other similar studies it may be concluded that a person's self-attitudes are susceptible to change by receiving information *concerning the person's task performance or personality characteristics* from an authoritative or significant other.

There are a variety of ways in which a student's self-attitude concerning academic achievement may be changed in a school setting. Most of these involve modifying the images and expectations that existing significant others hold of the student's abilities. Of the three significant others involved—parents, teachers, and peers—Brookover (1962) found that parents were seen by the majority of the students he studied as being "most important in their lives" and "concerned with how well they are doing in school." Rosenberg (1963), furthermore, demonstrated that when parents manifested indifference toward their children, the children later exhibited low degrees of self-esteem. In his study of the relationship between self-attitudes and achievement, Brookover counseled parents of low-achieving, ninth-grade students in the need their children had for expressions of their parents' faith in their children's ability to achieve. In cases where the parents changed their evaluation and the change was apparent to the children, a gain in grade point average was shown by 42 percent of the children. This study demonstrates that parents can affect a student's self-attitudes and, thereby, raise his academic performance. One way in which a school can raise the self-attitudes of underachievers, therefore, is to enlist the aid of the parents and have them express positive expectations about their children's ability to perform well academically.

Another approach has been to offer intensive counseling to those students with low self-attitudes concerning their ability to achieve. Dolan (1964) conducted a study aimed at improving the scores in reading of junior high school students by changing their self-attitudes of their ability through intensive counseling over a six-month duration. The experimental and control groups were both randomly selected from a population that was characterized by high ability, low achievement, and low self-esteem. Subjects in the experimental group were given intensive counseling aimed at raising their self-esteem. All groups were then retested in regard to both reading and self-esteem. The experimental group made significant gains over the control group in both areas.

On the college level Dickenson and Truax (1966) demonstrated that group counseling can raise the achievement of underachieving students. Other studies of counseling, however, have not had such good results. For example, Winborn and Schmidt (1962), in a study of college level students, used short-term counseling to try to affect an improvement in grade point average in a group of underachievers. Following six group counseling sessions the experimental group's grade point average showed no change whereas the control group's had increased. On the high school level Broedal and his associates (1960) also found no change in achievement due to group counseling.

The expectations of the teacher can have a great deal of influence upon a student's self-attitudes and, consequently, upon his academic performance. In an unusually exciting and provocative but often criticized study, Rosenthal and Jacobson (1968) demonstrated the power of teacher expectations. Their study and other supporting evidence will be discussed in detail in Chapter 8. It should be stated here, however, that the teacher's expectations toward the child as a learner will not always affect the self-attitudes of the child. Under some circumstances they will and under other circumstances they will not. It seems reasonable to state that only when the child has a need for social approval from adults or when the teacher has a warm, trusting relationship with the child will the teacher's expectations have the most powerful influence upon the child's self-attitudes. Some students, such as lower-class children, may not be adult-oriented when it comes to need for social approval or may not be able to develop the relationship with a middle-class teacher needed for the teacher's expectations to have much impact. In addition, a word of caution should be expressed toward lying about one's expectations to students in an attempt to promote change: it seems reasonable to generalize from the research of Rosenthal (1966) that only when the teacher really believes that the child is worthwhile and capable of achievement will his expectations affect the child's self-attitudes.

There are a wide variety of research studies that demonstrate that one's peers have a great deal of influence upon one's attitudes and behaviors. It is safe to state that if the student's peers began to bolster his self-attitudes and support academic achievement it would have a great deal of effect on the student. This material is discussed in detail in Chapter 12.

One study that contrasts the power of a warm and supportive teacher with the active assistance and support from a peer provides evidence that peer-group acceptance and support brought measurable increases in grade point average, while the warm teacher did not (Engle, Davis, and Meyer, 1968). One would suspect, however, that the power of the peer group and the teacher over the student's attitudes and behavior would vary as the age of the student varies, that is, younger children may be more influenced by the teacher and adolescents may be more influenced by their peers.

There are two other methods that have been used to affect a student's self-attitudes and, consequently, his achievement. One is to place the student in a series of situations where he receives support and recognition for success experiences in critical areas. Gillham (1967) cites a case study of twenty eighth-grade students who were poor readers with inadequate self-attitudes. She had them help in the kindergarten, making it clear to the children that the kindergarten teacher needed the help in reading and would welcome it. They selected the materials to be read and discussed the needs of their listeners. They were honestly praised and their activities were publicized in the school. Grades higher than the kindergarten asked for their help. As their abilities were recognized by others, they began to ask for help in correcting their own reading deficiences and raised their grade level in reading appreciably. This seems a powerful approach. Consistency theory, however, would predict that it would only be successful where the experiences are so overpowering that changing the student's self-attitudes restores balance to his attitude structure with less overall change than denying, distorting, or repressing the positive experiences the student has.

Finally, it has been hypothesized that by providing an appropriate model one may change a child's self-attitudes. Fox and Schwarz (1967) evaluated a program that paired students from two "slow" second-grade classes in a Harlem elementary school with students in two high achievement fifth-grade classes. It was hypothesized that by providing a successful model for the children their attitudes and performance in school would become more positive. The results of the study showed that the second graders improved in school attendance and reading achievement.

It may be possible, therefore, to modify a student's self-attitudes concerning achievement through modifying the expectations parents, peers, and teachers have toward the student as a learner and through group counseling, success experiences in critical areas, and appropriate models. It should be emphasized, however, that none of these methods will be successful in all cases. Under some circumstances each of them can be very effective, under other circumstances each of them will be ineffective. It should also be remembered that a person's self-attitudes are differentiated and have many different facets. A teacher does not have to change all the self-attitudes a student might have, but can concentrate upon the few that are especially relevant to the subject matter in which he wants to raise the child's achievement.

Finally, perhaps the safest approach for the teacher is to try everything at the same time. That is, the more support for the new attitudes and behavior that can be generated, the higher the probability of change. A teacher might enlist the aid of a student's parents and peers, express his own positive expectations more clearly, encourage the student to join a counseling group, and provide a variety of success experiences and possible models. Such a "shotgun" approach will be the most effective under most conditions.

Concluding Comment

It should be apparent from this chapter that achievement is not determined by intelligence alone, but is also affected by a wide variety of social-psychological factors, of which self-attitudes are one. The achievement of students can be increased through the manipulation of these social-psychological variables. The lack of achievement does not necessarily represent a lack of ability.

SUMMARY

Human beings characteristically act with self-awareness. As a child, an individual develops a conception of himself from the reactions of other individuals toward him. In the process of interacting with others, the individual comes to take-the-role-of-the-other, basing his beliefs, evaluations, and expectations of himself on the beliefs, evaluations, and expectations that significant people in his life have of him. The resulting self-attitudes function to direct behavior.

Applying the self-concept theory to academic achievement, we would postulate that a child's self-attitudes concerning achievement in general and in specific subjects have an influence upon his academic performance. There is empirical support for this postulated relationship from a large number of studies that have found a significant correlation between self-attitudes and academic achievement. Two qualifications, however, must be made to this empirical generalization: (1) a correlational relationship does not indicate causation and (2) it is necessary to specify under what conditions the relationship between self-attitudes and achievement will be high and under what conditions it will be low. A possible explanation of the relationship between self-attitudes and academic performance is found in the concept of the self-fulfilling prophecy.

Given the evidence that self-attitudes concerning achievement are related to academic achievement, it would be functional for educators to know exactly what factors affect self-attitudes and thus academic success. The evidence available indicates that a student's self-attitudes concerning his ability to achieve can be changed by modifying the academic expectations that parents, peers, and teachers have for the student and by providing successful experiences in critical areas and appropriate models. Again, however, one must take into account the exact conditions under which relationships will hold. For instance, under some conditions a teacher's expectations of a student's ability will have a significant influence upon the student's self-attitudes regarding his ability. But this situation will probably hold only when either the child has a need for social approval from adults or when the teacher has a warm, trusting relationship with the child. In addition, there is some evidence that it is only when the teacher really believes that the child is capable of achievement that his expectations affect the child's self-attitudes.

CHAPTER 6

ACHIEVEMENT MOTIVATION

Introduction

Why do two children with the same intelligence achieve at different levels? What determines the level of aspiration of a student? How does the expectation of success affect the academic achievement of students? What role do incentives play in motivating achievement behavior? These questions are dealt with in theories of achievement motivation developed by David C. McClelland (1961) and John W. Atkinson (1965) and their associates.

There are two important directions that the research on achievement motivation has taken. One, represented by Atkinson, deals with the scientific task of sharpening the psychological theory of motivation, of testing and refining it, and working it into a more useful conceptual tool. The other has been primarily concerned with the social origins and major social consequences of the need for achievement. This direction of inquiry has been guided by McClelland's elaboration of a hypothesis that the achievement motive is the mainspring of entrepreneurial activity fostering the economic development of a society.

In very simple terms, the achievement motive can be defined as the impetus to do well relative to some standard of excellence: a person with a strong need for achievement wants to be successful at some challenging task, not for profit or status, but merely for the sake of doing well. Using a projective test in which respondents would view a picture and then write a brief story about what is happening in the picture, McClelland (1965) defines the achievement motive as what is measured by coding an individual's spontaneous thoughts, as in the imaginative stories he tells, for the frequency with which he thinks about competing with a standard of excellence, or doing something better than before.

Other studies on achievement motivation have emphasized the subject's level of aspiration and his reaction to success or failure at a task. The sequence of events that is typical for many of these studies is as follows. First, the subject plays a game or performs a task in which he can obtain a score. An example of such a game is throwing darts at a target or trying to toss a ring over a stake. After playing the game and obtaining a given score, the subject is asked to estimate what score he will undertake to make the next time he plays; in other words, he sets his level of aspiration for future performance. He then plays the game again and achieves another score. The experimenter then measures the subject's reaction to his second performance, his feelings of success or failure, and the level of aspiration he sets for future performance at the game. From the subject's reactions to his performance and the way in which this affects his level of aspiration he can be classified as being high or low in achievement motivation. This will be explained in more detail later in this chapter.

Atkinson's Theory of Achievement Motivation

In a school there are times when the student performs a task specifically to be evaluated upon his performance; examinations are the typical example. There are other times, however, when the student may be performing a task on which he can neither succeed or fail and evaluation is quite inappropriate; reading library books, helping plan a special class event, eating lunch, going to one's locker between classes are all examples. The difference between working on a task for which striving for success and achievement is appropriate and one for which it is not is usually quite clear due to situational cues. Atkinson's (1965) theory of achievement motivation applies only when an individual knows that his performance will be evaluated (by himself or by others) in terms of some standard of excellence and that the consequence of his actions will be either a favorable evaluation (success) or an unfavorable evaluation (failure). The disposition to strive for achievement is presumed to be latent until aroused by situational cues which indicate that some performance will be instrumental to achievement. That is, a student with a high need for achievement will not seek success in every situation. It is only when he perceives that the situation is such that his behavior on some task will be evaluated against some standard of excellence will his motive to achieve be activated.

To discuss Atkinson's theory, three variables need to be defined: motive, expectancy, and incentive (Atkinson, 1965; Atkinson and Feather, 1966). An *expectancy* is a cognitive anticipation, usually aroused by cues in a situation, that performance of some act will be followed by a particular consequence. A student, for example, may have the expectancy that if he studies he will pass an examination. The strength of an expectancy can be represented as the subjective probability of the consequence, given the act. That is, the strength of the student's expectancy is the subjective probability that he will pass the test if he studies.

An *incentive* represents the relative attractiveness of a specific goal that is offered in a situation, or the relative unattractiveness of an event that might occur as a consequence of some act. For example, passing an examination offers some attractiveness relative to other uses of the student's time besides studying. In deciding whether or not to study the student has to weigh the relative attractiveness of passing the examination versus playing ball, dating, earning money, and the like.

A *motive* is a disposition to strive for a certain kind of satisfaction, a capacity for satisfaction in the attainment of a certain class of incentives. Motives are relatively general and stable characteristics of the personality that have their origins in early childhood experience. The general aim of one class of motives is to maximize satisfaction of some kind; the achievement motive is the disposition to approach success. The aim of another class of motives is to minimize pain—an avoidance motive represents the individual's capacity to experience pain in connection with certain kinds of negative consequences of acts. The motive to avoid failure is considered a disposition to avoid failure and/or a capacity for experiencing shame and humiliation as a consequence of failure.

Atkinson's theory states, therefore, that a student's need for achievement depends upon three variables: his motivation to achieve, the expectancy that by doing certain acts he will achieve, and the incentives available for achievement relative to the incentives for engaging in other competing activities. The actual achievement-oriented tendency of an individual, however, is conceived by Atkinson as being the resultant of two opposed tendencies: the tendency to achieve success and the tendency to avoid failure.

The tendency to achieve success depends upon the individual's motive to succeed, the strength of his expectancy that success will be the consequence of a particular activity, and the incentive for attempting the activity. The tendency to achieve success is strongest when a task is one of intermediate difficulty and when the person is highly motivated. A number of studies have demonstrated that persons in whom the tendency to achieve success is relatively strong will show greater preference for tasks of intermediate difficulty than will persons in whom the tendency to achieve success is relatively weak (see Atkinson and Feather, 1966). The theory predicts and there is supporting research evidence that when the task is of moderate difficulty, students with a relatively high tendency to achieve success will be more successful on the task and will persist at the task longer when faced with the option of engaging in some nonachievement-related activity.

Whenever performance is evaluated in relation to some standard of excellence, what constitutes the challenge to achieve for one individual poses the threat of failure for another. The tendency to avoid failure is aroused when there is an expectancy that some act will lead to failure, when one is motivated to avoid failure, and when there is an incentive for avoiding failure. The tendency to avoid failure inhibits the student from attempting a task on which he is to be evaluated, especially when the probability of success is intermediate. Students, however, whether dominated by the tendency to avoid failure or not, are forced into achievement-oriented situations. In such a case the student who is dominated by the tendency to avoid failure is likely to choose tasks with a very high or very low chance of success. Doing so minimizes his anxiety about failure for if the chance of success is very high he is almost sure not to fail and when the chance of success is very low no one can blame him for failing at such a difficult task.

Individuals who are dominated by the tendency to achieve success prefer tasks for which there is an intermediate chance of success. Individuals who are dominated by the tendency to avoid failure prefer very high or very low risk tasks. This has been found not only for specific tasks in the classroom but also for vocational choice. Men in whom the need to achieve success is dominant over their fear of failure more frequently have realistic, moderately high aspirations when choosing vocations. Men dominated by anxiety about failure are more frequently unrealistic in their vocational choice; they either set their vocational aspirations very low or too high for their ability (see Atkinson, 1965; Atkinson and Feather, 1966).

Expectancy of Success as a Motivational Variable

One of the most interesting implications for education of Atkinson's theory of achievement motivation has to do with the effects of success and failure of students on a task. It has been assumed for many, many years that if a student succeeds at a task and is rewarded he will repeat the task; this is the well-known *law of effect* that has been firmly established by learning theorists. Atkinson argues, however, that the law of effect is fundamentally inadequate as a guide to understanding the effects of success and failure in the domain of achievement-oriented activity. Success does not invariably strengthen the tendency to undertake the same activity on another occasion; it sometimes weakens the subsequent tendency to engage in the same activity.

When an individual undertakes an activity and succeeds, his expectancy of success at that task and similar tasks is increased; when he fails, his expectancy of success at that and similar tasks is decreased. Atkinson theorizes that the incentive to engage in a task is directly related to the expectancy of success and, therefore, a change in expectancy results in a change in incentive. It can then be shown mathmatically (see Atkinson, 1965) that when a student whose motive to succeed is greater than his motive to avoid failure has a success experience, instead of seeking to repeat his success on a similar task in the future, he will raise his aspiration level and look for a harder, more challenging task. When he has a failure experience, he will lower his level of aspiration and look for a task that is easier in the future. When a student whose motive to avoid failure is stronger than his motive to succeed, the law of effect does hold for when he succeeds at a task; he will repeat the task in the future as his expectation that he will succeed will be higher and, therefore, he will have less anxiety about failing. These theoretical predictions are supported by research conducted by Atkinson and his students. In terms of classroom teaching, if the teacher knows a student is dominated by the motive to succeed and he succeeds on an assigned task, to keep the student interested in academic achievement the teacher should then offer him a more challenging assignment. If the teacher knows that a student is dominated by the fear of failure and he succeeds on an assignment, the teacher should then offer him similar assignments or perhaps increase the difficulty of the tasks very gradually to keep him functioning successfully in the classroom.

Persistence after Continual Failure

Another area in which Atkinson's theory generates interesting implications for the classroom is the student's persistence at a task after continual failure. A person in whom the motive to succeed is dominant should be much more persistent following failure at a task that he believes initially to be easy than one he believes initially to be very difficult. A person in whom the motive to avoid failure is dominant will behave quite differently; he will be much more persistent following failure at a task that he believes initially to be very difficult than one he believes initially to be quite easy. When he fails at a task he believes initially to be quite easy his anxiety about failure increases and, therefore, he avoids the task in the future. But when he fails at a task he believes initially to be quite difficult his anxiety about failure will actually decrease, as no one can blame him for failing at such a difficult task and, therefore, his tendency to engage in the task will increase.

A teacher who knows Atkinson's theory should be alert for the student who is dominated by the motive to succeed failing at a task that he perceives as too difficult and give him something easier (and, therefore, more challenging) to do. The student who is dominated by a fear of failure, however, will have to be persuaded or influenced to give up a task too difficult for his abilities and settle on something easier. When the two fail at a task they thought would be easy, on the other hand, the teacher may let the former student work on his own as he will be motivated to continue trying to accomplish the task; the latter student will become anxious and wish to drop the task, which the teacher may or may not want to allow, depending upon the circumstances.

Achievement Motivation and Academic Performance

A number of studies have shown that individuals whose achievement motivation is high (and is stronger than their fear of failure) prefer tasks in which they have intermediate probability of succeeding, persist longer on achievement tasks, and perform at higher levels, when compared with students whose achievement motivation is low or is outweighed by their fear of failure. The implications of these findings have been explored in previous sections of this chapter. On the basis of these findings one would in general expect that students high in achievement motivation would perform well in school. There have been a wide variety of studies on the correlation between achievement motivation and academic performance. These studies have primarily been conducted on college students, although a number have also been carried out with elementary and secondary school students. For the most part these studies show a low and often nonsignificant relationship between the two variables. How then can this be explained?

These studies are, by and large, examples of educational research that, while claiming to test a major hypothesis, miss the boat completely in terms of a relevant testing of the theory. The theory of achievement motivation generated by Atkinson does not say that there should be a general relationship between achievement *motivation* and academic *performance*. On the contrary, it states that *under certain conditions* there will be a strong relationship, under other conditions there will be no relationship. Most of the studies finding negative results used large groups of students without attention to whether the conditions that mediate the relationship between the two variables were present or absent. Their negative findings can be interpreted as meaning that in most school situations, the appropriate conditions do not exist for achievement motivation to affect academic performance.

A student with a high need for achievement should achieve academically only when his fear of failure is weaker than his need for achievement and when the academic tasks assigned are challenging and represent an intermediate opportunity for success. If the class is too easy or too difficult he will not be motivated to achieve in it. If his anxiety about failing, on the other hand, is too great he will not work on a task unless it is very easy or very difficult.

What happens to a student with a high need for achievement when the classroom does not offer him the challenge which motivates him? Very simply, he will probably look elsewhere for a task to work on. This might be in extracurricular activities. If students who have a high need for achievement are not challenged in the classroom and they turn to extracurricular activities you would expect a low correlation between success in the two activities. Holland and Richards (1965) report that academic and extracurricular achievements have only negligible correlations with each other.

It should be noted that there are other possible explanations for the lack of correlation between need for achievement and academic performance. Mitchell (1961), in a study using eight different measures of achievement motivation, found that achievement motivation as customarily measured consists of several different dimensions or components, including academic motivation and efficiency, self-satisfaction, wish-fulfillment motivation, nonacademic achievement orientation, and external pressures to achieve. Thus, many measures of achievement motivation include nonacademic components that should not be correlated or expected to correlate with academic performance.

Apathy and Action

The theory of achievement motivation and level of aspiration give an interesting prediction about the reasons for apathy in the schools. According to the theory, people are not likely to attempt to achieve even highly valued objectives when they see no way of attaining them. That is, when the expectation of success is zero, the tendency to engage in the behavior will be zero. If people feel that they cannot achieve their objectives, they will have no motivation to attempt to do so. Coleman and his associates (1966), in a recent study on integrated education, found that the feeling that one had control over one's future fate correlated highly with achievement in school for minority-group students. Atkinson's theory would predict that when minority-group students feel that education will not open up opportunities for them in society they will have no motivation to achieve in school. If, however, they do feel that education will make a difference in future opportunities, then they will be motivated to achieve in school.

Similarly, the theory sheds some light upon why social revolution tends to occur only after there has been a slight improvement in the situation of oppressed groups. The improvement raises their level of aspiration, making goals which were once viewed as unattainable now perceived as realistic possibilities. Since the goals are now perceived as attainable, people work hard to achieve them in the immediate future. In other words, if minority-group students begin to feel that education is a realistic means to formerly unobtainable goals, they will become highly motivated to achieve academically.

Increasing Tendency to Achieve

From the theory that the tendency to achieve is determined by the motivation to achieve, the expected probability of success, and the incentive for achievement ($T_s = M_s \times P_s \times I_s$), one may conclude that there are two major ways in which to increase motivation in students. One is to increase the need for achievement (or conversely, lower the fear of failure) and the second is to increase the expected probability of success. Atkinson feels that the latter is the most feasible means of bringing about changes in a student's tendency to engage in achievement-oriented behavior, as, in his opinion, it is a much easier variable to change than are the personality characteristics of need for achievement and fear of failure. There are many ways to raise the expected probability of success, such as breaking the task down into subunits that the student can handle more easily or provide the skill training, help, and consultation the student needs in order to succeed at the task. McClelland (1965a, 1965b), however, has taken just the opposite route; he has developed a training program by which achievement motivation (or other motives) may be learned and increased. A discussion of his techniques for increasing achievement motivation appears in the next section of the chapter.

Other Motives for Academic Achievement

The theory of need for achievement does not make the claim that need for achievement is the only reason why a person achieves. There are other motives for achievement, such as the desire for social approval, the desire to conform to role expectations, the desire for reinforcements offered for achievement, and the desire to conform to informal and formal norms in an organization. When attempting to increase the achievement of a student, therefore, it is important for the teacher to tap other motives and external pressures for achievement as well as the need for achievement.

Implications

Knowing Atkinson's theory of achievement motivation enables a teacher to diagnose the achievement needs of his students and to plan a rational change program for a student if it is needed. For example, if anxiety concerning failure is deterring a child from achievement-oriented behavior, then the teacher can plan a strategy for decreasing the student's anxiety and bringing other sources of motivation for achievement into play, such as the desire for approval from the teacher. If a student is high in need for achievement and is not being challenged by the work assigned in the class, the teacher can adopt a much different strategy based upon offering the student a more challenging task. Several other teacher strategies have been pointed out in this chapter.

Perhaps the major implication of this chapter and the other chapters on the student role, however, is that experience and social factors are determinants of ability and performance. Educators often oversimplify and see students as doing well because they are intelligent and doing poorly because they are stupid or because they do not try. Too often the situation or circumstance that leads a person to behave as he does is ignored, and even less attention is given to the effect of the student's previous experience on his performance. Teachers and other educators should resist the temptation to write off certain children as hopeless and to label others as capable of only mediocre performance, and instead try to determine the situational conditions under which the children can succeed in school.

McClelland's Theory of Achievement Motivation

David C. McClelland and his associates have taken a quite different approach to achievement motivation than has the Atkinson group. McClelland has been interested in the development of achievement motivation in individuals and the consequences for a society of having a large number of achievement-oriented members. In what follows, we will focus on McClelland's work on the behavior of individuals with high achievement needs, the child-rearing practices that affect one's need for achievement, the effect of achievement-oriented individuals on the development of a society, and the development of high need for achievement in adults, teenagers, and children.

Behavior of Students with High-Achievement Needs

There have been a number of studies on the difference in behavior of individuals with high-achievement needs and those with low-achievement needs. In comparison with individuals who score low on achievement-motivation measures, individuals with high-achievement needs show a greater preference for moderately difficult tasks, they enjoy taking carefully calculated risks (that is, moderate risks in which skill or ability—not chance—is involved). They are more self-confident than are persons with low-achievement needs, they have confidence in themselves and their abilities, not in luck or fate. They do not become motivated to do well unless the task is challenging to them. They are very much interested in concrete measures of how well they are doing in performing a task. They are not motivated by money *per se*, but will seek money when it is used as a symbol of attainment, a measure of success. They have the ability to defer gratifications. Finally, they will seek out occupations in which they have a moderate chance of succeeding rather than those in which they have complete certainty or little possibility of success.

The Development of Achievement Motivation: Child-Rearing

One of the most crucial studies on achievement motivation for the later development of the theory was Marian Winterbottom's (1953) study of the childhood origins of achievement motivation. She obtained achievement-motive scores from twenty-nine boys, aged eight to ten. In addition, she interviewed the boy's mothers, asking questions about how children ought to be raised. The most significant part of the interview was a questionnaire concerning demands for independent action. Each mother was asked to tell by what age she expected her child to be able to do such things as: (1) know his way around the city, (2) try new things for himself, (3) do well in competition, and (4) make his own friends. She found that the mothers of the children with high needs for achievement expected the accomplishment of the above four tasks at a markedly earlier age than did the mothers of low-scoring (in terms of achievement motivation) boys. It seems that mothers of children with high-achievement motivation are concerned that a boy should begin early to move out on his own, to acquire skills, and explore possibilities. Through such attitudes it is inferred that the mothers gave the boys early independence training. In contrast, the mothers of the boys scoring low in achievement motivation believed in more restrictions on behavior and kept those restrictions on until a later age. When the mothers were asked how they rewarded their sons for doing what was expected of them it turned out that mothers with sons with a high need for achievement were more likely to use primary physical manifestations of affections, such as hugging and kissing. This study also provides some evidence that middle-class mothers tend to emphasize mastery and independence training in the rearing of their sons to a greater extent than do lower-class mothers. This finding helps to explain the greater achievement motivation found among middle-class boys than among lower-class boys. From this study it may be concluded that early training in independence and mastery contributes to the development of strong achievement motivation.

From Winterbottom's study we know what mothers report about their child-rearing practices. This, however, may or may not be congruent with their actual behavior. Rosen and D'Andrade (1959) went into private homes to observe how parents reacted to their sons when the sons were trying to achieve on prescribed tasks. They visited forty families of which twenty included a son with a high score on need for achievement and twenty a son with a low score. The boys were between the ages of nine and eleven and were matched for age, race, and IQ. Each boy was seen in his home by two observers. He was asked to perform five tasks at the kitchen table in the presence of both parents. The whole performance was recorded on an observation schedule. The tasks were designed so that the parents could choose to assist the boys or not. For example, in one task each boy was asked to build a tower out of some very irregularly shaped blocks; the task was made difficult by blindfolding boy and restricting him to the use of one hand. His father and mother were allowed to look on and to say anything they liked, but were forbidden to touch the blocks. The parents were told that the "average" boy could, in these circumstances, build a tower of eight blocks. The parents were asked to estimate in advance, and confidentially, how high they thought their son could build the tower.

From the above measure the investigators found that the parents of the high-achievement boys had higher aspirations for him to do well at any task in comparison with parents of the low-achievement oriented boys. In addition, they seemed to have a higher regard for his competence at problem solving. They set up standards of excellence for the boy even when none were given, or if a standard was given they expected him to do "better than average."

When the blindfolded boy worked at the tasks the parents urged him on, gave him directions, exploded in happy laughter when he succeeded. But there were differences in the character of this behavior for the parents of the two kinds of sons. Parents of the high-achievement oriented boys, especially the mothers, worked up a lot of hopeful encouraging tension over the performance and when it went well poured out happiness and warmth. When he performed poorly the mothers tended to react with disapproval. The mothers stressed achievement training and were frequently dominating rather than allowing their sons self-reliance. The mothers were themselves striving, competent persons and apparently expected their sons to be the same. They became very involved in their sons' work, giving them constant emotional feedback of warmth and rejection.

For the low-achievement oriented boys, the fathers tended to give specific directions, and to make decisions for the child, to urge them on, and react with irritation when things did not go well. It appears that a father who is domineering and authoritarian in behavior is not likely to have a son with high-achievement motivation. The fathers of the high-achievement motivated boys, although they set high standards for their son and had high expectations for his performance, tended to be less rejecting, less pushy, and less dominant than were the mothers.

Achievement Motivation and Economic Growth

The emphasis upon early independence training led McClelland to characterize differences between total cultures. His general plan was to assess the two variables, training for independence and achievement motivation, on the cultural level. A problem immediately arose about what kind of data to use; obviously it would require great effort and expense to administer the standard measures to a representative sample of persons belonging to a culture. McClelland and Friedman (1952) argued that for simple nonliterate cultures one might reasonably score popular folktales and take the average score as characteristic of the culture. They found a significant positive relationship between the amount of stress on early independence training and the level of achievement motivation in the eight cultures they studied. Using refined techniques, Child, Storm, and Veroff (1958) selected twelve folk tales from forty-five primitive cultures and coded each story for signs of achievement motivation. The societies were also classified as to whether people in them engaged in full-time entrepreneurial activities (traders and independent artisans, for example). A significant relationship was found. Even though the cultures varied over a wide range of economic and social systems, the groups high in achievement motivation, as indicated by the folk tales, were much more likely than the lower-achievement groups to have such entrepreneurial occupations. The data indicated, furthermore, that it was direct training for achievement rather than a

113

stress on independence or self-reliance that was related to the motivation levels revealed in the folk tales of the cultures. This and other studies raised questions about the exact dimension of parental behavior that is effective in producing achievement motivation in children. On the basis of the above-reported research, it seems safe to state that it is somewhere in a cluster having to do with independence, achievement, aspiration, and self-reliance. It should also be noted that the evidence so far presented has not proved that the childhood correlates of achievement motivation are actually the childhood sources, since there are no data adequate to establish a cause and effect relationship.

These findings led McClelland to make one of the more audacious investigations in the history of the social sciences. Taking Max Weber's (1904) famous thesis that the rise of Protestantism caused the rise in capitalism in the Western world, McClelland suggested a mediating social-psychological mechanism. He stated that the Protestant ideology should cause parents to stress achievement, self-reliance, and self-denial. If child-rearing worked in the past as it seems to work in the present, the Protestant family should have produced sons with high-achievement motivation. And this motivation may have found its expression in entrepreneurial enterprise and led to the rapid economic growth found by Weber in England, Germany, Switzerland, and the Netherlands.

McClelland promptly tested his hypothesis. In an ingenious study comparing national levels of achievement motivation with national rates of economic growth for two periods, 1920–1929 (twenty-three countries studied) and 1946–1950 (forty countries studied), McClelland (1961) found that the level of achievement motivation is predictive of a subsequent increase in the rate of economic growth. This research and subsequent studies provide strong evidence that a motivational variable, achievement motivation, plays a role in the economic development of a country. Much work, primarily in developing better measures, needs to be done before this hypothesis is fully confirmed. It is safe to tentatively conclude, however, that although there are undoubtedly many other variables involved, achievement motivation seems to be related to economic development. The educational implications of this finding are staggering. It seems that the schools, by developing high levels of achievement motivation in their students, can influence the future economic growth of a country.

The Development of Achievement Motivation: Resocialization

The question of whether one can change or develop new motives in an individual has received a great deal of attention in psychology, with no clear answers. Various change programs have been tried, such as psychotherapy, group counseling, and sensitivity training. All education can be seen as a process of reeducation, where individuals learn new behaviors and new ideas that replace old behaviors and old ideas. At present, however, there is no clear research evidence that shows the conditions under which change programs will work successfully. Most educators and psychologists are, however, convinced that one can develop new motives as a result of educational or training experiences. McClelland (1965a; 1965b) is convinced that achievement motivation can be developed through a training program. Much of his initial interest came from a study by Burris (1958), who undertook a counseling program in which an attempt to elicit and reinforce achievement-related fantasies proved to be successful in motivating college students to get better grades.

McClelland has in recent years conducted a series of training programs with business personnel aimed at increasing their achievement motivation, in the United States and in several foreign countries. He has also conducted similar training programs with lower-class populations in the United States. His basic thesis is that in underdeveloped countries and in lower-class populations in the United States, increased opportunity for advancement will not in itself motivate individuals to achieve more. There must also be a program of attitude or personality change that develops a high motivation to take advantage of the new opportunities open to them. His training program sets goals for the participants to develop a high need for achievement, it teaches them to think clearly in "need-for-achievement" terms, it provides cognitive and group supports for a high need for achievement through which the motive becomes integrated into the participant's self-attitudes, and it provides practice in high need for achievement behavior. McClelland (1965a) lists nine phases of his training program:

1. Create expectations that the person can, will, and should change as a result of the training experience.
2. Show that the desired change is consistent with the demands of reality and reason.

115

3. Have the trainee develop a clear conceptualization of the behavior or motive.
4. Have the trainee relate the newly developed conceptualization to related actions.
5. Have the trainee relate the newly conceptualized associate-action complex to events in his everyday life.
6. Have the trainee perceive the newly conceptualized motive as an improvement in his self-image.
7. Have the trainee perceive the motive as an improvement on prevailing cultural values.
8. Get the trainee to commit himself to achieving concrete goals in life related to the newly formed motive.
9. Have the trainee keep a record of his progress toward achieving goals to which he is committed (related to the motive).

In addition, McClelland (1965a) lists three overall characteristics of his training program:

1. The interpersonal atmosphere of the training should be one in which the individual feels warmly but honestly supported and respected by others as a person capable of guiding and directing his own future behavior.
2. The setting of the training should dramatize the importance of self-study and lift it out of the routine of everyday life.
3. The new motive (and new behavior) should be a sign of membership in a new reference group.

McClelland (1965b) gives an account of one such training program conducted in India. The goal of this training program was to push a whole community into an economic "takeoff" by training a significant number of its business leaders in achievement motivation. Fifty-two men from one city were trained in a ten-day residential course in groups of twelve to fifteen members each. The group was composed predominately of small-business men. He describes this training program as follows. First, the training program is "sold" to the participants in a way which makes them interested in participating and convinced that they can and will change in a positive way from participation in the program. In other words, he creates a strong positive expectation that the training program will be beneficial and successful, thus setting up the possibility of a favorable self-fulfilling prophecy. Second, the participants are given a quick course in achievement motivation, learning in detail exactly how it is related to certain types of successful entrepreneurial performance. This teaches the participant that becoming a high achievement-motivated person will help him function better in reality. Third, the participants are taught how to score instruments used in measuring achievement motivation. The purpose of this is to teach them to think constantly in achievement-motivation terms and to differentiate achievement motivation from other needs, such as the need for affiliation and the need for power. It also helps the participants to conceptualize clearly the need for achievement.

Next, the participants tie thought to action by playing business games in which they practice high need for achievement behaviors and watch other participants portray the behavior. From these games the training moves to "case histories" of real business problems, in order to link the activitites to everyday life. Fifth, discussions are held on how high need for achievement fits into the prevailing cultural values in order to integrate achievement-motivated behavior into the dominant culture of the society. Through these discussions and the training program it is hoped that the participants will become identified with each other and the training experience, forming a new reference group that supports the goals of the training for each other. The training program ends with each participant preparing a written document outlining his goals and life plans for the next two years. These plans are supposed to be quite specific and realistic. The purpose is to obtain commitment to achievement behavior in the future. Finally, over the following two years the participants are sent a questionnaire every six months that serves to re-arouse many of the issues discussed in the training and to provide them with information on how far they have progressed toward achieving their goals.

McClelland (1965b) again emphasizes that during the training the instructors act as warmly, honestly, and nonevaluatively as possible because this creates the type of authority that seems to develop individuals with high-achievement needs. Furthermore, the reward structure of the training program is such that the participants reward those trainees who best learn to have high needs for achievement. That is, peer support and recognition is given for adopting the behaviors desired by the training staff.

The training methods McClelland (1965b) used can be summarized into four main areas. The first is *goal setting*. This takes the form of creating the belief that the participant *can* and *should* change through "prestige suggestion" in which high-status staff members express their beliefs and the evidence for the possibility and desirability of change. At the end of the program the participant plans and describes his goals for future behavior, with the emphasis upon making his goals specific, realistic, and practical. The second area is learning the *language of achievement*. Emphasis is placed upon having the participant learn to think, talk, act, and perceive others like a person with a high-achievement motive. By learning how to score his fantacies, thoughts, and actions on the degree of achievement motivation they express, the participant learns to engage in behavior and thinking that are characteristic of high achievement-oriented persons. By learning to think in achievement-motivation terms the participant is equipped to evaluate his future behavior in regard to achievement motivation.

The third area is the use of *cognitive supports* for engaging in achievement-oriented behavior. The new cognitive structure must be integrated into old cognitive structures, such as (1) what kind of person he thinks he is, (2) what is reasonable, logical and scientific to him, and (3) what is important and valuable in his life. In addition, the assumptions of the culture are discussed in order to integrate one's need for achievement with one's culture. The fourth area is the use of *group supports* in order to provide emotional as well as rational support for the changes involved in the training program. Emotional support is given by the instructors who maintain throughout an accepting, nonmanipulative attitude. The message they attempt to convey by word, thought, and deed is: "Whoever you are, we accept you as worthy of our respect. Whatever you decide you want to be, we will respect your choice—including the possibility that you may decide the achievement motive is not for you." In addition, the experiences in group living and the discussions in small groups facilitate building a new reference group that supports achievement-motivated behavior.

At the time McClelland (1965b) published his article on the training program in India, he stated that it was too soon to know what the long-range results of the program would be, but between six and ten months after training, two thirds of the men had become unusually active in business in some readily observable way; for example, they had started a new business, expanded their old business, greatly increased profits, or taken active steps to investigate a new product line. Only one third of these men had been unusually active in similar ways in the two years prior to taking the training program. In short, it would appear that the training program doubled the natural rate of unusual entrepreneurial activity in the group studied.

Implications

The implications of McClelland's work for the classroom and the school are as follows. First, it provides evidence that achievement motivation can be developed in students through training programs carried out by the school. If the school chooses to do so, it can increase the achievement motivation of many if not all of its students. Second, the general program for inducing achievement motivation can be applied to other motives which the school might want to induce in students, such as self-reliance, independence, or self actualization. Any school initiating a program on achievement motivation, however, should remember that an essential part of it will be to provide the student with the tools to engage in achievement-oriented behavior, but the choice to do so is still with the student. As McClelland emphasizes, the choice of how he wants to be is given to the student, but the development of the skills and behaviors that provide the student with real alternatives lies with the school.

Conclusion

From the work of McClelland it is evident that the schools can systematically develop a high need for achievement in those students for which it would be agreeable. It can be argued that schools should do so in order to facilitate the continued development of our society. It can also be argued that schools should do so for individual well-being, as there is some evidence that indicates that persons with high needs for achievement lead more vigorous, interesting, productive, less anxious lives. Creating a high need for achievement among students will not result in conforming individuals who accept the present nature of schooling as perfect and labor mightily in this Garden of Eden. Certainly, having more students with high needs for achievement would mean that the schools would have to provide more meaningful challenges for students; as among other things, there is preliminary evidence that high need for achievement may be correlated with certain types of creativity, and developing a high need for achievement in students may markedly increase student and teacher unrest and dissatisfaction with the present nature of educational organizations. Such dissatisfaction is, of course, the major impetus for creative and productive change.

From the theory of achievement motivation, a person can learn how to take moderate risks, how to be challenged by moderately difficult tasks, how to have self-confidence in one's abilities to solve long-range problems, how to look for feedback on one's long-range performance, how to defer gratifications until tomorrow or the day after, how, in short, to have a high need for achievement and behave like high achievers do. The more "hip" among us, however, might take a cool look at the achievement motive and think of what John Dryden would say to those square enough to "dig" McClelland:

> Happy the man and happy he alone,
> He who can call today his own.
> He who secure within can say,
> Tomorrow do thy worst, for I have lived today.

SUMMARY

Motivation for achievement can be defined as the impetus to do well relative to some standard of excellence. Two important contributions to understanding this phenomenon are found in the works of John W. Atkinson and David C. McClelland. Atkinson deals with the scientific task of developing a systematic formulation of the determinants of achievement motivation. There are three fundamental variables in Atkinson's schema: (1) *expectancy*, a cognitive anticipation or subjective probability, usually aroused by cues in the situation, that performance of some act will be followed by a particular consequence, (2) *incentive*, the relative attractiveness of an event that might occur as a consequence of some act, (3) *motivation*, a general, stable disposition to strive for a certain kind of satisfaction.

The tendency to achieve in any situation is conceived by Atkinson to be a function of two opposed tendencies, the tendency to achieve success minus the tendency to avoid failure. The resultant achievement-oriented tendency is positive when the disposition to achieve is greater than the disposition to avoid failure and negative when the opposite is true.

The tendency to achieve success is assumed to be a function of the general motive to achieve success, the subjective probability that success will be the consequence of a particular activity, and the incentive value of success.

The tendency to avoid failure is associated with the anxiety posed by the threat of failure. This tendency is assumed to be a function of the general motive to avoid failure, the subjective probability of failure, and the negative incentive value.

Atkinson's theory has many implications for education. For one, it adds an important qualification to the long-established *law of effect,* which states that if a student performs successfully on a task and is rewarded, he will repeat the task on another occasion. First, according to Atkinson's theory, we have to take into account the relative strengths of the tendency to succeed and tendency to avoid failure. If an individual's motive to succeed is greater than his motive to avoid failure, then success at a task will strengthen the tendency to undertake the same activity, but only if an individual believes the initial task was difficult; whereas if he believed the initial task was easy or of intermediate difficulty, success would weaken the subsequent tendency to engage in the same activity. In the case where the motive to avoid failure is stronger than the motive to succeed, the law of effect will only hold if the task is believed to be easy.

Atkinson's formulation might also explain why a large number of studies have found a low and often nonsignificant correlation between achievement motivation and academic performance. According to the theory, a student with a high need for achievement should achieve academically only when his anxiety about failing is weaker than his need for achievement and when the academic tasks assigned are not too easy or too difficult.

Finally, there are two major ways in which one may increase achievement motivation in students: one is to increase the general need for achievement (or conversely, lower fear of failure) and another is to increase the expected probability of success. Atkinson

90823

believes that the latter is most feasible, since he feels that it is an easier variable to change than are the personality characteristics of need for achievement and fear of failure.

McClelland approaches the problem of achievement motivation from another, yet complementary point of view. McClelland has been concerned with the social origins and major social consequences of the need for achievement. Earlier studies investigating what child-rearing practices contribute to the development of strong achievement motivation found that emphasis on early training in independence and mastery over one's own fate were related to a strong achievement motivation in children. McClelland and his associates substantiated this finding at the cultural level; that is, they found a significant positive correlation between the amount of stress on early independent training as expressed in popular folk tales and the level of achievement in eight nonliterate cultures.

McClelland also investigated the effects of achievement-oriented individuals on the development of a societies. Taking Max Weber's thesis that the rise of Protestantism caused the rise in capitalism in the Western world, McClelland suggested a mediating social-psychological mechanism. Basically, he hypothesized that the stress Protestant parents placed on early independence and mastery training lead to high-achievement motivation in their sons and this, in turn, found its expression in entrepreneurial enterprise. McClelland provided evidence in support of this hypothesis by finding a significant relationship between the level of achievement motivation in twenty-three countries and a subsequent increase in their rate of economic growth during the first part of the twentieth century.

Another area of interest for McClelland is the development of a high need for achievement in adults and students. He feels this can best be accomplished through a training program of attitude and personality change. Specifically, he presents evidence that achievement motivation can be increased through a training program with the following characteristics: (1) create expectations that the person can, will, and should change in a positive way as a result of the training experience; (2) have the trainee develop a clear conceptualization of the behavior or motive and learn exactly how achievement motivation is related to successful performance; (3) show that the desired change is consistent with demands of reality, everyday events, his own self-image, and cultural values; (4) get the trainee to commit himself to achieving concrete goals in life related to the newly formed motive; (5) have the trainee keep a record of his progress toward achieving goals to which he is committed; and (6) the overall inter-personal atmosphere of the training should be one in which the in-dividual feels warmly but honestly supported and respected by the instructors and other group members as a person capable of guiding and directing his own future behavior.

CHAPTER 7

LEADERSHIP

Introduction

Within the classroom there are two primary roles, the teacher and the student, whose relationships to one another and to the school affect the manner in which classroom activities are conducted. Organizationally, the way in which the teacher and the students relate to each other is important. In this chapter one of the variables which influences the interrole relationships in the classroom is examined: leadership.

Definition of Leadership

In the social psychological literature leadership has three major meanings: as the attribute of a position, as a characteristic of a person (the trait approach), and as a category of behavior (the functional approach) (Katz and Kahn, 1966). The literature on leadership as a characteristic of a person and as a category of behavior are discussed in this chapter. The view of leadership as an attribute of a position, however, is not discussed, as it is by and large an inadequate definition: it defines leadership as holding a position in the authority hierarchy. The use of authority will be discussed in Chapter 11. According to the role definitions within a school, all teachers are created equal in regard to the legitimate power of their position and the rewards and sanctions that they can use to influence students. They do not, however, remain equal. Some teachers show strong leadership, others do not. Some teachers use their position power more effectively than others; one may use it to maximize his influence in the classroom and school whereas another may fail to use it appropriately and thereby decrease his influence. Leadership, therefore, does not mean routine role performance; it is the amount of influence a person exerts over and above the mechanical compliance with the routine directives of the organization. More specifically, *leadership constitutes an influence relationship between two or more persons who depend upon one another for the attainment of mutual goals within a group situation* (Hollander and Julian, 1969). The group situation involves variables such as the group's task, size, structure, resources, and history.

Leadership is a relationship concept implying two types of people, the leader who influences and the followers who are influenced. Without followers there can be no leader. The relationship between leaders and followers is built over time and involves an exchange or transaction between leader and led in which they both give something and get something. The leader receives status, recognition, esteem, and other reinforcements for his contributing his resources toward the accomplishment of the group's goals. The followers obtain the leader's resources and his ability to structure the group's activities toward goal attainment in return for deferring to his influence and reinforcing him for successful leadership. Since both the leader and the led control resources the other wants, they both influence each other's behavior. The relationship between dependence upon another and influence will be discussed at length in Chapter 11. The important point for now is that while leadership is defined in terms of successful influence upon the other members of the group, the followers also influence the leader. As Homans (1961) puts it, "Influence over others is purchased at the price of allowing one's self to be influenced by others." Homans feels that to be influential, authority depends upon esteem; thus one's followers can control one's behavior to a certain extent by giving or denying esteem. There is a series of research studies demonstrating that symbolic manifestations of esteem activate leadership, that is, encourage a person to take on the leader role. One study demonstrated that individuals who were low on leadership behavior were led to behave far more actively in leadership behaviors by the group's evident support for their assertions; other individuals known earlier to be high on leadership behaviors were affected in precisely the opposite way by the group's evident disagreement with their statements (Pepinsky, Hemphill, and Shevitz, 1958). It seems that the group's reinforcement of an individual's influence-attempts substantiates his position of authority within the group. Other studies demonstrated that the use of lights as reinforcers of leadership behavior exerts a significant effect on the target person's proportion of talking time as well as his perceived leadership status; the lights not only produced a heightening of leadership acts, but also created the impression of greater influence with the implication of legitimacy as well (Bavelas et al., 1965; Zdep and Oakes, 1967).

Given the above definition of leadership and the discussion of the leadership relationship, this chapter will now focus upon the view of leadership as a personal trait and as a category of behavior. The nature of leadership in groups and organizations will then be examined.

Trait Approach

The earliest approach to research on leadership concentrated on the physical, intellectual, and personality traits commonly found in leaders. Leaders were usually operationally defined as people holding positions of authority. Many studies contrasted characteristics of leaders with those of followers (Cartwright and Zander, 1968). It has been reported, for example, that leaders tend to be somewhat bigger and brighter than the rest of the members of a group. They also seem to show better adjustment on various personality tests. This approach has proved to be unsatisfactory and has yielded contradictory results. The traits found in leaders are also found in followers, and the different requirements of diverse leadership positions demand very different qualities in effective leaders. Finally, leadership is too often dependent upon the nature and environment of the group to depend solely on possession of certain and specific traits.

Leadership, therefore, is not a personal quality inherent in certain people. Leaders are indistinguishable from nonleaders in personality, ability, and background variables. This is not to say that certain people such as John F. Kennedy or Malcolm X do not have a quality known as "charisma" that inspires others to support and to follow them. We cannot all be John F. Kennedys, however. Leadership, by and large, is a matter of competence and skill, not charisma.

Functional Theory of Leadership

Dissatisfaction with the trait approach to leadership has given rise to research studies concentrating more upon the leader's skills or what he does than upon the nature of his deeper personality. This approach to leadership seeks to discover what actions are necessary if a group is to achieve its goals under various conditions and how different group members take part in these group actions. The performance of acts that help the group achieve its goals is termed leadership. The functional approach to leadership stresses the performance of these acts, termed *group functions*. Leadership functions include setting goals, helping the group proceed toward these goals, and providing necessary resources. Other functions not directly related to goal achievement, such as improving the stability of the group and insuring the satisfaction of individual members are also part of the leadership role. According to this approach, leadership is seen as function-centered rather than position-centered and, therefore, groups should be flexible in assigning leadership functions to various members as conditions change. Only those group members who are sensitive to the changing conditions and who can adapt to these conditions can be effective leaders for any period of time. In principle, leadership may be performed by one or many members of the group.

The concept of functional leadership includes two basic ideas

(Cartwright and Zander, 1968): (1) any member of a group may become a leader by taking actions that serve group functions and (2) any leadership function may be served by various members performing a variety of behaviors. Leadership is thus specific to a particular group in a particular situation. It can depend on the background of the group members, the nature of the goals, or the organization of the group. It can also depend upon outside expectations or pressure exerted on the group to behave in certain ways. All of these influence the nature of leadership behavior and the choice of which members will perform these behaviors.

According to the functional approach to leadership, under specific circumstances any given behavior may or may not serve a group function. Under one set of conditions a certain behavior may be beneficial, under another set of conditions that same act may be dysfunctional. For example, when a group is trying to define a problem, suggesting a possible solution may not be helpful, but when a group is specifying alternative solutions to a defined problem, suggesting a possible solution may be quite helpful.

The skills possessed by a designated leader or the holder of an office may, furthermore, make him well qualified to perform important group functions under certain conditions and poorly qualified under others. A bomber pilot, for example, may be an excellent leader for the crew while the plane is in the air, but may be totally inadequate for survival leadership if the plane crashes (Cartwright and Zander, 1968). A change in the task of the group often demands a new set of leadership skills, and the same individual may not be able to alter his own actions to meet the demands of the new situation.

Finally, the functional approach to leadership assumes that leadership is a learned set of skills that anyone with certain minimal requirements can acquire. Effective group membership and leadership depend upon flexible behavior, the ability to diagnose what behaviors are needed at a particular time in order for the group to function most efficiently, and to fulfill these behaviors or to get other members to fulfill them. A skilled member or leader, therefore, has to have diagnostic skills in order to be aware that a given function is needed in the group and he must be capable of flexibilities in his behavior in order to provide diverse types of behaviors that are required under different conditions. In addition, he must be able to utilize other group members and obtain their cooperation in providing needed group functions.

Two Basic Types of Group Functions

It is useful to distinguish among various group functions according to the type of group objective to which the function contributes. *Goal achievement* and *group maintenance* are generally considered to be the two basic categories of group objectives (Bales, 1958; Cartwright and Zander, 1968). Examples of member behaviors that help in the achievement of the goals of the group are "initiates action," "keeps members' attention on the goal," "clarifies the issue," "develops a procedural plan," "evaluates the quality of the work done," and "makes expert information available to the group." Acts that contribute to maintenance or improvement of the group are examplified by the following: "keeps interpersonal relations pleasant," "arbitrates disputes," "provides encouragement," "gives the minority a chance to be heard," "stimulates self-direction," and "increases the interdependence among members."

Any given behavior in a group may affect both goal achievement and group maintenance. Both may be served simultaneously by the actions of a member, or one may be served at the expense of the other. Thus, a member who helps the group work cooperatively on a task may simultaneously help the group reach its goal and increase group solidarity. On the other hand, a member who pushes for task accomplishment may help the group accomplish its task, but in a way that creates frictions among members so that the future existence of the group is endangered.

Supervision and Group Effectiveness

The nature of a group's leadership influences many aspects of its functioning. A classic study on group leadership conducted by Lewin, Lippitt, and White (1939), although it has many shortcomings, demonstrates strikingly that the same group of people will behave in markedly different ways when operating under leaders who behave differently. In this study, clubs of eleven-year-old children were run by leaders who adopted each of three styles for a specified period of time: autocratic (themselves planning for and directing the children), democratic (joint planning with group decisions), or laissez-faire (no leader intervention).When the clubs were under an autocratic leader, they were more dependent upon him and more egocentric in their peer relationships. When rotated to a democratic style of leadership, the same children evidenced more initiative, friendliness, and responsibility. These children continued to work even when the leader was out of the room. Their interest in the work and in the quality of their product was higher. Aggressive acts were more frequent, furthermore, under the autocratic and laissez-faire leaders than they were under a democratic leader.

Since the leadership style of a supervisor affects the group's functioning, it is important that he adopts a style that contributes to both task effectiveness and group maintenance. Supervisory effectiveness has been studied by many different behavioral scientists. Deutsch and Hornstein (in preparation) state that work-group effectiveness is positively correlated with the degree to which the supervisor is perceived by his subordinates as (1) defining roles and organizing functional structures, (2) allowing sufficient individual autonomy, and (3) being considerate of their welfare. Kahn and Katz (1960) summarized the findings of several studies that investigated the performance of a variety of work groups in relation to the characteristic behaviors of each group's supervisor and concluded that the supervisors of more effective groups: (1) played a differentiated role better than the supervisors of the less effective groups, and they spent more time in planning what was to be done, in providing necessary materials, and in initiating next steps; (2) delegated authority to others more than the poorer supervisors; (3) checked up on the subordinates less often and were more supportive in their manner than the less effective ones; and (4) developed cohesiveness among their associates more than did the supervisors of poorer functioning groups. On the basis of a review of Likert's (1961, 1963) work on supervision, Watson (1966) states that five characteristics of good supervisors have appeared with considerable consistency: (1) they spend their time in supervisory rather than in production work; (2) they are more person-centered and more considerate; (3) they encourage subordinates to speak their minds freely; (4) they usually react supportively rather than punitively to mistakes of subordinates; and (5) they supervise less closely, that is, they enlarge the area of responsibility left to subordinates. Watson notes, however, that one important exception to the effectiveness of this kind of supervision is encountered when top management does not support supervisors and foremen in a person-centered approach. Pelz (1958) found that a supervisor's influence on subordinates depended greatly on his status with his superiors. If his friendliness toward employees runs counter to what the top administrators believe and practice, he loses their respect and also that of his own subordinates, and his effectiveness is diminished.

Likert (1961) has summarized many of these findings into what he calls the principle of supportive relationship: "The leadership and other processes of the organization must be such as to ensure a maximum probability that in all interactions and all relationships within the organization each member will, in the light of his background, values, and expectations, view the experience as supportive and one which builds and maintains his sense of worth and importance."

Cartwright and Zander (1968) report that the factor-analytic studies of Halpin and Winer (1952) and Fleishman, Harris, and Burtt (1955) resulted in two factors which account for most behavior of leaders in large organizations: *consideration* and *initiating structure*. Consideration involves human qualities such as warmth, respect, empathy, and approachability. Initiating structure defines leader behaviors such as subordinate role definition, establishment of channels of communication both up and down, and development of organizational patterns for goal achievement. Every supervisor combines these two factors in some way. The optimal balance between the two is largely determined by the nature of the goals and the membership of the group. Fleishman, Harris, and Burtt (1955) found that the employees of a large industrial organization liked working under foremen who were high in consideration and disliked working under those who were high in initiating structure. Proficiency ratings of the foremen based solely on the output of their subordinates revealed, however, that in production divisions the foremen with higher proficiency ratings were those who showed more initiation of structure, while in the nonproduction divisions those with the higher proficiency ratings manifested more consideration. In the production divisions, however, employee absenteeism was found to be positively related to foremen's initiating structure and negatively related to consideration. Thus, the most effective leader is not necessarily the one preferred by his subordinates.

In summarizing the total available evidence, Shartle (1956) concludes that a pattern of leader behavior high in both consideration and initiation of structure tends to increase group effectiveness. In a recent study in Japan, Misumi and Tasaki (1965) confirmed this hypothesis. It is a difficult task to be high in both consideration and in initiating structure and, therefore, in many groups the two areas of leadership are informally divided between two different individuals.

Hemphill's (1955) study is one of the few that attempts to relate these research findings to supervision within an educational organization. He studied twenty-two college departments, ranking them on the extent to which they were perceived as being administratively effective. He found that there was high agreement ($r=0.94$) about the departmental reputations for administrative effectiveness. When he compared members' descriptions of the chairmen of the departments reputed to be highly effective with those descriptions of the chairmen from members of the departments reputed to be low in effectiveness, he found that the effective departmental chairmen were seen as being relatively more initiating of structure and more considerate than were the ineffective chairmen.

Since the vast majority of the research done on supervision and group effectiveness is correlational, any application of the findings must be cautious as no cause-and-effect relationship has been demonstrated. It should be remembered, furthermore, that under some conditions the relationship between the supervisor's style and group effectiveness should be quite high and under other conditions it may be low. Merei (1949) demonstrated that when a leader is placed in a group which has well-established norms and traditions, he has to adapt his style of leadership to conform to the norms and traditions of the group in order to gain influence. Finally, having a considerate supervisor who initiates structure may increase group effectiveness under some conditions but not under others. Fiedler (1958) presents evidence that an overconsiderate, nondiscriminating supervisor is *less effective* than one who differentiates between competent and incompetent workers and who is critical of incompetent workers. In a more recent article (Fiedler, 1968) he also presents evidence that the leaders of more effective groups tend to be those who are concerned with successful completion of the task if the situation is either very easy or very difficult: when the situation is of intermediate difficulty, the most effective leader is one who devotes his attention primarily to friendly interpersonal relations.

Organizational Leadership

Much of the social psychological literature on leadership has a non-organizational quality and has been negligent in describing the operation of leadership processes in social systems. There are, however, a few exceptions. Argyris (1962) defines organizational leadership as being related to the organization's abilities to achieve its objectives, maintain itself internally, and adapt to its external environment. He sees leadership within organizations as being composed of two inter-related but analytically separable components: (1) intellectual, rational, technical competence and (2) interpersonal competence. Argyris is primarily concerned with interpersonal competence. He states that interpersonal competence tends to increase: (1) as one's awareness of problems increases, (2) as the problems are solved in such a way that they remain solved, (3) with a minimal deterioration of the problem-solving process. Based upon a sound theoretical model and a great deal of research within organizations (primarily on executive decision making), Argyris states that if these three criteria of interpersonal competence are to be met by an individual, he will have to: (1) own up to his ideas and feelings (that is, identify his ideas and feelings, communicate them, and accept responsibility for them), (2) be open to new ideas and feelings (that is, permit and encourage the reception of new information from himself and others), and (3) take risks and experiment with his behavior. In addition to engaging in these types of behaviors an interpersonally competent person will help others to engage in these behaviors and support group norms which facilitate members engaging in the above types of behavior, such as norms of trust, concern for each other, and freedom for everyone to be an individual.

A basic requirement for interpersonal competence is self-awareness (Argyris, 1962): unless a person is aware of how his behavior comes across to others he will not know how "competent" his interpersonal behavior really is. But how does an individual become more aware of his self? One way is to receive feedback from others as to how they see his behavior and how it affects them; a person can increase his self-awareness by receiving valid information from others. In order for feedback to be most useful both the giver and the receiver should be minimally defensive, because the more defensive a person is the higher the probability that he will distort his perceptions of the other's behavior. Although self-awareness is essential for interpersonal competence, it is not easy to find situations in which there is enough trust, acceptance, and concern that feedback can be given and received in maximally effective ways. One way in which individuals can receive feedback on their behavior under ideal conditions is to participate in a sensitivity-training group or an encounter group. When run by competent professionals, such as the members of the National Training Laboratories Institute of Applied Behavioral Science, a sensitivity-training group experiment can be a very rewarding and productive experience. Sensitivity training is discussed as a procedure for personal and organizational change in Chapter 14.

In discussing leadership within social systems Katz and Kahn (1966) state that there are three types of leadership behavior that occur in organizational settings. The first is the introduction of structural change or policy formation. This is perhaps the most challenging of all organizational tasks, but unfortunately rarely occurs without strong pressures from outside the organization. As stated in Chapter 2, as the members of the organization and the environment change, organizational structures often become inappropriate for accomplishing the organization's goals. Unfortunately, however, there is a marked tendency for many people to become more committed to the structures within which they function than to the goals toward which they are working. Leadership within organizations necessarily strives to keep the organization's structure flexible enough to adapt it to changes in the environment and clientele; thus keeping the structure appropriate to the organization's goals.

The second type of leadership behavior in organizations deals with embellishing upon its formal structure in creative ways (Katz and Kahn, 1966). Every problem the organization faces is in some aspects unique, while every policy statement deals only with the general issues across all problems. Thus the present policy of the organization is not always applicable to the unique qualities of the current problems and so must be either circumvented or modified. During the Second World War, army sergeants were infamous for their ability to circumvent the bureaucratic structure of the army when they felt it was necessary. Often school secretaries can also cut much of the red tape involved in working within the bureaucratic structure of the school.

Finally, the use of the structure formally provided to keep the organization in motion relates to leadership behavior within organizations (Katz and Kahn, 1966). The use of the existing structure to influence others is commonly thought of as administration, which will not be discussed here. The use of the authority system within the organization, however, will be discussed in Chapter 11.

When members have been influenced to engage in organizationally relevant behavior, leadership has occurred within the organization. When no attempt has been made to influence others, there has been no leadership. Katz and Kahn (1966) note, however, that the important thing for organization effectiveness is not just whether influence attempts are made or not, but rather when they occur and whether they have the effects which the leader intended. Thus two important aspects of competence for leaders are being able to diagnose what member behaviors are needed within different situations and having the content of one's influence attempts accurately perceived by others. The latter depends upon receiving feedback from others as to how they see one's behavior in order to find out what misperceptions, if any, are taking place and to improve one's communication skills.

Leadership and Power

The functional approach to leadership is at this time the most concrete, direct approach to improving the effectiveness of a group. It ignores, however, the fairly primitive, prerational aspects of leadership and followership and the realities of how power is often handled. Ever since the days of Machiavelli there have been theorists who conceive of leadership essentially in terms of possession and exercise of power for self-enhancement. To some extent they are right: leadership inevitably involves the ability to influence other people in some way, but in order for a person to be an effective leader he must exercise his power in a way which moves the group toward its task and maintenance goals. Many people in leadership positions turn out to be poor leaders because they are motivated primarily to have and use power rather than to improve the effectiveness of the group. In a democratic organization and in organizations with a strong production emphasis such leaders are usually replaced rather quickly with ones who are more concerned about the group's and organization's needs. In an organization such as a school, however, which is not democratic and not production-oriented, such leaders may be more difficult to replace. Power will be further discussed in Chapter 11.

Leading a Discussion Group

The functional theory of leadership can be applied to leading a discussion group in two areas—diagnosing the effectiveness of a group and intervening in ways to increase its effectiveness. A teacher needs to be able to diagnose which behaviors are needed in the group in order for it to accomplish its task and maintain itself over time. This will involve such things as identifying which functions are being met and which are not, which norms are present or absent in the group, and what is the current learning climate of the group. In order to make such a diagnosis the teacher needs to know how to obtain valid and reliable data from the group on its functioning. In diagnosing the ongoing process of a discussion group, a person needs to have some criteria against which to evaluate the present level of functioning and some idea of the behaviors needed to fulfill the task and maintenance functions of the group. A few criteria for judging the effectiveness of a discussion group are: (1) the prevalence of a warm, accepting, nonthreatening group climate that makes it safe for students to risk exposing their ignorance and to ask questions, (2) a cooperative approach to learning in which students give mutual aid in developing understanding of the material being discussed, (3) participation and leadership behaviors distributed across the group with the responsibility for making the group operate successfully shared by all members, and (4) the successful learning of the material being covered. The major types of behavior needed in order for a discussion group to function effectively are: (1) initiating and contributing ideas, (2) giving and asking for information, (3) giving and asking for opinions and reactions, (4) clarifying, synthesizing, summarizing, and giving examples, (5) evaluating effectiveness of the group and diagnosing difficulties in group functioning, and (6) encouraging and supporting participation of all members.

After a diagnosis of the group's functioning is made, the teacher needs the skills necessary to intervene effectively in the ongoing process of the group. Intervention skills depend primarily upon self-awareness and flexibility of behavior. Through an awareness of how he is behaving and how his behavior is perceived by the members of the group, the teacher establishes control over his behavior. For example, when a teacher wishes to give support to a student who is having a difficult time participating in a discussion group, he needs to be aware of the cues he uses to communicate his support and how they are perceived by the students. A person's behavior is quite often misinterpreted; a simple supportive comment such as "Thank you for your contribution, John," can be misconstrued as being sarcastic and punishing. As a result of one's awareness of his behavior, he can modify it to communicate his intent more clearly. An awareness of and control over his behavior enables a teacher to behave flexibly according to the demands of the situation and the characteristics of the group members. A teacher who is locked into one style of behaving in groups, such as a democratic or autocratic style, will not be able to function effectively under a variety of conditions. At times a group may need a strong, directive leader, and at other times it may need a moderator who only initiates a discussion topic and then sits back and lets the group members do the rest.

Both the teacher and the students are responsible for behaving in ways that will help the group accomplish its task and maintain itself in good working order. There are, however, two major roles the teacher will perform that are difficult for students to assume. The first is an instructional role of resource expert; the teacher in most situations will best know what materials, information, and readings are most relevant and helpful for the group. The second is a group-performance role of teaching the students the group skills they need to function effectively in a discussion group. This may involve skill sessions in which students are given practice in fulfilling different roles in the group and/or periodical evaluations of the functions present in the group and those needed to improve the quality of the group's functioning.

Finally, in a discussion group the members should clearly understand what is expected of them. The teacher's expectations and the procedure that the group is going to follow should be as clear as possible. Goal-directed behavior cannot be achieved in the absence of perceived goals. If the goals are not clear, even the most highly motivated student will have difficulty being effective, because he has no conceptual model or clear understanding of the kind of behavior that would contribute to building a good group. This does not mean that the teacher should impose a clear structure upon the students, but that the teacher and the students need to develop a clear understanding of what the objectives of the group are, of the criteria against which the performance of the group can be evaluated, and of what behaviors are needed in order to insure an effective learning group.

SUMMARY

Leadership may be defined as an influence relationship between two or more persons who depend upon one another for the attainment of mutual goals within a group situation. The earliest approach to leadership focused upon the conception of leaders as people who possess certain distinctive traits. This approach has proved unsatisfactory, however, as research indicates that leaders are practically indistinguishable from nonleaders on personality, ability, and background variables. Dissatisfaction with the trait approach gave rise to a view of leadership that stresses the characteristics of the group and the situation in which the group exists. Leadership is viewed as the performance of those acts that help the group achieve its goals. Such acts are termed group functions. Defined as such, any member of a group may be a leader in the sense that he may take actions that serve group functions. The functional approach to leadership stresses the ability to adapt to changing situations. Situational factors such as the nature of the group's goals, the structure of the group, the attitudes or needs of the members, and the particular requirements of the group's ongoing tasks, influence the specific leadership behavior needed to perform group functions at a given time and who among the members will perform them.

The main conclusion that can be drawn from much of the research on leadership is that the pattern of leader behaviors that is high on both the dimensions of consideration and of initiation of structure tends to increase group effectiveness. Groups functioning under different conditions, however, may need different emphases on the two factors. There is evidence, for example, that if the task is either very easy or very difficult the leader who focuses primarily upon initiating structure is effective, while if the task is of intermediate difficulty, consideration is the more important leadership behavior.

Finally, leadership behavior in the classroom was discussed as dealing with the ability to diagnose what actions are needed in order for the classroom groups to accomplish their tasks and maintain themselves over time and the ability to intervene effectively in the on-going group process of the classroom. As is discussed elsewhere in this book, diagnostic skills are based upon the conceptual schemes one uses to analyze the classroom; many of the concepts a teacher could use in diagnosing classroom functioning are presented in the different chapters of this book. Intervention skills are based upon self-awareness and interpersonal competence, which can be best gained in such activities as sensitivity-training groups, which are discussed in the chapter dealing with innovation and change within organizations.

CHAPTER 8

INTERPERSONAL EXPECTATIONS AND ACADEMIC PERFORMANCE

Introduction

The role of the student is to adhere to the organizational norms of the school and classroom and to apply himself to the accomplishment of the school's objectives. One of the school's objectives is to have the student achieve academically, and there are a variety of school and classroom norms that support this objective. In organizational settings, role expectations and norms direct the behavior of members. Role requirements are based upon the expectations of complementary positions, with the expectations of occupants of positions higher in the authority structure usually having more influence than the expectations of positions lower in the authority structure. Norms refer to the common beliefs of an evaluative type that make explicit the forms of behavior appropriate for members of the social system, and refer to the expected behavior rewarded or punished by the social system. The very existence and functioning of organizations demonstrate the power of role and normative expectations in controlling, directing, and coordinating behavior of individuals. Perhaps the basic law of social organization is that individuals will usually conform willingly to the expectations of others. In a classroom, therefore, a teacher's expectations of student role behavior should have considerable effect upon student behavior.

In addition to behavior within organizations, the expectations of others, especially if they are especially significant in an individual's life (that is, his parents, friends, and so forth), are powerful influences upon his behavior. In this chapter these expectancy effects upon behavior as well as the role and normative expectancy influences will be subsumed under the concept of "interpersonal expectation." An interpersonal expectation is an expectation held by one individual concerning the behavior of another individual.

The Effect of Expectation upon Behavior Change

In addition to the material discussed in Chapter 6, there is evidence from a variety of sources that the expectations of a "significant other" influence a person's behavior (McClelland, 1965a). Hovland, Janis, and Kelley (1953) conducted a series of studies on prestige-suggestion, which showed that people will believe or do what prestigeful sources suggest. Roethlisberger and Dickson (1939) coined the term "Hawthorne effect" for the fact that people who feel that they are especially selected to show an effect will tend to show it. Frank (1963) talks about the "Hello-Goodbye" effect in psychotherapy, in which patients who merely have contact with a prestigeful medical authority improve significantly over waiting list controls and almost as much as those who get prolonged therapy. Rosenthal (1966) demonstrates that experimental subjects will often do what an experimenter wants them to do, even though neither he nor they know he is trying to influence them. Kausler (1959) and Mierke (1955), in a series of studies on goal setting, showed that setting goals for a person particularly in the name of prestigeful authorities like "science" or "research" improves performance. Finally, parent-child studies (for example, Rosen and D'Andrade, 1959) show that parents who set higher standards of excellence for their sons are more likely to have sons with high-achievement needs. The common factor in all of these studies seems to be that goals are being set for the individual by sources he respects, goals that imply that his behavior should change for a variety of reasons and that it can change. The belief in the possibility and desirability of change are tremendously influential in changing a person.

The Power of Interpersonal Expectations

In his book on the psychology of human conflict, Guthrie (1938) gives the following case to illustrate how the expectations of others and the subsequent treatment an individual receives from others may modify his self-attitudes and change his behavior.

> A small group of college men . . . agreed to cooperate in establishing a shy and inept girl as a social favorite. They saw to it . . . that she was invited to college affairs that were considered important and that she always had dancing partners. They treated her by agreement as though she were the reigning college favorite. Before the year was over she had developed an easy manner and a confident assumption that she was popular. These habits continued her social success after the experiment was completed and the men involved had ceased to make efforts in her behalf. They themselves had accepted her as a success. What her college career would have been if the experiment had not been made is impossible to say, of course, but it is fairly certain that she would have resigned all social ambitions and would have found interests compatible with her social ineptitude.

Such expectancy effects have been well documented in folklore and rumor, one of the most notable being a theme of the play *Pygmalion* by Bernard Shaw. Furthermore, the use of placebos in medicine and research on psychotherapy has long indicated how expectations can affect psychological and physiological processes. Frank (1963) notes:

> Comparison of the effects of psychotherapy and placebos . . . suggests that certain symptoms may be relieved equally well by both . . . and raises the possibility that one of the features accounting for some of the success of all forms of psychotherapy is their ability to arouse the patient's expectation of help.

Self-Fulfilling Prophecy

In a variety of settings and under a wide range of conditions inter-personal expectations can set up a self-fulfilling prophecy. As previously noted, a self-fulfilling prophecy is, in the beginning, a *false* definition of the situation evoking a new behavior that makes the originally false conception come true. Some self-fulfilling prophecies are benign; for instance, the child's expectations that his new school-mates will be friendly can help considerably to create friendly peer relationships. Other self-fulfilling prophecies are malignant; such as when a child is falsely defined as being of inferior ability and the power of the expectations help to create an underachiever. The problem for the teacher is to support benign prophecies and intervene in ways that terminate malignant self-fulfilling prophecies. It is possible that the highly skilled and successful teacher is good at helping make her prophecies come true.

The Effect of Expectations upon Achievement-Oriented Behavior

Perhaps the most famous case of the effect of expectations upon behavior is that of a horse known as Clever Hans (Rosenthal and Jacobson, 1968). By means of tapping his hoof Hans could add, subtract, multiply, and divide. He could spell, read, solve problems of musical harmony, and answer personal questions, all through tapping his foot. His owner, a German mathematics teacher, seemed unlikely of having any fraudulent intent, as he did not profit financially from his horse's talent. In a brilliant set of experiments it was discovered that Hans could answer questions only if the questioner himself knew the answer and was visible to the horse during his foot-tapping of the answer. It was finally discovered that whenever people asked Hans a question, they leaned forward very slightly the better to see Hans' hoof. That, it turned out, was the unintentional signal for Hans to begin tapping. Then, as Hans approached the number of hooftaps representing the correct answer, the questioners would typically show a tiny head movement. That almost imperceptible cue was the signal for Hans to stop tapping, and Hans, once again, gave the correct answer. The questioner, by communicating his expectations to Hans through subtle nonverbal cues, was actually telling Hans the right answer.

In the 1960s a social psychologist named Robert Rosenthal began to systematically study expectancy effects in both animals and humans. His animal experiments typically followed a set procedure. He would ask a class in experimental psychology to perform an experiment with animals. The students were told of studies that had shown that maze-brightness and maze-dullness could be developed in strains of rats by successive inbreeding of the well and the poorly performing maze runners. He would then assign a perfectly ordinary laboratory rat to each student and would tell half the students that their rats were maze-bright while the other half were told that their rats were maze-dull. The student then gave his rat a chance to learn a maze correctly, giving the rat a number of trials for a number of days. The results of the experiments are quite clear (Rosenthal, 1966). Beginning with the first day and continuing on through the experiment, animals believed to be better performers became better performers. These experiments took place in a variety of learning situations, such as mazes, Skinner boxes, and troughs. They demonstrate that the expectation of the experimenter can affect the performance of an experimental animal.

Rosenthal then moved to demonstrating the same phenomena with human subjects. In an experiment that has been replicated several times, ten students served as experimenters in a psychological experiment in which they each asked twenty students to rate a series of ten photographs of people's faces on the degree of success or failure shown in each face. The photographs had been carefully preselected as being faces that were seen as neither successful nor unsuccessful. Half of the experimenters were told that subjects generally rated the photos as being of successful people and half were told that subjects rated the photos as being of unsuccessful people. Although each experimenter was given identical instructions (except for his expectation about how subjects would probably respond) and were given identical instructions to read to their subjects, every experimenter who had been led to expect ratings of the pictures as sucessful obtained a higher average rating of success than did any experimenter expecting ratings of the pictures as less successful. Thus Rosental demonstrated that on a highly controlled person-perception task, the expectations of the experimenter significantly affected the performance of the subject. He then turned to a school situation to see if the same expectancy effect could be demonstrated in a field situation.

The basic experiment (Rosenthal and Jacobson, 1968) was to administer an intelligence test to all students of an elementary school (grades one through six), randomly choose a certain number of students to serve as an experimental group, and inform the teachers that the results of the test indicated that these students would make unusual strides in intellectual development during the coming year. The teachers had previously been informed that the intelligence test had been developed to predict forthcoming "spurts" in intellectual growth. The intelligence test was then readministered to the children after a semester, after a year, and again after two years. The major finding of the study was that the experimental children on the average increased in performance 12.2 points in IQ during the year, while the undesignated children (that is, the control group) increased in performance an average of 8.4 IQ points. Statistical tests suggest that this difference was one that could not reasonably be ascribed to chance variation alone and, therefore, the investigators concluded that teachers' expectations do affect the intellectual growth of students. The difference between the experimental and control group, however, was greatest during the first two years of school. Data from questionnaires completed by the teachers participating in the study indicate, furthermore, that there may be real costs for the student who does not conform to the teacher's expectations. The teacher evaluations of the children in the control group who gained intellectually during the year indicate that such children were regarded as *less* well-adjusted, *less* interesting, and *less* affectionate than the children in the control group who did not gain intellectually. Students in the experimental group who gained intellectually, on the other hand, were very favorably evaluated. Thus, when children who are not expected to develop intellectually do so, they seem either to show accompanying undesirable behavior or at least are perceived by their teachers as showing undesirable behavior. This was especially true for children placed in the lower-ability tracts. It appears that in at least the classrooms which Rosenthal and Jacobson studied, unpredicted intellectual growth is hazardous.

It is a very difficult task to conduct such a study under controlled conditions. Rosenthal and Jacobson's study has been severely criticized on the basis of such factors as the validity of the tests used and the validity of the pretest data, which was used in calculating the extent of the expectancy effects. Gumpert and Gumpert (1968) even went so far as to reanalyze the data, but concluded that the study provides a perfectly satisfactory demonstration that the teacher-expectation effects hypothesized do indeed take place. Rosenthal (1967) reports three replications of the study in the midwest and the east, which corroborate the Rosenthal and Jacobson results. Beez (1967), furthermore, conducted an excellent study of the short-term effects of teacher expectations. In his study, sixty preschool pupils were taught the meaning of a series of symbols by one teacher. Half the sixty teachers had been led to expect good symbol learning and half had been led to expect poor symbol learning. Twenty-three percent of the children alleged to have poorer intellectual prospects learned five or more symbols while 77 percent of the children alleged to have better intellectual prospects did so. Such a result would occur by chance only two times in a million. The effect of expectation upon teacher effort was equally astonishing. Eight or more symbols were taught by 87 percent of the teachers expecting better performance, but only 13 percent of the teachers expecting poorer performance tried to teach that many symbols to their pupil; this result would occur by chance only one time in ten million.

The Rosenthal and Jacobson study needs to be replicated successfully several more times before it can be fully accepted. Taking the research on experimenter-expectancy effects and the research on teacher-expectancy effects as a whole, however, one can safely conclude that teacher expectations do have powerful short-term effects and perhaps have powerful long-term effects on the students' intellectual functioning.

A point that should be emphasized is that the teachers and the experimenters were not aware that their expectations were communicated to the students, rats, and subjects. It appears that a person who is in a position to exercise over another the subtle interpersonal influence contained in expectation may do so without being aware either of the content of the message he transmits or the ways he transmits it. The recipient of the expectations may be equally unaware that any transaction other than the obvious overt one is taking place; he may well do what is expected of him without even realizing that a demand on him is being made.

Gumpert and Gumpert (1968) note that the manner in which one person influences another is not determined entirely in advance by previously existing attitudes and beliefs. Expectations may change, vary, increase, or decrease, depending on the nature of the ongoing social interaction and the reciprocal influence that two people have upon one another. In the classroom the teacher's behavior toward a child is based not only upon initial expectations, but also by what occurs between them.

Nor is expectation an isolated variable. During interaction with the child the teacher builds up many impressions, attitudes, and reactions of the child. Initial expectations, however, may make the teacher more sensitive to the child's potential and sensitize the teacher to perceive the child's capabilities and ignore some of his shortcomings.

Explanation of Expectancy Effects

As common and powerful as interpersonal expectancy effects seem to be, virtually nothing is known about how they are communicated. Rosenthal's research has dramatically demonstrated that a person's behavior is affected, often in very subtle ways, by the expectancies of others. But it does not lead to the specification of the conditions under which expectancy effects are most powerful nor to an understanding of the processes that mediate their effectiveness. He found very exciting ways to demonstrate the existence of a phenomena, but he has not contributed to the understanding of the phenomena or the advancement of social psychological theory in the area, though his ongoing research is attempting to isolate, identify, and explain just what factors (verbal and nonverbal) are at work in the communication of teacher expectancy. One of the major problems of social psychology is the profusion of concepts which represent essentially the same phenomena. As noted in the introduction of this section, Rosenthal's expectancy effects are related to the work in role expectations and conformity to normative expectations. By neither relating his research to the already existent research and theory in these and other areas nor subsuming other work under his concepts, Rosenthal has perhaps introduced an unnecessary confusion to the area of interpersonal expectations.

The literature on conformity to normative expectations is discussed in Chapter 12 and, therefore, will not be discussed here. Gumpert and

Gumpert (1968), in their discussion of the Rosenthal and Jacobson study, raise the possibility that one of the processes that may mediate the effect of interpersonal expectations is the effect of expectations upon perception. There are literally hundreds of studies conducted in a variety of contexts that are relevant to the notion that a person's attitudes, set, or expectation will affect his perceptions and behavior. This research demonstrates that expectation affects perception through momentary and enduring sets derived from past experiences (Postman and Brown, 1952; Foley and MacMillan, 1943). Such sets sharpened one's ability to perceive barely distinguishable stimuli (Neisser, 1954) and resulted in interpreting ambiguous events in such a way as to confirm the expectations derived from the set (Minturn, 1954). Two people with different sets can observe the same event and interpret it quite differently (Dearborn and Simon, 1958). In other words, an expectation that a certain student will improve in achievement during the school year can serve as a mental set that increases the probability that the teacher will notice very small indications of improvement and will interpret ambiguous responses by the student as being "bright." It is possible that two teachers given different sets toward a student would interpret his behavior quite differently. When the teacher finds his expectations being confirmed, furthermore, he is likely, either subtly or overtly or both, to alter his treatment of the child, intensifying his efforts to reach him, changing his behavior and attitudes toward the child in such ways as alterations in body posture when conversing with the child, tone of voice, perceived interest, facial expression, or verbal praise. This in turn will reward the student for achieving and encourage him to increase his motivation, attention, and so on. It becomes a benign cycle of the self-fulfilling prophecy.

Conditions under Which Expectancy Effects Are Strongest

Under cooperative conditions, a teacher is defined as an ally who has one's best interests at heart. Under competitive conditions a teacher is defined as an enemy who is trying to force one to engage in undesired behavior. It would seem logical that teacher expectations would have a positive effect, therefore, only when the student sees himself in a cooperative relationship with the teacher. When the student sees the teacher as an enemy it will become a matter of prestige and strength to behave opposite to what the teacher expects. Teacher expectations, in other words, may boomerang in conditions where the student sees a competititive relationship existing between himself and the teacher.

The personality of the student seems another variable that influences the effectiveness of teacher expectations. Frank (1963) found that placebo successes occurred most often with patients who tended to be dependent, emotionally reactive, conventional, and more trusting than other patients. Students, furthermore, who are adult-oriented, who have a high need for social approval from adults, or who are "other-directed" will probably be more affected by teacher expectations than will students who are peer-oriented, independent, and "inner-directed."

It also stands to reason that some teachers will be better at expressing expectations in ways that affect student behavior than are other teachers. Rosenthal (1966) presents some evidence that such things as the physical appearance, confidence, warmth, friendliness, amount of experience or competence, interest, and status of the person affect the extent to which his expectancies are influential. It is possible that the teacher who is warm, friendly, and sure of himself will be more effective in expressing expectations that affect student behavior than will a teacher who is cold, distant and unfriendly, and unsure of himself. There is evidence that warmth of the examiner, for example, may affect performance on achievement tests.

Gordon and Durea (1948) found that when the examiners behaved more warmly toward their eighth-grade subjects, the IQ scores obtained were over six points higher than when they behaved more cooly toward their adolescent subjects. Crow (1964) found that even with college-age subjects, those who were treated more warmly performed better at a coding task that was very similar to one of the subtests ("Digit Symbol") of the Wechsler Adult Intelligence Scale. An experiment by Ware, Kowal, and Baker (1963) on subjects in the military in which the performance required was that of detecting signals demonstrated that the subjects were significantly more alert in the detection of signals when the experimenter was warmer, and less alert when the experimenter was cooler toward the subjects. Finally, Sacks (1952) found that more warmly treated nursery-school children showed a net profit of nearly ten IQ points relative to more indifferently treated children.

A recent study provides additional information about the effect of warmth upon behavior when it is paired with rewarding remarks. Canavan (1968) distinguishes between two general styles that can be used by a person to attempt to maintain satisfaction in his environment: reward orientation and cost orientation (see Thibaut and Kelley, 1959). A reward-oriented individual is one who attempts to act in his environment to obtain satisfying things for himself. In viewing the world he pays more attention to potential rewards than he does to potential costs. He is usually confident, outgoing, and relatively skillful at controlling the environment. A cost-oriented individual, on the other hand, maintains his satisfactions by keeping his standards for satisfaction relatively low and by using his energy to avoid costs and failures; he attends more to the potential costs in the environment than to the rewards that may lie in it. He tends to feel unconfident, constricted, and relatively powerless to influence the environment. Often he has fewer skills for handling the environment than does the reward-oriented person. Canavan suggests that individuals who hold special significance for an individual, such as his parents, teachers, and friends, teach a person to adopt a reward or a cost orientation to life or to certain situations.

It seems reasonable to assume that to risk new ways of doing things or new levels of task difficulty or to raise one's level of aspiration may be useful for the development of new skills as well as for feelings of mastery and self-confidence. If the above theory is correct, reward-oriented individuals will be more achieving students and will have higher levels of aspiration and take more risks in testing the limits of their abilities than will cost-oriented people. Schools, therefore, may wish to attempt to develop students who are more reward-oriented than cost-oriented.

In her experiment, Canavan demonstrates that children who are rewarded by warm, complimentary remarks for correct responses will choose more difficult problems to work on in the future, and will make fewer errors on those problems in spite of their difficulty than will children punished for incorrect responses by cold, uncomplimentary remarks by an adult who ignores correct responses. Subjects who are rewarded, furthermore, will tend to be more confident that they will do well on similar tasks in the future and will be less bothered by their failures than will children who are punished.

Conclusion

Expectations of teachers are affected in many overt and covert ways in a school. The things one hears from other teachers, the records of the student, the opinions of the counselor, the previous academic performance of the student, all affect a teacher's expectations about how a student will behave. Perhaps the most powerful influence upon expectancies is ability grouping, which institutionalizes expectancies for the children placed in each tract. Ability grouping is discussed in detail in Chapter 10. It is important that school personnel be aware of the powerful influence interpersonal expectancies can have and attempt to intervene in instances where a malevolent self-fulfilling prophecy may be operating.

SUMMARY

In this chapter we have examined the concept of "interpersonal expectation," that is, the expectations held by one individual concerning the behavior of another. Subsumed under this concept are role and normative expectations and the expectations of significant others. It is the basic hypothesis of the chapter that these expectations of others have a great deal of influence over the actual behavior of an individual.

A number of studies have shown that people will believe or do what prestigeful others suggest. Probably the most concentrated and systematic investigation of expectancy effects however, was undertaken in a series of studies conducted by Robert Rosenthal. Starting at the level of animal behavior, he had students train rats to run a maze and found that the group of students who worked with animals they expected to perform well, actually performed better than the animals of students who expected a poor performance from their animals. Moving on to human subjects, Rosenthal demonstrated that, on a highly controlled person-perception task, the expectations of the experimenter significantly affected the performance of the subject.

He then turned to a school situation. Teachers of a number of elementary-school students, designated as the experimental group, were informed that test results indicated that these students would show a sudden intellectual growth during the coming year. A control group of students was also set up about which no information was given. The major finding of the study was that the average increase in IQ of the children in the experimental group was significantly greater than the average increase in the control group, leading Rosenthal to conclude that teachers' expectations do affect the intellectual growth of students. In addition, the teachers were not aware that their expectations were communicated to the students and, although not examined in this study, students may be equally unaware that any transaction is taking place.

Rosenthal's research has substantiated the fact that a person's behavior is affected, often in very subtle ways, by the expectations of others. He has not, however, specified the conditions under which expectancy effects are most powerful nor indicated the processes which mediate their effectiveness. One possible explanation may be found with the framework of role theory. That is, given the student's role in the classroom social system is subordinate to that of the teacher, interpersonal expectancy effects may merely reflect conformity to the legitimate role expectations of one who occupies a position of higher authority. Another possible mediating process is that an expectation that a certain student will improve in achievement increases the probability that any given academic performance on the part of the student will be perceived as improvement. Finding his expectations confirmed, the teacher will be more likely to reward the student for achieving. This in turn will increase the student's expectations of success and thus his academic motivation that, subsequently, would lead to a higher IQ score.

This chapter also specifies certain conditions under which expectancy effects are likely to be strongest. With respect to students, these effects will be most powerful when students see themselves in a cooperative relationship with the teacher and when they have a high need for social approval from adults or tend to be other-directed. From the point of view of teachers, their expectations are more likely to affect student behavior when they are warm, friendly, and sure of themselves.

CHAPTER 9

COOPERATION, COMPETITION, AND CONFLICT RESOLUTION

Introduction

Matthew Arnold once said:

> . . . the world which seems
> To lie before us like a land of dreams,
> So various, so beautiful, so new,
> Hath really neither joy, nor love, nor light . . .
> And we are here, as on a darkling plain
> Swepth with confused alarms of struggle and flight,
> Where ignorant armies clash by night.*

Man as a species is standing in a maze of conflicts between nations, races, and generations, any one of which could start a third world

* From "Dover Beach."

war. Man as a species has had for the last twenty years or so the technology and raw materials to destroy the entire world or, at the very least, to kill every living thing upon the earth. This technological capacity has made war and other forms of violence obsolete as means of resolving conflicts. Yet the basic answer man seems to have to conflict situations is "kill" or repress by force. If man as a species is to survive he must learn to handle conflicts constructively. Perhaps the most important question facing the world today is whether or not man can do so.

To make a prediction about how successful man will be in handling conflicts constructively, imagine yourself to be a visitor from another planet, engaged in a field study of man. You survey his technological capacities for self-destruction, his stock piles of weapons, you look at his past and present behavior in conflict situations, then you make a prediction about his survival. What would it be? Lorenz (1963) says the following:

> An unprejudiced observer from another planet, looking upon man as he is today, in his hand the atom bomb, the product of his intelligence, in his heart the aggressive drive inherited from his anthropoid ancestors, which this same intelligence cannot control, would not prophesy long life for the species. . . .
>
> We approach a crossroad at which we either educate ourselves, allies and enemies alike, in the nature of human behavior, using this knowledge to promote future behavior, or we continue along a road leading to the extinction of our species. And this, in the evolutionary view, will be about as significant as the extinction of the icthyosaur. (p. 49)

Broadly, the question of how conflicts are handled involves the survival of man as a species. This chapter, however, will not attempt to deal directly with such a broad issue, but rather will deal with how organizational and interpersonal conflicts are and can be handled within the school. Every social relationship contains elements of conflict, disagreement, and opposed interests. The relationships between the students in the classroom and between the students and the teacher are no exception. One of the most important aspects of classroom life is how conflicts are handled, and one of the key ways of ensuring that conflicts are handled constructively is to build cooperative relationships among students and between the students and the teacher.

Perhaps the leading theorist in the field of cooperation, competition, and conflict resolution is Morton Deutsch; it is primarily his research and theory, therefore, that this chapter discusses.

Conflict within Organizations

The role definitions and the norms and values of organizations are not fixed entities that never change. In many respects they are constantly changing and can be viewed as compromise outcomes of antagonistic forces within the organization. Organizations function by means of adjustments and compromises among conflicting elements in their structure and membership. Within the membership of an educational organization there may be conflicts between members who aggressively advocate innovation and change and members who favor the present approaches to education. Inherent areas of conflict within the organizational structure may exist between different subsystems who compete for the same resources or between various levels in the hierarchy of power, privilege, and rewards. Within universities for example, different departments may compete for the same resources, such as students, money, and facilities. Almost inevitably, furthermore, there are conflicts within organizations between members who have power and authority and those who do not; those who are low on the hierarchy of power, privilege, and rewards want to distribute them more equitably while the members who are high in the hierarchy want to keep the status quo. Finally, in organizations such as schools, whose major input is people, many conflicts result from major changes in the type of students attending the school. When the nature of the student body changes, the old structures for educating students may be inappropriate and ineffective, therefore giving rise to conflicts within the organization.

Two common ways of resolving conflicts within organizations are through public review of grievances by impartial individuals and through an appeals system through which members can challenge actions of their superiors. Neither method is often used, however, within educational organizations. Students and parents with felt grievances against school personnel have almost no recourse to review by impartial bodies. Teachers' accountability for their behavior is only occasionally to their students or communities. For the most part teachers are accountable to colleagues or supervisors within their profession. Most often attempts on the part of parents and members of the community to influence teachers' classroom behavior is resisted and resented by teachers.

Scott (1965) points out that appeals systems that bypass the chain of command are a necessary and fruitful procedure for conflict resolution in most organizations. Although procedures to insure members' redress against the arbitrary use of authority is common in most medium- and large-size industrial organizations and public agencies, within school systems there is a notable absence of judicial and appeals systems. Students are seldom granted the right to appeal the teacher's use of his authority. In order for an appeals system to be effective, furthermore, members must be aware of the process by which it is used, of the breadth of their rights to use it, and the degree of separation between the judicial and other management functions. In many schools students may find a sympathetic administrator, but lack of general awareness of procedures for appealing teacher actions negates any effective appeals system.

Conflicts between Students and School Personnel

Perhaps the major area of conflict within the public schools and many colleges and universities involves the redistribution of decision-making power among students and school personnel. The roots of this area of conflict lie in the increasing student alienation from the school and in the control orientation found in most schools.

From a review of the literature, Chesler and Franklin (1968) conclude that urban and suburban public schools may increasingly have students who, for a variety of reasons, are likely to be rebellious against adult controls or insistent upon personal and social autonomy. Schools are primarily based upon the premise that a good education increases the chances of being successful in future life; for students who are not highly motivated for future success many of the school activities are irrelevant and distasteful. There are, in addition, a growing number of students who actually perceive the school as an obstacle to their own goals; many minority-group students, for example, see the present educational system as promoting racism and inequality in American society. Stinchcombe (1964) states that student alienation is most likely to occur when students' future status is not clearly related to present school performance and when adolescents lay claim for personal autonomy and status more typically conferred on adults. Kvaraceus (1965) states that for the Negro child, there is very little apparent connection between what goes on in the school and the present or the future life of the learner. For many reasons, therefore, students are becoming disenchanted with and alienated from the public schools and the universities. Such students will no longer gullibly accept the notion that everything in the school, including repressive teachers, is benevolently intended for furthering their best interests and aspirations.

The organizational life of public schools is dominated by a concern with controlling students. This control orientation largely springs from the fact that public schools cannot select their clients and students cannot refuse to attend. The major concern of teachers seems to be classroom control and the competence of teachers is often judged by their peers on the basis of how well they control their classes. Ziegler (1967) notes that the maintenance of the superior-subordinate relationship between teachers and students leads to personal rigidity on the part of teachers and that the teachers' fear of loss of authority makes security their dominant need. The need for security, for clear authority that the students do not challenge, leads to attempts to impose controls on students' behavior. Kvaraceus notes that teachers in urban schools, where there are numbers of reluctant or recalcitrant learners, are dominated by fear, anxiety, and anger. Perhaps the popularity of behavior-modification techniques reflects an attempt by school personnel to regain control over students; by reinforcing students for desired behaviors the teacher is in control of the student, with clear guidelines on how to "shape" his behavior.

The emphasis of the public schools on the control of student behavior makes students vulnerable to the arbitrary, or apparently arbitrary, use of authority. The lack of public review of the use of authority by school personnel and the absence of any judicial or appeal system highlights the students' lack of power. As Chesler and Franklin note, the lines between "rulers" and "ruled" are overt, visible, and liable to attack within public schools. Since the role characteristics of students constantly remind them of their lack of influence and lower status, a general potential for conflict exists. Kvaraceus states that the school's heavy stress upon external and adult controls tends to deepen the minunderstanding and resentment that exist between students and school personnel. He notes that when strong controls are successful in forcing students to conform to school regulations, a reluctant and recalcitrant conformist living close to the letter of the law results; when the controls are unsuccessful an overt aggressive student who is ready to join any rebellion results.

Students almost never have direct representation in the policy making of the school and are rarely consulted for advice. Student councils, student courts, and student newspapers all overtly or covertly controlled by the faculty and administration, represent a mockery of democratic political processes, and students know it (Kvaraceus, 1965). When large numbers of students resent and distrust the control mechanisms of the school, the collective and legitimate authority of the school personnel is undermined. When students no longer believe that school personnel will act in the students' immediate behalf, or adapt the educational program to their present and long-run needs and best interests, they are likely to directly attempt to change the school. Since students have few legitimate channels for the exercise of influence or control over school life, they are forced to use disruption to force negotiations with school personnel. Perhaps the only clear power students have is to organize and so disrupt the ongoing activities of the school that they close it down.

Chesler and Franklin, in examining the causes of conflicts between students and school personnel, concluded that many such conflicts originate in student concerns about the lack of personal communication with school personnel, the dehumanizing way in which students are treated, the lack of student power to legitimately change the situation, and the failure of the school to make good on its pronouncements concerning the formation of an educational program that encourages self-actualization and develops personal autonomy, independence, and self-reliance.

On the whole, public school administrators have responded in three general ways to student rebellions (Chesler and Franklin, 1968). They often deny that there are problems within the school and attempt to ignore the evidence of student discontent and to gloss over the issues. Frequently they distort the position and grievances of students. Finally, they often attempt to repress the student unrest by suspending or expelling the students involved or bringing police forces into the school. As Chesler and Franklin note, sometimes students' requests are quite legitimate and should be considered carefully and openly. The above methods of dealing with students requests confirm students' preconceptions of the school and the society as being closed and inaccessible to change.

While schools as organizations need to make structural changes to increase the decision-making power of the students, it is primarily within the classroom that conflicts arise and are dealt with. Thus, taking a closer look at the definition of a conflict, this chapter now moves to the discussion of cooperation, competition, and the management of interpersonal conflicts within the classroom.

The Nature of Conflict

To understand the nature of conflicts within schools it is necessary to define what a conflict is, to specify its source, and to evaluate its potential functional and dysfunctional consequences. A *conflict* exists whenever incompatible activities occur (Deutsch, 1969); an action that is incompatible with another action prevents, obstructs, interferes with, injures, or in some way makes that action less likely or less effective. The incompatible actions may originate in one person (intrapersonal), one group (intragroup), two or more persons (interpersonal), or two or more groups (intergroup). A conflict may arise from a variety of sources, some of which are (1) differences in information, beliefs, values, interests, or desires, (2) a scarcity of some resource such as money, power, time, space, or position, and (3) rivalries in which one person or group competes with another (Deutsch, 1969).

A superficial reading of many social psychological theories with their emphasis on tension reduction, dissonance reduction, good balance, and good form would seem to imply that the psychological utopia would be a conflict-free existence (Deutsch, 1969). Many discussions of conflict cast it in the role of causing psychopathology, social disorder, and war. Yet it is apparent that most people seek out conflict through such activities as competitive sports and games, plays, television, and books, and through interpersonal activities such as teasing. Deutsch (1966) notes that conflict is often of personal and social value and is certainly a pervasive and inevitable aspect of life; in addition, it can have many useful functions: (1) it prevents stagnation, (2) it stimulates curiosity and interest, (3) it is the me-

159

dium through which problems can be solved, (4) it is the root of personal, organizational, and social change, and (5) it is often part of the process of testing and assessing oneself and, as such, it may be highly enjoyable as one experiences the pleasure of the full and active use of one's resources.

The question, therefore, is not how to eliminate or prevent conflict, but rather how to make it productive, or at the very least, how to prevent it from being destructive. A social psychologist would phrase the question as, what are the conditions under which the participants in a conflict will resolve it in productive rather than destructive ways.

Cooperation and Competition

As will be discussed in more detail later in this chapter, whether the relationships in the classroom are cooperative or competitive is of great importance both in terms of how conflicts are handled and in terms of student learning. The nature of cooperative and competitive relationships, therefore, needs to be defined.

In a cooperative social situation the goals of the separate individuals are so linked together that there is a positive correlation between their goal attainments (Deutsch, 1962a). Under pure cooperative conditions, an individual can obtain his goal if and only if the others with whom he is linked can obtain their goals. An example of a cooperative relationship is a football team; its goal is to win the football game and in such a team sport if one person accomplishes the goal then every member of the team also accomplishes the goal.

From the definition of cooperation it follows that when any individual behaves in such a way as to increase his chances of goal attainment, he increases the chances that the others with whom he is linked will also achieve their goals. Deutsch (1949, 1962a) states that the psychological consequences of such a state of affairs are: (1) substitutability—the actions of members in a cooperative relationship are interchangeable; if one member has engaged in a certain behavior there is no need for others within the relationship to repeat the behavior; (2) positive cathexis—if the actions of one member in a cooperative relationship move the individuals toward their goal, his actions (and he as a person) will be favorably evaluated by the others; and (3) inducibility—if the actions of a person in a cooperative relationship move the others toward their goal, the others will be receptive to his attempts to induce them to engage in behavior which will facilitate his actions.

In a competitive social situation the individuals' goals are so linked that there is a negative correlation between their goal attainments (Deutsch, 1962a). Under pure competitive conditions an individual can obtain his goal if and only if the others with whom he is linked cannot obtain their goals. An example of a competitive situation is an athletic contest between two teams; both their goals are to win and if one team wins the other team has failed to accomplish its goal. In a competitive relationship, when any individual behaves in such a way as to increase his chances of goal attainment, he decreases the chances that the others with whom he is linked will achieve their goals. One may expect just the opposite of substitutability, positive cathexis, and positive inducibility if a person perceives another's actions are decreasing rather than increasing his chances of goal attainment (Deutsch, 1962a). That is, he will hinder rather than facilitate, be negatively rather than positively influenced, dislike rather than like, correct rather than be satisfied with the other's actions.

One may expect, therefore, radically different types of behavior in cooperative and competitive situations, depending upon whether the actions of the individuals involved are seen as increasing or decreasing the chances of goal attainment. Deutsch (1962a) emphasizes that an individual will tend to facilitate the actions of others when he perceives that their actions will be promotive of his chances of goal attainment, and will tend to obstruct their actions when he perceives that they will be detrimental to his goal attainment.

There is often a basic confusion between the terms "conflict" and "competition"; although competition produces conflict, not all instances of conflict reflect competition (Deutsch, 1969). In conflict derived from competition, the incompatible actions of the individuals involved reflect incompatible goals. Conflict, however, may occur even when there is no perceived or actual incompatibility of goals. Two individuals, for example, could be in conflict over the means to be used to accomplish a single goal that they both desire and can jointly share; such controversy over the means to achieve a mutually desired goal is a common part of cooperation. Conflict of this type is not competitive so long as the cooperators are motivated to select the best means to their mutual goal rather than insisting on the ones which they initially advocated. The distinction between conflict and competition is an important one for Deutsch as it is his contention that conflict can occur in a cooperative or a competitive context and the processses of conflict resolution which are likely to be employed will be strongly influenced by the context within which the conflict occurs.

The Context of Classroom Relationships, Conflict, and Learning

Relationships within the classroom, ways of dealing with conflict, and learning activity all can occur in either cooperative or competitive contexts and are all likely to be influenced strongly by the context within which they do occur. The processes of cooperation and competition, furthermore, tend to be self-confirming, so that the experience of cooperation will induce a benign spiral of increasing cooperation and the experience of competition will induce a vicious spiral of intensifying competiton. What then are the effects of the differences between cooperation and competition upon the classroom?

Deutsch (1949) compared the effects of cooperative and competitive grading systems in experimental sections of an introductory college psychology course. In half of the sections the students were graded cooperatively; that is, all students in the same group received the same grade on the basis of how well the group's discussion and analysis of a human-relations problem compared with other similar groups. In the other half of the sections, the students were graded competitively; they were told that the student who was judged to have contributed the most to their section's discussion and analysis of a human-relations problem would get the highest grade, the next most productive student the next highest grade, and so on. Thus, in the competitive sections individuals competed against fellow group members for grades (a situation similar to most classrooms); in the cooperative sections individuals cooperated with their fellow group members to enable the group to do as well as possible in its competition with other groups. The results of the experiment indicated that the two different grading procedures had definite and predictable effects upon behavior in the classroom. Groups that were cooperatively interdependent with respect to grades were characterized by much friendlier discussions; they learned each other's names more rapidly, were more satisfied with their discussions, were more attentive to and more influenced by what their fellow group members said, and they felt more secure personally. In the groups that were competitively interdependent with respect to grades, students behaved in more aggressive, obstructive, oppositional, and self-defensive ways; there was less sense of being listened to and of being understood, and there were more misunderstandings and more frequent need for repetition of what had just been said. In both types of situations the students seemed equally and strongly motivated to do well in the course and no significant differences in individual learning were obtained.

A number of studies have replicated Deutsch's findings in both actual classrooms and laboratory experiments. A study that attempted to extend the findings to specify the conditions under which cooperation will result in more student achievement than competition was conducted by Haines and McKeachie (1967). Haines and McKeachie theorized that the variable mediating the effect of cooperative or competitive goal interdependence upon classroom performance is the amount of tension generated by the task which is reduced or increased by the actions of the other group members. Since in the cooperatively interdependent classrooms there is high substitutability, there is much greater probability that cooperative group members will have tensions associated with the task reduced by the action of other members; this reduced tension will result in higher performance in the classroom. In the competitively oriented classrooms, the actions of the other members will increase the tension associated with the task, resulting in decreased performance in the classroom.

The investigators compared cooperative and competitive techniques of teaching discussion sections of general psychology at the college level with respect to their effects on student anxiety, student achievement, and student satisfaction. Students in the four classes studied participated in class discussions conducted in a competitive manner for two weeks and in a cooperative manner for two weeks. Two of the classes received the cooperative treatment first and two received the competitive treatment first. Given a task that arouses achievement anxiety, students in competitive-discussion situations became more anxious, displayed a greater incidence of self-oriented needs, and found themselves losing self-assurance. Furthermore, they were less able to perform effectively in recitation, and they became dissatisfied with the discussion method. When the discussion was

163

structured cooperatively, students felt less tense, displayed more task-oriented behavior, worked more effectively, and enjoyed the discussion. Although the researchers found that in daily recitation students covered more material in the cooperative sessions than they did in the competitive sessions, the examination performance of the two groups did not differ significantly. From this study one may conclude that, given a task that generates tension, cooperative goal interdependence reduces the tension while competitive interdependence increases the tension. Although daily performance is greater in cooperative groups than in competitive groups, actual examination performance seems to be based more upon the individual's actual motivation to achieve than upon the way in which his discussion group is structured. The results of the Haines and McKeachie study are corroborated by a study conducted by Naught and Newman (1966), who found that competition increased anxiety in students performing a motor-steadiness task.

There is some ambiguity in the interpretation of the Deutsch and the Haines and McKeachie experiments due to the confounding of cooperation among individual group members and competition among groups. In their experiments individual competition was compared with intergroup competition, the members within each group being cooperatively interdependent. Other studies have tried to determine if the particular effects attributed to cooperation might have been due to the competitive intergroup relations rather than due to the cooperative relations that existed among the group members, with conflicting results. Gurnee (1968) contrasted competition between two individuals with cooperation (with no competition between dyads). He found that the rate of learning in a maze was significantly more rapid under instructions to collaborate than under instructions to compete. Members of the dyad with inferior learning ability generally benefited much more from collaboration than did the members with superior learning ability. More than two thirds of the subjects reported the collaborative situation as being more pleasant than the competitive situation. Julian and Perry (1967), however, found that group members were more highly motivated and more productive under both individual and intergroup competition than in a purely cooperative condition where individual group members cooperated without their group competing with other groups. Pure cooperation did, however, generate the most favorable interpersonal relations among group members. There was also some indication that if the cooperative groups had had more time in which to work (the experiment lasted only two hours) they would have improved their performance.

Deutsch (1949) was concerned with group members working parallel to each other to accomplish a common goal. In such a case each person's efforts help the others attain their goal and, therefore, substitute for their efforts. Besides being cooperatively interdependent in terms of striving for a mutual goal, two or more individuals can be cooperatively interdependent through a division of labor (Thomas, 1957). In a division of labor one's efforts do not substitute for another's, if one person does not perform his part of the task then others cannot perform theirs. Unless the departmental secretary duplicates a test, the teacher cannot give it. Unless the teacher presents the material he wants students to learn, either through a lecture or text materials, the students will not learn it. Cooperation is facilitated in the classroom through setting mutual goals or through a division of labor.

Finally, there is some evidence that individuals in cooperative relationships will imitate others more than individuals in competitive relationships (O'Connell, 1965). If the teacher is concerned with inducing students to imitate certain desired behaviors of both the teacher and other model students, he should strive to develop cooperative relationships in the classroom.

In order for relationships within the classroom to be optimally rewarding, in order for conflicts to be handled in productive ways, and in order for learning to be most facilitated, the teacher should develop cooperative interdependencies within the classroom. This can be done through a division of labor and through setting mutual goals. In addition the teacher may wish to minimize the interpersonal compeitition aspects of classroom life; many behavioral scientists have noted the destructive aspects of interpersonal competition within the classroom. Sexton (1961) states:

> The present, highly competitive, system of marks, exams, and comparisons of sorts should be replaced by other types of incentives to learning. If there is to be competition, emphasis should be on group, rather than on individual competition. Marks and grades hurt more than they help; they discourage students from studying "hard" subjects or taking good but tough teachers; they discourage really independent and critical thinking.

Resolving Conflicts in the Classroom

Most destructive classroom conflicts can be avoided if the classroom is structured so that the relationships within it are predominantly cooperative. Under many conditions, however, this is difficult, especially when the teacher and the students come from different social class or cultural backgrounds. Within any classroom, furthermore, there are times when dysfunctional competition may develop or when conflicts will begin to escalate in competitive ways. To resolve a conflict productively there must be clear perception of the other's position and motivations, accurate communication, a trusting attitude toward the other, and a definition of the conflict as a mutual problem. Whether the predominant context of the classroom is cooperative or competitive affects the members' perceptions, communication, attitudes, and task orientation in conflict situations (Deutsch, 1966). Each of these areas will be discussed in following sections. Much of the research discussed, however, has been conducted on situations in which the parties involved were of equal power. In the classroom the teacher has power superior to the students' due to his position in the authority hierarchy. The following discussions, however, can be adapted to such a situation.

Perception in Conflict Situations

In conflict situations there are often perceptual distortions and misperceptions concerning the opponent's position and motivations. Many of these are so common that they can be found in almost any conflict situation which takes place in a competitive context; they include the mirror-image, the mote-beam mechanism, the double standard, and the tendency to oversimplify self- and enemy-image.

The *mirror-image* can be defined as the situation where two competing parties hold similar but directly opposite views of each other. The concept was formulated by Bronfenbrenner, (1961), a social psychologist who was allowed to travel alone in Russia, without a guide, during the summer of 1960. He devoted much of his time to striking up conversations with Russians in public conveyances, parks, stores, restaurants, or just on the street, making sure that he talked with individuals who did not take the initiative as well as those who did. For example, he would decide before entering a restaurant to sit at the third table on the right and interview whomever was sitting there. During his conversations he would inquire about how the individuals felt about America and Americans. At first he was deeply disturbed by the distorted view the people he talked with had of America, but gradually he developed an even more disturbing awareness. The Russian's distorted picture of America was curiously similar to the American's view of Russia. Both Russians and Americans saw the other country as a dangerous aggressor and the government of the other as exploiting and deluding its people. Both thought that the mass of the people of the other country was not really sympathetic to the regime they lived under, that the other country could not be trusted, and that the policies of the other country verged on madness. Thus, both Russians and Americans felt threatened by the other country and both felt innocent—*they* want war, *we* want peace, *we* are right, *they* are wrong, *we* are good, *they* are evil. The perceptions of each country were the mirror-image of the other's.

The *mote-beam mechanism*, similar to projection, consists in perceiving certain characteristics in others that one does not perceive in himself (Icheiser, 1949). These characteristics are perceived as though they were peculiar traits of the other and, hence, the differences between the other and oneself are accentuated. Since the traits we are unable or unwilling to recognize in ourselves are usually traits we consider to be undesirable, the mote-beam mechanism results in a view of the other as peculiarly shameful or evil. Since the mote-beam mechanism works on both sides, there is a tendency for each side to view the other as peculiarly immoral and for the views to mirror each other. This perceptual distortion, which is common in highly competitive conflicts, takes its name from a Bible verse, "Thou hypocrite, first cast out the beam (a large piece of timber) out of thine own eye; and then shalt thou see clearly to cast out the mote (a small particle of dust) out of thy brother's eye" (Matthew, 7:5).

The *double standard* is the process whereby ingroup or personal virtues become outgroup or opponent vices. It means simply the same action is evaluated good for oneself and bad for the opponent. A recent study by Oskamp (1965), for example, demonstrated that American students are likely to rate more favorably an action of the United States directed toward the Soviet Union than the identical action directed by the Soviet Union toward the United States; the placement of U.S. missile bases near Russia, for instance, was evaluated much more favorably than the placement of Russian missile bases near the United States.

Finally, there is commonly an *oversimplified view of oneself and the opponent* in competitive conflicts; one sees himself or his group striving for humanitarian goals, as being totally good, with "God on his side." The opponent, on the other hand, is perceived as striving for illegitimate goals, as being criminal, immoral, and the representative of the devil.

The above perceptual distortions can be found to varying degrees in almost any competitive conflict, whether it is between countries, generations, a wife and a husband, or between two students. Such distortions contribute to basic misunderstandings between the parties involved in a conflict, which in turn contribute to escalation and inhibit resolution. A few principles of perception explain many of the underlying roots of these perceptual distortions (Deutsch, 1962b).

First one's perception of the opponent's behavior is determined both by the perception of the behavior itself and by the perception of the context in which the behavior occurs. The contexts of behavior are often quite ambiguous in conflicts, so one tends to impose his context upon the opponent's behavior. Thus the opponent's and one's own behavior may be interpreted quite differently depending upon from whose frame of reference one is viewing the behavior. When the two parties in conflict are from different cultures, the misunderstandings can be phenomenal. An example of such a misunderstanding is as follows:

> The scene was a small square in the city of Hue, South Vietnam, on a summer day in 1965. The place was known as a rendezvous for American GI's and Vietnamese girls. A couple of military police were on duty to keep order. On this day, one of them had supplied himself with some candy for the children who played in the square and crowded around the Americans. As he started his distribution in a *friendly mood,* a swarm of youngsters jumping and reaching, pressed about him. With a laugh he tossed the candy out on the cobblestones. Immediately the children descended like locusts, each intent on grabbing a piece. A young Vietnamese school teacher happened by at this moment, and seeing the scrambling children, he spoke to them in stern and emphatic tones. He told them to pick up the candy and give it back to the American. After some hesitation, they sheepishly complied. Then, facing the soldier and speaking in measured English with a tone of suppressed

anger and scorn, he said, "You Americans don't understand. You are making beggars of our children, prostitutes of our women, and Communists of our men!"*

In the above example the two parties were allies, but their interpretations of the American's behavior were astonishingly different. To the American he was being generous and helpful, to the Vietnamese he was reinforcing the children for begging and dependency. Such misunderstandings are the rule, not the exception, in conflicts when the parties use their own frame of reference to interpret their opponent's behavior and they contribute to the mirror-image effect.

Second, one's perceptions are influenced greatly by his expectations and preconceptions. If one expects the opponent to act aggressively, then any action he takes may be seen as being aggressively motivated. Finally, intense threat, fear, or conflict tends to impair perceptual and cognitive processes. When tension increases beyond an optimal, moderate level, it reduces the range of perceived alternative actions, reduces the time perspective in such a way as to focus on the immediate rather than the overall consequences of the perceived alternatives, and polarizes thought to a simplistic view of the conflict. In addition, it leads to stereotyped responses, increases defensiveness and conformity to group norms, and leads to increased distortion of information and actions.

Perhaps the most tragic result of perceptual distortions is that they are so difficult to clarify once the conflict becomes highly competitive. Deutsch (1962b) gives three reasons for the perpetuation of distortions. First, parties in conflict often make major psychological investments in the distortions and there is a high cost in giving up the distorted view of the opponent, such as loss of social face, guilt over past actions toward the opponent that no longer seem justified, ambiguity concerning how one should relate to the opponent, and personal instability. Certain distorted perceptions perpetuate themselves because they lead the individual to avoid contact or meaningful communication with the opponent. This will be discussed in more detail in the next section, which deals with communication, but there are many examples of communication being cut off in conflict situations, such as the wife who goes home to mother after a quarrel with her husband, the cutting-off of diplomatic channels between two countries

* From *Peace in Vietnam* by the American Friends Service Committee, 1966, p. 1.

involved in a dispute, or the segregating of Negroes or Indians in areas of the United States that are dominated by white racists. Finally, distortions are often perpetuated because they evoke a self-fulfilling prophecy—because one views the opponent as being vindictive, one treats him in such a way as to evoke vindictiveness, which confirms the original misperception.

Deutsch's (1966) research indicates that the extent of misperception in conflict situations depends upon whether the context in which the conflict occurs is primarily cooperative or competitive. In a purely cooperative situation individuals seem to have increased sensitivity to similarities and common interests, while minimizing the salience of differences. Cooperation seems to stimulate a convergence of beliefs and values and biases one toward seeing the other's actions as benevolently intended. In a purely competitive situation, on the other hand, individuals seem to have increased sensitivity to differences and threats, while minimizing their awareness of similarities. Competition seems to stimulate a sense of complete oppositeness and biases one toward misperceiving the opponent's neutral or conciliatory actions as malevolently motivated.

Communication in Conflict Situations

Whether a conflict takes place in a cooperative or a competitive context has great influence upon communication between the parties involved (Deutsch, 1966). In a purely cooperative situation the communication of relevant information is open and honest with each party being interested in informing as well as being informed by others. In a purely competitive situation, however, there is either a lack of communication or misleading communication, and conflict resolution is thereby inhibited (Sherif, 1966; Blake and Mouton, 1962; Newcomb, 1952; Deutsch, 1949, 1962a, 1965). Competition gives rise to espionage or other techniques to obtain information about the other that the other is unwilling to communicate and at the same time to attempts to communicate information that discourages or misleads the other about oneself.

In order for a conflict to be handled constructively, there must be a means to communicate with the opponent, either overtly or tacitly. Effective and continued communication is of vital importance in resolving a conflict (Rapoport, 1960; Douglas, 1957). Deutsch and Krauss (1962) have conducted a series of classic studies on the effects of communication on bargaining. A *bargaining situation* can be defined as one in which the participants have mixed motives toward one another; on the one hand each has an interest in cooperating so that they reach an agreement, on the other hand they have competitive interests with regard to the nature of the agreement they reach. In effect, the cooperative interests of the bargainers must be strong enough to overcome their competitive interests in order for an agreement to be reached. The investigators found that, given the opportunity to communicate, individuals participating in a bargaining game under competitive conditions refused to do so. When the experimenters required them to communicate, they often communicated lies and threats as well as promises and trustworthy statements. They concluded that communication that is effective in inducing bargainers to reach cooperative agreements is characterized by being compulsory, by reflecting a norm of fairness, and by being introduced after the bargainers have experienced the destructive effects of mutual competition.

Finally, one of Deutsch's students, Loomis (1959), conducted a study that indicates that communication is likely to be effective in inducing cooperation in a bargaining situation to the extent that it: (1) expresses one's intentions, (2) expresses one's expectations for the other's behavior, (3) expresses one's planned reaction to violations of one's expectations, and (4) expresses a means of restoring cooperation after a violation of one's expectations has occurred.

Role Reversal

Given the tendency in competitive conflict situations to distort one's perceptions of the opponent's behavior and motivations and the difficulties in communicating in ways that have low probabilities of being cut off or misunderstood, there is a need for procedures that reduce distortions in perception and ensure effective communication. A procedure that has had marked success in various applied settings in eliminating misunderstandings, perceptual distortions, and defensive adherence to one's point of view is role reversal.

Role reversal is a procedure in which one or both of two persons in a discussion present the viewpoint of the other. It is "taking the role of the other" in a specific situation where the other person is present. That is, given that A and B are in a discussion, A presents B's point of view and/or B presents A's point of view. Although first proposed as a procedure to ensure accurate communication in negotiations by Cohen (1950, 1951) and elaborated by Rapoport (1960) and Deutsch (1962b), role-reversal theory has centered around the work of Carl Rogers (1951, 1952, 1965). Rogers discusses role reversal as a means of facilitating communication between two individuals. He states that the major barrier to mutual interpersonal communication is the human tendency to judge, to approve or disapprove, to evaluate the statement of the other person. This evaluation is done from the individual's own point of view. The tendency to evaluate another's statements from one's own frame of reference is heightened in situations where feelings and emotions are deeply involved; the stronger the feelings, the less the likelihood of real communication. According to Rogers, the tendency to react to any emotionally meaningful statement by evaluating it from one's own frame of reference is the major barrier to interpersonal communication. This evaluative tendency is avoided when a person is able to achieve the frame of reference of the other, that is, when he sees the expressed ideas and attitudes from the other's point of view. Role reversal is suggested as the primary means of understanding the other's ideas, attitudes, and behavior from the other's frame of reference. By role reversing, furthermore, one communicates that he is attempting to understand the other's frame of reference, which reduces the other's feelings of defensiveness and of being threatened, by convincing him that he has been clearly heard and understood. According to Rogers' theory, however, it is not the routine reflection of what the other is saying that increases the cooperativeness and trust in the situation. Through role reversal one needs to communicate that he is: (1) accurately understanding the other's "inner world," (2) feeling a nonpossessive warmth for and acceptance of the other as a person, and (3) behaving authentically and genuinely in the situation (Truax and Wargo, 1966). Truax and Wargo present considerable evidence that accurate understanding, nonpossessive warmth, and authenticity are essential for growth and development in the therapy relationship.

Despite the promise of role reversal as a communication technique for inducing cooperation in interpersonal and intergroup conflict situations, there has been no research on its use until very recently. Johnson (1967) examined the respective effects of role reversal and the direct presentation of one's position upon the participants in a highly competitive intergroup-negotiation situation. He found that role reversal resulted in more understanding of the opponent's position than did self-presentation without role reversal. Mutual understanding of the other's position, however, does not mean that agreement will be easier to reach by the two parties. Some misunderstandings cloud real differences between individuals, the clarification of which would increase the competitive forces in the situation by removing any possible benevolent misunderstandings. Other misunderstandings cloud similarities and points of agreement between the parties; the clarification of these would lead to the resolution of the conflict. When role reversal was adequately performed, Johnson found that when legitimate opposed differences were clarified, conflict increased, and when misunderstandings and false expectations were clarified, conflict decreased.

Attitudes toward the Other in Conflict Situations

The attitudes one has toward the other in conflict situations influences greatly how one behaves. When an individual, for example, distrusts his "opponent," he will often hide information or communicate misleading information; when he trusts his "partner," he will be open and honest in his communication of information. Deutsch (1966) states that cooperative relationships lead to a trusting, friendly attitude toward the other and increase one's willingness to respond helpfully to the other's needs and requests; competition, on the other hand, leads to a suspicious, hostile attitude toward the other while increasing one's readiness to exploit the other's needs and to respond negatively to the other's requests. Thus in a classroom dominated by cooperative relationships, the teacher and the students will respond helpfully to each other's needs and there will be a high level of mutual trust, liking, and influence. In a classroom dominated by competitive relationships, however, the teacher and the students will exploit each other's needs, revolt against each other's influence attempts, and distrust and disdain each other.

Productive interpersonal attitudes may be developed in many different ways. The literature is too voluminous to be discussed here. It is apparent, however, that under most conditions trust is built by the teacher behaving in trustworthy ways; if the teacher likes the students the students will reciprocate, and if the students can influence classroom life they will become more committed and involved.

Task Orientation in Conflict Situations

Whether a conflict takes place within a context that is predominately cooperative or competitive will influence several aspects of task orientation (Deutsch, 1966). If the context is predominately cooperative, individuals will tend to recognize the legitimacy of each other's interests and search for a solution that is responsive to the needs of each side; if the context is predominately competitive, individuals will deny the legitimacy of the other's interests and attempt to achieve a solution that is only responsive to their own needs. In a predominately cooperative situation individuals will attempt to influence each other through persuasion, striving to enhance mutual power; in a predominately competitive situation individuals will attempt to coerce each other while attempting to increase one's own power and to decrease the power of others. Perhaps the most important aspect of task orientation in conflict situations, however, is how the conflict is defined.

There are a number of research studies that indicate that those who define the causes, type, and size of a conflict specify the way in which it should be handled. Many conflicts in schools, for example, are defined as being caused by maladjusted, deviant students; this implies that the way in which the conflict should be handled is to expel the "sick" students, send them to a special school, or get them into therapy. Rebellious student behavior that is consistently defined as being caused by personal pathology not only labels the misbehaving students as being sick, but also protects the school from admitting or investigating its own shortcomings. This is often a clear organizational defense, for if the school's organizational pathologies became defined as the cause of student misbehavior and failure, the legitimacy and effectiveness of the school would be brought into question.

The way in which conflicts are labeled often influences the ease with which they are resolved. Deutsch (1966), for example, discusses a study conducted by one of his students where a bargaining game was presented as a game of "chicken" and as a problem-solving situation. When the situation was described as being a test of who would "chicken out" first, the bargainers were very highly competitive; when the game was described as a mutual problem the two bargainers had to solve, they were basically cooperative.

Finally, the smaller the conflict the more easily it is resolved (Deutsch, 1966). Participants often have a choice of defining a conflict as being large or small and usually the larger the definition the harder it is to resolve. A conflict can be reduced by defining it as being between two individuals rather than between two groups, as being over the application of a principle rather than over the principle itself, as representing a small procedural precedent rather than a large one, and as representing a small substantive issue rather than a sizeable one. Any expansion of the definition of the size of a conflict increases its motivational significance to the participants and intensifies their emotional involvement, which makes a limited defeat less acceptable or more humiliating than mutual disaster. A reduction of the definition of the size of a conflict decreases its motivational significance to the participants and their emotional involvement. Thus they are more willing to compromise to reach an agreement.

Conflicts will be easier to resolve if the legitimacy of each side is not questioned, if both sides rely primarily upon strategies of persuasion, if the conflict is not seen as being caused by the pathologies of the individuals on the other side, if it is labeled as a joint problem-solving situation instead of a win-lose game of "chicken," and if it is defined as being of small size. Such a problem-solving orientation to the conflict is much more easily obtained when the conflict takes place in a predominately cooperative context. If, however, a conflict between students and school personnel becomes predominately competitive, participants can facilitate its resolution by attempting to define it as a small, joint problem-solving situation.

The Initiation of Cooperation

There are, in addition to the principles already discussed, several conclusions from the literature on conflict resolution that may be helpful in dealing with conflicts in the classroom. First, the use of threat in a conflict situation to intimidate another person will increase the competitive aspects of the situation and will often provoke the events at which it attempts to deter, especially if the threatened party sees the threat as an illegitimate attempt to make him yield (Deutsch and Krauss, 1962). Threat is an aggressive behavior and the most probable response to aggressive acts is counteraggression. Under most conditions, in order to induce cooperation in others threats and other attempts at intimidation should be avoided.

A number of studies have dealt with the behavioral strategies for inducing cooperation in an opponent (Deutsch, 1966). The types of strategies usually compared are: (1) unconditional cooperation, where no matter what the opponent does one responds cooperatively; (2) unconditional competition, where no matter what the opponent does one responds competitively; and (3) conditional cooperation, where whatever the opponent does, one matches his behavior. The most effective strategy for inducing cooperation is the conditional cooperative one. The least effective is often the unconditional cooperative strategy; bargainers often exploit unconditionally cooperative opponents with very little guilt. Deutsch (1966) concludes that what seems to be most effective in inducing cooperation is a strategy that is generously responsive to the other's cooperative behavior, does not reciprocate hostility, but does not allow hostility to be rewarding.

Finally, the teacher in the classroom may restructure a competitive situation as a cooperative one by bringing in a superordinate goal. Superordinate goals are goals that cannot be easily ignored by two antagonistic parties, but whose attainment is beyond the resources and efforts of one party alone; the two parties, therefore, must join in a cooperative effort in order to attain the goals (Sherif, 1966). In a series of studies on intergroup competition, Sherif compared the effectiveness of several different techniques of conflict resolution; he found that the most successful technique for resolving intergroup conflict was the use of superordinate goals. An example of a superordinate goal used by Sherif is a staged breakdown of a truck on its way to pick up food for a picnic for two adversary groups; in order for the groups to eat, the truck had to be started. It took the joint efforts of both groups to push the truck fast enough for it to start, thus uniting them in a cooperative effort that resolved much of the conflict between them. In Sherif's studies the superordinate goals were introduced by a third party. A later study by Johnson and

Lewicki (1969), however, indicates that such superordinate goals are not as successful when they are initiated by a party involved in the conflict.

Intergroup Conflict

In the classroom there are often many instances of intergroup conflict as well as instances of interpersonal conflict. In a later chapter dealing with classroom norms it is recommended that teachers structure the classroom so that groups of students compete against each other. Regardless of whether intergroup conflict in the classroom is initiated by the teacher to promote learning or whether it arises against the teacher's wishes, the teacher needs to understand its dynamics in order to control or resolve it. In a series of studies on intergroup conflict, Sherif (1966) and Blake and Mouton (1962) have found that competition between two or more groups has certain definite and very predictable effects on intragroup relations, intergroup relations, and negotiations between groups.

Within the group there is a strong upward shift in group cohesion as the group members join together to defend their group against defeat. There is a refinement and consolidation of the ingroup power structure as militant leaders take control. Values and norms governing ingroup behavior change. During the competition, personal reputations merge with the group reputation, and personal stakes become involved. There is high member satisfaction and identification with the group and the group's position on the issues involved in the conflict. At the same time, the opposing group and their position are belittled and devalued. Conformity is demanded from the group members. Finally, a task-oriented approach is adopted by the group.

Between the groups, an attitude of hostility and inaccurate and uncomplimentary sterotypes form. Interaction and communication decrease between the members of the competing groups. When given a chance to clarify the position of the other group, the situation is used to belittle the competitor's position, to cast doubt on its validity, and to demonstrate its inferiority in relation to the position of one's own group. This intensifies the conflict. High distrust exists between the groups. Finally, as the group elevates its own position, it downgrades the other group and its position.

In negotiations there are distortions of judgment concerning the quality of the competing solutions, with one's own solution perceived as "good" and the other group's solution perceived as "bad." Negotiators are relatively blind to points of commonality between their own and contending proposals and tend to emphasize the differences. The orientation of both negotiators is to win for their group, not to reach a mutually satisfying agreement. This results in the "hero-traitor" dynamic, in which a negotiator who "wins" for his group is seen as a hero and one who "loses" for his group is seen as a "traitor." When a neutral third party decides who is "right" and who is "wrong," the winner perceives the third party as being impartial and objective; the loser perceives the third party as being unfair, biased and thoughtless. Both sides see themselves as objective and rational and the other side as irrational—the only loyalty is to one's own group position; this excludes any questions of objectivity from negotiations. The common result of negotiations is deadlock. Finally, the representative is caught in a conflict between his own beliefs and perceptions and the mandates given to him by his group.

SUMMARY

One of the most important aspects of classroom life is how conflicts are handled. A conflict exists whenever incompatible actions occur. Conflicts can have both functional and dysfunctional consequences and, therefore, are most effectively resolved when their functional consequences are maximized and their dysfunctional consequences are minimized. Conflicts can occur in a cooperative or a competitive context; the processes of resolution will usually be strongly influenced by the context within which the conflict occurs. A cooperative context is one in which the individuals' goals are positively correlated. A competitive context is one in which the individuals' goals are negatively correlated. The psychological consequences of cooperation are substitutability of the actions of the individuals involved, positive cathexis to the behaviors of others, and influencibility. The opposite psychological consequences result from competition. Under most conditions, an individual will tend to facilitate the actions of others when he perceives that they will be promotive of his goal attainment, and will tend to obstruct their actions when he perceives that they will be detrimental to his goal attainment.

There is considerable evidence that if the relationships within the classroom are perceived to be predominantly cooperative, communication is likely to be relatively open and undefensive, a trusting and responsive attitude will exist, the members will perceive themselves as having similar interests, beliefs, and attitudes, and they will be more likely to face disagreements and conflicting interests as mutual problems to be solved openly with recognition of the importance of being responsive to the needs of both sides in a dispute. The opposite sort of conditions will hold if the relationships are perceived to be basically competitive. An emphasis upon cooperative relations within groups that compete with one another is, therefore, perhaps the most facilitative context in which interpersonal relationships, conflict resolution, and learning can take place.

When conflicts arise in the classroom and become defined in competitive ways, communication is often broken off or distorted. There is a tendency for one to impose his own frame of reference upon the other's behavior, to perceive one's own behavior as more benevolent and legitimate than the opponents, and, subsequently, for the conflict to escalate. A procedure that has been proposed to facilitate accurate communication and decrease defensive adherence to one's position in such situations is role reversal. In addition, conflicts will be easier to place within a cooperative context when the use of threat and intimidation are avoided, when they are defined as problem-solving situations and as being specific, small issues, and when the teacher rewards cooperative behavior, does not reciprocate hostility, but does not allow hostility to be rewarding. Finally, the teacher may resolve many conflicts by introducing a series of superordinate goals that restructure the context of the conflict from competition to cooperation.

CHAPTER 10

ABILITY
GROUPING

Introduction

There are basically three types of ability grouping that have been used by schools: interschool grouping, intraschool grouping, and intraclass grouping. Interschool grouping exists when students of different measured IQ or achievement are sent to different schools, such as academic high schools or vocational high schools. Intraschool grouping is what is commonly termed "tracking" or in England, "streaming." It consists of separating students of different measured IQ or achievement into different classes within the school. Intraclass grouping is the practice of subgrouping students within the same class on the basis of achievement in certain areas. In this chapter the practices of interschool and intraschool grouping are examined; the following discussion does not necessarily apply to intraclass grouping.

The Theory, Rationale, Assumptions, and Evaluation of Ability Grouping

Ability grouping was first proposed as a means for separating students in order to make basic changes in teaching methods and course content. The hypothesis advanced by the proponents of ability grouping was that the differentiation of teaching methods and course content made possible by ability grouping would result in higher achievement by all ability levels. This can be represented as follows:

INDEPENDENT VARIABLE	MEDIATING VARIABLES	DEPENDENT VARIABLE
Ability -------------- Grouping	Differentiated Teaching ----- Practices and Course Content	Increased Achievement for All Ability Levels

The rationale for grouping by ability states that narrowing the ability range in a classroom facilitates the provision of more appropriate learning tasks, makes more teacher time available to pupils of a given ability level, and stimulates the teacher to gear his teaching to the level of the group (Goldberg, Passow, and Justman, 1966). Pupils of each ability level, therefore, should do better academically as a consequence of being in classes where the ability range is limited. In this rationale and hypothesis there are a number of "common sense" beliefs (Goldberg, Passow, and Justman, 1966):

1. Intellectual ability, as measured by intelligence tests, is the prime factor which distinguishes between more and less "rapid" and more or less "successful" learners.
2. The average ability level of the class prompts the teacher to adjust materials and methods and to set appropriate expectations and standards. Thus, the ability of the children in large measure determines what is taught and how it is taught.
3. When the range is narrowed, the teacher can more readily adapt both content and method to the abilities of the children.
4. In the absence of ability extremes, which require special planning and instruction, each pupil can receive more teacher time and attention.
5. When the range is narrowed, the children are faced with more realistic criteria against which to measure themselves. They compete with their peers, so to speak, rather than having to

181

compare their own achievement to that of far brighter or far duller pupils. (pp. 150, 151)

These assumptions are all very dubious. Take the first assumption for example. The belief that intellectual ability distinguishes between individuals who can and cannot learn is based on the further assumption that intelligence is largely determined by hereditary factors and can be accurately assessed at a fairly early age. Yates (1966) states that rigid forms of grouping, such as the organization of different types of secondary schools or the provision of distinct streams or tracks within a school, was clearly defensible when such assumptions were made. The research and development within the fields of cognition and intelligence, however, have led to a substantially revised conception of the nature of intelligence. Intelligence is now regarded as a fluid collection of skills whose development is demonstrably affected by early experience and subsequently by the quality and duration of formal education. In these circumstances the early segregation of pupils on the basis of apparent differences in intellectual capacity, especially when this involves accordingly different kinds of educational treatment to the groups so formed, is scarcely justifiable.

According to Yates, if ability grouping is to be justified, it must be on the grounds that it allows teachers to deal appropriately with children who have different educational needs and capacities. For if children are separated into tracks on the basis of differences in learning ability, there seems to be little point in confronting them all with exactly the same curriculum and teaching them by identical methods. There is, however, little evidence that such differentiation of curriculum materials and teaching methods have taken place in very many classrooms.

Goldberg and her associates (1966) state that despite seventy or eighty years of practice and at least forty years of research, many of the issues concerning ability grouping remain unresolved and most questions are still unanswered. Yates (1966) states that there has been a considerable volume of research devoted to the problems associated with ability grouping but that it has made limited contribution to the solution of the problems due to defects in its design and conduct. It seems that despite the years of research and evaluation, the proper studies on ability grouping have not been carried out in a competent way.

Most investigators researching and evaluating ability grouping have focused on the wrong question; that is, they have focused on whether ability grouping per se will result in increased achievement. They have *not* investigated whether ability grouping results in differentiated curricula and teaching practices, which effectively increase the achievement of students in all ability levels. Consequently, we still do not know the conditions under which ability grouping may be used to increase the achievement of different levels of students.

After eighty years of practice and forty years of multitudes of research studies it is bewildering as to why so few people have conducted decent studies on ability grouping. Perhaps one of the major reasons is that ability grouping soon became an end in itself and was applied widely without any attempt to change teacher behavior, to provide new skills and knowledge for the teachers involved, or to arrive at curriculum developments that were aimed at different levels of students. Ability grouping has by and large been overgeneralized, has been applied uncritically using insufficient data on the students, and has not been accompanied by basic changes in classroom practice and course content. In the absence of properly conceived and operating programs utilizing ability grouping, it is difficult to evaluate it as an educational practice.

The Reliability and Flexibility of Grouping

In order for ability grouping to be effective as an educational practice the reliability of the measures by which students are grouped must be verified and a means for correcting mistakes in placement must be demonstrated. Yates (1966) states that studies carried out mainly in Britain and West Germany on the efficiency of methods of selection for academic secondary-school courses have demonstrated that a sizeable error, affecting some 10 percent of the pupils, is involved even when the best known techniques are employed. In addition, statistical evidence has been collected that shows that when selection is abandoned or when its effects are modified the general level of attainment has tended to rise. The basis on which students are grouped, therefore, is not very reliable. The unreliability of the measures can be compensated for if there is a flexible means by which students can be reclassified in order to correct for the mistakes made due to the unreliability of the measures. Jackson (1964), however, has shown that once a student is placed in a particular ability classification, there is a very high probability that he will remain there. On the basis of normal shifts in intelligence test scores, about 40 percent of the children in the various ability levels ought to be transferred from one ability level to another. The actual rate of transfer in Jackson's study, however, was from 1 to 5 percent.

There is a great deal of evidence which demonstrates that ability grouping as it is commonly used contains a social-class bias. Eash (1961) states that ability grouping at an early age seems to favor unduly the placement of children from the higher socio-economic class in higher ability groups. Yates (1966) states that intergroup school grouping based on assessments of intellectual potential involves segregation with respect to social class. Goldberg et al. (1966) found that because of the consistently positive correlation between IQ and socioeconomic status, ability grouping often acts to separate pupils by social class as well as ability. They add that in some cases, the behavioral patterns, appearance, language, and dress of students deviating markedly from those of middle-class pupils bar their admission to selected, high-ability classes. In a study of grouping practices in Sweden, Husen and Svensson (1960) reported that children of lower-class status, despite high achievement, did not find their way into classes for able students at early transfer points as frequently as did children of higher socio-economic status. Finally, Douglas (1964) states that children who come from well-kept homes and who themselves are clean, well clothed, and well shod stand a greater chance of being put in the upper tracks than their measured ability would seem to justify. Once there they are likely to stay and to improve in performance in succeeding years.

Not only are the procedures used to assign students to ability levels unreliable and the probability of a student who is misplaced being reassigned very low, but the system seems to discriminate against the lower class so that they are most often placed in lower-ability tracks, no matter what their true ability is.

Effects of Ability Grouping on Academic Performance

As previously noted, ability grouping has been practiced by the schools for the past seventy to eighty years and has been extensively researched for the past forty years. Although there was a large quantity of research on ability grouping prior to the 1960s, the quality was generally very poor and the results were inconclusive. In a review of the previous reviews of the literature on ability grouping, Goldberg and her associates (1966) found no consistent evidence that ability grouping was effective in raising academic performance of students. Eash (1961), in another extensive review of the literature, concluded that ability grouping in itself does not produce improved achievement in children and may even be detrimental to children in the average- and lower-ability groups, as it deprives them of the intellectual stimulation of the brighter students. The brighter students, on the other hand, do not seem to suffer intellectually when left with the average- and lower-ability students, at least through the elementary school. Finally, Eash concluded that the research indicates that college achievement is not improved by ability grouping in high school.

In the past few years there have been several major studies of the effects of ability grouping upon achievement. Svensson (1962), in a major study of ability grouping in Stockholm, Sweden, found that early segregation of children on the basis of their levels of ability did not significantly affect their subsequent attainments. Millman and Johnson (1964) analyzed more than 8000 gain scores for pupils in 327 class sections in 28 schools, in a study of the relation of the ability range of students in a classroom to their achievement gains in mathematics and English. From their analyses they concluded that, "whatever the potentialities may be for increasing achievement through narrowing the ability range of classes, such improvement is apparently not taking place." Borg (1964) studied the consequences of two grouping systems, one involving ability grouping with the curriculum differentiated by speeding or slowing the presentation of materials and the other consisting of random grouping with curriculum enrichment. In general, he found that the grouping patterns had no consistent effects on achievement at any grade level.

Goldberg, Passow, and Justman (1966), in one of the most thorough studies of the effects of ability grouping, studied 2200 children in 86 classes in 45 different schools. The schools studied were almost all in the more affluent areas of New York City and, by and large, serviced a predominantly white, middle-class population (the conclusions of their study, therefore, can be generalized only to similar populations). At the beginning of the study the children were entering the fifth grade. Each child was assigned an intelligence level on the basis of his IQ; five intelligence levels ranging from an IQ of 130 (gifted) to an IQ below 99 (low and below average) were used. The children were placed in classes with varying ranges of ability: narrow-range classes included only one or two IQ levels, medium-range classes three levels, and broad-range classes four or five levels. At the end of the sixth grade (two years after the beginning of the study), those children who had been in their assigned classes for two full years were retested to assess changes in academic achievement, interests, attitudes toward school, attitudes toward themselves, attitudes toward pupils with greater and lesser ability, and teacher appraisal.

The effects of grouping were minimal on all the variables Goldberg and her associates studied. Differences in achievement growth over the two-year period did not support the proposition that narrowing the ability range or separating the extreme groups enables teachers to be more effective in raising the pupils' achievement level. The presence of the gifted pupils was consistently upgrading to the other students only in science, while the only consistent effect of the presence of the "slow" children was in raising the arithmetic achievement of the other students. Overall observed increments in achievement tended to favor the classes within which there was a broad range of ability among the students.

Goldberg and her associates note, however, that the evidence from their study indicates that teachers did not adjust the content and method of their teaching to any greater degree when confronted by narrower rather than broader ranges. Where such adjustments were made there was a tendency to teach less of certain subjects to pupils in the lower-ability levels and to set lower standards for achievement in the lower-ability-level classes. Lower-ability students in the broader-range classrooms, furthermore, appeared to benefit from exposure to the content probably intended for the brighter pupils. The investigators conclude that narrowing the range of ability (on the basis of group intelligence tests) per se, without specifically designed variations in program for the several ability levels, does not result in consistently greater academic achievement for any group of pupils, nor does it affect the academic interests of the pupils or their attitudes toward school.

Effects of Ability Grouping
on Personal and Social Development

Grouping students on the basis of their IQ or performance on achievement measures has effects in nonacademic areas. There is evidence that ability grouping affects the self-attitudes of students and their attitudes toward other ability groups, racial groups, and socioeconomic classes.

Self-Attitudes

Eash (1961), in his summary of the research on grouping, stated that the evidence is fairly conclusive that grouping practices in a school can assist in developing social situations that influence the student's perception of self, his sense of dignity and worth, and his attitudes toward other children. Borg (1966) states that the self-concept of both the average and the slow pupil suffers markedly in schools where ability grouping is practiced. Pupils, especially girls, in randomly grouped classes had more favorable attitudes toward self and higher self-acceptance than those in ability-grouped sections. In addition, there were fewer pupils in the randomly grouped classes who were designated social isolates on sociometric tests. Goldberg, Passow, and Justman (1966), on the other hand, in their study of middle-class white pupils, found that the effect of narrowing the range or separating the extreme levels of ability was to raise the self-assessments of the slow pupils, lower the initially high self-ratings of the gifted, and leave the intermediate levels largely unaffected. The slow pupils also showed the greater gains in their "ideal image" when the gifted were absent than when they were present.

Attitudes toward Others

There is growing evidence that under the conditions with which ability grouping is usually used it affects attitudes toward other students in ways that are detrimental to a democratic, pluralistic society. There are indications that ability grouping results in an intellectual

187

snobbery where students designated as high ability avoid associating with students designated as low ability. There is evidence that the racial and class biases of ability grouping promotes racial and class prejudice. Finally, there have been instances where ability grouping has been openly adopted as a means of segregating students along racial lines within the school.

Eash (1961) states that grouping practices that separate students on the basis of ability as determined by group IQ or standardized tests reduce the likelihood that students will be exposed to a broader range of ethnic and cultural differences; this affects the development of general attitudes of acceptance of differences needed by citizens in a democracy. He warns that schools should be alert to the fact that by grouping students they may be assisting in maintaining and promoting social and racial biases that militate against the general educational objectives, equal educational opportunities and the development of each person as an individual. Yates (1966) states that the available evidence lends support to the view that grouping procedures can effectively serve either to maintain the structure of a society or to bring about changes in the distribution of privileges and opportunities within it. He states that there is strongly suggestive evidence that grouping based on distinctions such as measured ability and membership in a social class, racial group, or religious denomination helps to emphasize or even to exaggerate these distinctions. The gulf that separates able and less able children appears to widen if they are assigned to separate schools or to separate tracks within a school. Goldberg and her associates (1966), on the other hand, found that grouping by ability did not seem to affect students' attitudes toward other children in the predominantly white, middle-class student bodies they studied.

There is an additional body of research that indicates that heterogeneous grouping is desirable for the development of democratic social attitudes such as acceptance of individuals from different races and backgrounds. Singer (1967), in a series of studies comparing fifth graders in suburban schools near New York City who had high or low exposure to children of other races, concluded that there is no substitute for exposure to children of other races in developing democratic attitudes. She concludes that integration is the most vital factor in acceptance between the races, in more realistic judgments and knowledge about one another, in wiping out stereotypes, and allowing for greater acceptance and appreciation for individuality. It also helps the Negro child build up his self-image and understand himself and whites better. For both black and white students, greater exposure resulted in greater realism in racial attitudes, greater cognitive differentiation, and greater appreciation of the worth of the individual and of the necessity to get along together.

Furthermore, when properly used, heterogeneous grouping within the classroom can be used to socialize deviant students into the values and attitudes necessary for successfully completing an education. Coleman et al. (1966) suggest that in heterogeneous schools, children who come from backgrounds not usually supportive of the values of formal education may profit considerably from being exposed to children whose values incline them toward school achievement.

Self-Fulfilling Prophecy

In the literature on ability grouping there is common recognition that placing a student in a certain ability-level class often operates as a self-fulfilling prophecy. Yates (1966) states that because of the tendency for grouping to exaggerate the differences on which it is based and because the expectations of teachers and the morale of pupils are both affected by those forms of grouping that can be interpreted as global judgments of ability and potential, such practices as ability grouping often seem to be justified by their results. The prediction of relative success or failure, even when based on psychometrically dubious procedures, is often borne out in practice, largely because children are obliging creatures and are inclined to produce the standard of work that elders regard as appropriate.

Considerable support for the effects of the self-fulfilling prophecy in ability grouping comes from studies carried out in England (Douglas, 1964). Able pupils placed in the high-ability-track classes tended to improve their scores between ages eight and eleven, while pupils of equal ability at age eight who were placed in lower-track classes deteriorated. Pupils of lower ability placed in the high-ability-track classes at age eight gained, while classmates of equal potential placed in the lower-track classes lost. In the high track, the slower the pupil, the greater the improvement; in the lower track, the brighter the pupil, the greater the loss.

The self-fulfilling prophecy demonstrated to exist in ability grouping is undoubtedly related to teacher expectations. Tillman and Hull

(1964) state that teachers in school systems with ability grouping tend to develop rigid opinions concerning individual differences in children. They divide children into types—the bright, the average, and the dull—and these types are thought of as enduring attributes of the children: immutable, unchangeable, and unassailable. Wilson (1963) found that within a single elementary-school district, teachers in predominately working-class schools came to expect less of their students than teachers in more middle-class schools and keyed their teaching to these expectations. The result was that by sixth grade the level of the subject matter taught in class varied widely between the two kinds of schools.

The children who suffer the most from the self-fulfilling prophecy involved in ability grouping are those who are placed in low-ability classes or schools. The fact that pupils of relatively low ability can achieve quite successfully in classes where expectations are high (Goldberg et al., 1966) suggests that teachers generally underestimate the capabilities of pupils in the lower-ability classes, expect less of them, and, consequently, the pupils learn less.

Finally, there is evidence that even when students are placed in a lower-track class on criteria other than ability, a decrease in academic performance results (Himmelweit and Wright, 1967). These investigators compared two schools with different policies regarding assignment to tracks. In one school, assignment to a track was based upon ability. In the other, assignment was based on criteria other than intellectual ability. Yet the effect of track placement on further academic advancement and final performance was identical for the two schools. Thus, the effects of grouping seem to be a more powerful determinant of performance than are the attributes that led to the pupils' initial placement in tracks. It seems that membership within a track carries with it self-fulfilling prescriptions for achievement behavior, no matter what criterion was used for placing the students.

Effects on Teachers

Although little research has been conducted on the effects of ability grouping of students on teachers three conclusions can be supported. The first is that teachers prefer homogeneous classes (Rock, 1929; Otto, 1941). When given homogeneous classes of students, furthermore, teachers do not seem to change or adapt their teaching methods or the content of their classes (Goldberg et al., 1966). Finally, the placement of a student in an ability level creates a rigid stereotype of the student's ability in the teacher's mind (Tillman and Hull, 1964; Wilson, 1963). Thus, it seems that while teachers are more satisified teaching students who have been labeled high ability and that they by and large support the practice of ability grouping in spite of the evidence of its undesirableness, they do not see it as an opportunity to adapt their teaching methods to the level of their students, and their expectations and stereotypes of student ability facilitate the self-fulfilling prophecy aspects of ability grouping.

Conclusion

In conclusion, there seems to be no evidence that ability grouping, under the conditions with which it has been commonly used, is effective in raising the achievement of any group of students. The research on the social effects (effects on self-attitudes and attitudes toward others), furthermore, indicate that ability grouping can have undesirable effects on children's self-attitudes and attitudes toward other children. With more recent advances in classroom technology, such as teaching machines, which aid the teacher in individualizing instruction within the classroom, there seems to be no rationale for its use.

As Goldberg and her associates (1966) state, however, it should be remembered that ability grouping is inherently neither good nor bad. It is neutral and its value depends upon the way in which it is used. When the use of ability grouping grows out of the needs of the curriculum, when it is varied and flexible, and where differences in content, learning pace, and materials are carefully planned, ability grouping may have some merit. The evidence for such use of ability grouping, however, has as yet not been found.

SUMMARY

It has been hypothesized that the differentiation of teaching methods and course content made possible by ability grouping will result in higher achievement at all ability levels. The actual application of ability grouping, however, has been to group students according to ability, expecting that this arrangement, in and of itself, will result in greater achievement for all groups. The research indicates that ability grouping per se does not result in consistently greater academic achievement for any group of pupils; although it can have undesirable effects on students' self-attitudes and attitudes toward other children.

There are a number of problems with using ability grouping in the schools. One is that the measures used to assign students to ability levels are unreliable, and socio-economic status, in many cases, is used as the major basis for assignment. Once a student is assigned to an ability level there is little chance of his ever being reassigned; thus any mistakes in assignment made are rarely corrected. It is very likely that ability grouping functions in some instances as a self-fulfilling prophecy.

CHAPTER 11

AUTHORITY
AND POWER IN
THE CLASSROOM

Introduction

Moore (1964) describes a classroom that he says is "in a fair state of confusion." Several children are lined up at the teacher's desk while the teacher is checking their work. Although they are supposed to be working on an assignment several other children are walking or skipping around the room; others are working at their desks or just sitting and talking to one another. The teacher orders one of the students who is running around and being somewhat loud to the back of the room, where he stays only for a few moments. Another girl is going around the room accusing students of taking her nickel. The teacher tells the class to all put their heads down on their desks; no one obeys her. The teacher threatens both individual students and the class as a whole with cutting their play period if they are not quiet, but students do not pay much attention and continue talking, shoving each other, and wandering around the room.

As discussed in the previous chapters, from the viewpoint of the school, the accomplishment of the school's objectives depends upon the fulfillment of the school's organizational role requirements. This depends upon a process of learning the expectations of others, accepting them, and reliably fulfilling them. In the classroom, the student *ideally* learns what is expected of him by the teacher, accepts the teacher's expectations as legitimate, and fulfills them as reliably as possible and to the best of his ability. The student, however, needs to retain a great deal of autonomy to insure that he is not manipulated by the school in ways that benefit the school without also benefiting him as an individual. In the example above, the teacher is not in complete control of the classroom, the students are not fulfilling an effective role requirement, and little learning is taking place. Many variables affect the extent to which students fulfill their role requirements—past experience, peer-group norms, the effectiveness of the school's socialization processes—but perhaps the most crucial variable is the teacher's control of the classroom. Unless the teacher is able to influence and control student behavior, he cannot direct and supervise the learning within the classroom. In this chapter the research and theory concerning the use of authority and power within the classroom are discussed.

Authority

According to the formal structure of the classroom, the teacher's basis of power resides in the authority of the role of teacher. Authority is legitimate power, power that is vested in a particular person or position, that is recognized as so vested, and that is accepted as appropriate not only by the wielder of power but by those over whom it is wielded and by the other members of the social system (Katz and Kahn, 1966). Since there is no more pervasive law of organization than that the occupants of certain roles shall respond to and obey certain kinds of requests from occupants of certain other roles, compliance with authoritative requests becomes a generalized role expectation in organizations.

Katz and Kahn (1966) note that an authority system can exist only if the majority of the people in the social system recognize and accept

the authority structure. This does not mean, however, that everyone will accept it or that everyone will accept it all the time. Authority is always backed, therefore, by the power of reward and punishment. Through an ancillary system of rewards and punishments,
exemplary fulfillment of role requirements is usually rewarded by
bonuses, special privileges, and recognition; failure to fulfill role requirements is punished by withholding of rewards, fines, suspen-
sions, and restrictions. The ultimate punishment that an organization
can impose is expulsion from the system, permanent exclusion from
its benefits. It is usually considered vital in organizations to get the
nonperforming, uninfluenceable member out of the system before his
performance failure does systematic damage.

The logic of the authority system is as follows (Katz and Kahn,
1966). For every organization certain activities must be performed if
the organization is going to survive and function effectively. For
schools to function effectively students must be taught cognitive skills
and knowledge, be socialized into industrial society, and realize their
distinctive potential as human beings. The primary means the organization has to ensure the performance of these activities is to stipulate
them as role requirements. Within schools the role of the student is
usually defined as that of learning the information, skills, and values
needed to function effectively in an adult role in society. An initial
condition for membership becomes the acceptance of the role. Next,
a set of supervisory roles is created to see that the requirements of the
basic organizational roles are fulfilled. In other words, the role of
teacher is created to ensure that students are educated; the role
of principal is created to ensure that the teachers function effectively,
and so forth. With the creation of supervisory roles on several levels
the conventional pyramid of authority in organizations appears. To
ensure that the admonitions of the supervisors are obeyed an organizational law is established: subordinates should obey their designated
supervisors with respect to matters of role performance, that is, students should obey teachers, teachers should obey principals, and so
forth. Finally, to ensure effectiveness of the organizational law, a
system of rewards and punishments is established under control of the
authority structure. Teachers, for example, have control over students' grades and promotions, and principals have control over
teachers' class size, type of students, and promotions. To ensure
that authority is not misused, organizations usually stipulate that au-

thority is role-relevant and can be used only in role relationships.

Within the role relationship, refusal to accept influence from a supervisor on some legitimate matter is invariably defined as a serious failure in role performance. Within organizations such as schools, where there is involuntary membership, however, the legitimacy of the authority structure and the school's goals may not be recognized. The result is that the teacher and the students operate on two different assumptions about the legitimacy of the teacher's authority. When the teacher's authority is denied, his exercise of power may be perceived as illegitimate.

French and Raven (1959) define a legitimate power relationship as one in which the students acknowledge the teacher's right to exert power over them; an illegitimate power relationship is one in which the teacher's right to exert power is not acknowledged by the students. Studies on the use of illegitimate power indicate that it will produce negative attitudes toward the wielder (Raven and French, 1958a, 1958b; French, Morrison, and Levinger, 1960; French, 1964). Since attraction is an important source of influence, the decrease in attraction due to the illegitimate use of power reduces the ability to influence. French (1964), in a summary of his research, further notes that a legitimate leader has more influence than an illegitimate leader, the use of illegitimate power sometimes produces effects opposite than those intended (an illegitimate leader sometimes gets less production if he tells his group to speed up), and the illegitimate use of coercion arouses more resistance than the legitimate use of coercion.

In other words, it is important that students recognize the legitimacy of the teacher's authority. Consequently, a major part of the student's socialization into the school deals with the acceptance of the legitimacy of the school's goals and authority structure. In classes that are considered hard to control, often a major part of the time is spent in establishing the legitimacy of the teacher's authority in the classroom.

In most schools the student is permitted almost no direct recourse to the way the teacher uses his authority. Students do have, however, both direct and indirect sources of control over the teacher. Indirectly, they have access to parents who may be willing to put pressure upon the school and the teacher. Directly, they can organize themselves to present opposition to the teacher and the school. They can reject their role requirements, refuse to value the educational goals of the school, and lower the teacher's interpersonal rewards by obstructing his role performance. These strategies, however, seem ultimately self-defeating as they exclude the students from receiving the rewards of having completed their education, given the assumption that what the schools offer is not irrelevant, worthless, or harmful. Other direct-influence modes such as currying the teacher's favor are demeaning for the student and usually are ruled out by strong peer-group norms against such behavior. Gordon (1957), however, found that in Wabash High School students would strive to develop a friendly relationship with their teachers, which they used in conjunction with their possible benevolent or malevolent influence over their peers to press for particularistic treatment by the teacher, such as being given good grades without doing the required work.

Power and Dependency

The complementary roles of the teacher and the students in the classroom make them dependent upon each other. Due to the hierarchical structure of the classroom the students are more dependent upon the teacher than the teacher is upon the students.

Most contemporary theories of power recognize, either implicitly or explicitly, that the power of person A over person B depends upon the dependence of B upon A for his need satisfaction and upon the alternatives for need satisfaction open to B. Emerson (1962), for example, states that the dependency of B upon A is (1) directly proportional to B's motivational investment in goals mediated by A and (2) inversely proportional to the availability of those goals to B outside the A-B relationship. In other words, the power of the teacher over the student resides in (1) the students' motivation to achieve the system goals mediated by the teacher and (2) the availability of the system goals or their equivalents outside the classroom.

The ancillary reward structure under the control of the teacher makes the student dependent upon the teacher to the extent to which the student wants to achieve within the classroom and advance through the educational system. If the student does not value the educational goals presented by the classroom or if he can obtain their equivalent somewhere else, he is relatively independent of the teacher's power. It is important, therefore, that the school socialize the students into the system in such a way that they come to value the rewards offered by the school for successful completion of the requirements of the system, or alter the rewards it gives to something valued by the student.

Teacher Use of School's Reward System

Within an authority structure there is an ancillary system of rewards and punishments. The basic rewards within the classroom include both the primary rewards of grades and promotions and secondary rewards such as praise from the teacher. The secondary rewards often are more useful in controlling student behavior as they can be applied on a day-to-day basis, whereas the primary rewards only appear periodically during the school year.

According to French and Raven (1959) reward power resides in B's belief that A has the ability to mediate rewards for him. If the student believes that the teacher has the ability to mediate rewards for him then the teacher has reward power. The use of reward power by the teacher rests on the students' belief that the teacher possess some resource that they value and that they can obtain if they conform to the teacher's standards of classroom behavior. The strength of reward power increases as (1) the amount of the reward and (2) the students' estimate of the likelihood of attaining the reward if they conform increase. Because the students' conformity is based upon being rewarded, use of reward power depends upon the teacher's ability to observe the students' behavior. When the teacher's influence is based solely on reward power, the students will conform to the teacher's standards only in those instances where the teacher's power is salient. Over time, reward power is likely to increase the attraction of the students toward the teacher and increase their identification with the teacher.

The use of positive reinforcement directly relates to the teacher's reward power. To briefly review, a reinforcement is any event that follows a student's response and makes it more likely that the response will be repeated (Deutsch and Krauss, 1965). Reinforcement can be continuous (every correct response is always reinforced) or intermittent (only a certain number of correct responses are reinforced). Intermittent reinforcement may be given at certain intervals of time (that is, every five minutes) or only after a given number of responses (ratio reinforcement). The time interval or response ratio may be fixed, as in the examples above, or varied around an average amount of time or number of responses. Continuous reinforcement results in more rapid acquisition of responses, but once learned, the behavior is more stable and more resistant to extinction if it has been acquired on an intermittent schedule. A general law in reinforcement theory is that the more immediately the reinforcement follows the desired response, the more effective it is in increasing the frequency of the desired response.

Within the classroom most reinforcement is out of necessity intermittent and variable; a teacher cannot observe all the behavior of each student and reinforce it continuously or at a fixed interval or ratio. In addition, in order to give the reinforcement as close to the desired student response as possible, the teacher needs to develop effective secondary reinforcements that can be applied at any moment in the classroom.

Bandura and Walters (1963) discuss several complementary methods of using reward power. The simplest method is giving a positive reinforcement for the desired behavior. They state that this approach has been used successfully with delinquents (paying them to behave in socially acceptable ways), severely withdrawn schizophrenics (giving them candy and cigarettes for behaving more appropriately), and autistic children (rewarding them for talking). In socializing students into the classroom, where you want them to adopt a set of values and norms which facilitate learning, this has proven to be an effective technique.

The counterpart of dispersing reinforcements for desired behavior is withholding reinforcements when a student engages in undesirable behavior. Many disruptive behaviors in the classroom are often subtly or unconsciously reinforced by such behaviors as the teacher noticing and paying attention to the deviant child. Several studies show that there is a rapid decline in the frequency of persistent disturbing behavior when attentive reinforcing reactions to the deviant behavior are withheld (Williams, 1959; Ayllon, 1960; Ayllon and Michael, 1959).

The most effective method for eliminating deviant behavior while at the same time promoting socially desired changes involves the active reinforcement of incompatible behaviors (Bandura, 1962). If a child, for example, cannot stay in his seat and is constantly wandering around the classroom, then the teacher reinforces the student for sitting quietly in his seat.

These three methods of reinforcement have been used successfully in changing behavior in a variety of situations ranging from minor disturbances in the classroom to severe mental illness (Bandura and Walters, 1963). An example within the urban elementary classroom is presented by Becker and his associates (1967). They identified, through a series of classroom observations, two problem children in each of five classrooms. The five classroom teachers participated in a workshop and seminar on the application of rewards in the classroom. The teachers were given the following general rules for classroom management:

1. Make rules for each period explicit as to what is expected of children.
2. *Ignore* (do not attend to) behaviors that interfere with learning or teaching, unless a child is being hurt by another. Use punishment that seems appropriate, preferably withdrawal of some positive reinforcement.
3. Give *praise* and *attention* to behaviors that facilitate learning. Tell the child what he is being praised for. Try to reinforce behaviors incompatible with those you wish to decrease. In general, give praise for achievement, prosocial behavior, and following group rules.

In fourteen weeks, on the average, the amount of disruptive behavior engaged in by the ten children was cut in half. One of the classroom teachers stated the results of the program this way:

> Albert was a very noisy, disruptive child. He fought with others, blurted out, could not stay in his seat, and did very little required work. I had to check constantly to see that the minimum work was finished. He sulked and responded negatively to everything suggested to him. In addition, he was certain that he could not read. If I had planned it, I could not have reinforced this negative behavior more, for I caught him in every deviant act possible and often before it occurred. I lectured him and, as might be expected, was making only backward motion. . . . I began to use the (ignore and praise) technique. He quickly responded and his deviant behavior decreased to ten percent, the lowest recorded (in the class). Along with the praising and ignoring, I attempted to establish a

calmer atmosphere in which to work, and carefully reviewed class behavior rules. A good technique with Albert was to have him repeat the rule because "he was following it." (p. 11)

There are children who are not motivated by such social rewards as the praise and attention of the teacher. Sgan (1967), for instance, found that working-class boys were less influenced by adult praise than were working-class girls and middle-class boys and girls. If social reinforcements are not powerful enough to induce the desired behavior, other reinforcements that do motivate the students need to be developed. Examples of reinforcements that have been used successfully with students who did not respond to social reinforcements such as teacher praise are candy, playing with a desired toy, earning tokens that can be traded for toys, and food (such as cookies and cupcakes).

Teacher Use of Punishment

In addition to the teacher's ability to administer rewards for students conforming to the classroom goals and norms, the teacher can administer punishments for nonconforming behavior.

French and Raven (1959) define coercive power as B's belief that A can mediate punishments. Coercive power is similar to reward power in two ways. First, its strength increases as the punishment becomes more negative to the student and as the likelihood of the student being punished increases. Second, for its effective use the teacher must keep the students under surveillance at all times. An important determinant of the students' reaction to the teacher's use of coercive power is perceived legitimacy; if the students feel that the teacher has the legitimate right to coerce them they will resist the teacher's influence less than when they feel that the teacher does not have the legitimate right to coerce them.

Closely related to French and Raven's discussion of coercive power is the research on the use of punishment. Punishment is defined as the presentation of an adversive stimulus in the presence of the undesired behavior. According to Bandura (1962) relatively severe punishment is ineffective in eliminating undesired behavior; this has been found to be true in research on both animal and human subjects. Bandura presents several reasons why punishment is relatively ineffective. First, punishment gives rise to conditioned anxiety that often motivates and reinforces patterns of behavior that are more socially undesirable than the ones that punishment was intended to suppress. For example, a child who is consistently punished for misbehavior in the classroom, through conditioned anxiety over his classroom behavior, may withdraw psychologically or avoid school altogether. Second, punishment is very likely to condition avoidance of the teacher, which reduces the teacher's future effectiveness in modifying the student's behavior. Third, teacher use of physical punishment provides the student an aggressive model for imitation, the influence of which may counteract any temporary inhibitory effects of punishment on the performance of aggressive behavior. Finally, there is evidence that unless the punished behavior is weakly established or punishment is extremely severe, its use tends to increase the frequency and amplitude of aggressive behavior. Aggression, in other words, results in counteraggression, if not against the teacher then through displacement against someone less powerful.

In a more recent review of the literature on punishment Walters and Parke (1966) conclude that punishment, if well-timed, consistent, and sufficiently intense, effectively suppresses undesirable behavior. The more immediate the punishment, the higher its intensity, and the more continuous it is, the more effective it will be. In addition, most of the available evidence indicates that the existence of a close, affectionate relationship between the agent and recipient of punishment enhances the effectiveness of the various kinds of disciplinary procedures for producing social compliance.

Reasoning increases the effectiveness of punishment. Reasoning includes describing the consequences that the person's behavior may have for others, explicit instructions on how to behave in specific situations, and explanations of motives for punishing the person's behavior. Reasoning is commonly used to prevent undesirable behavior. The clarity with which the reasoning is communicated is important, as is the degree to which the reasoning is supported by group norms and general rules for behavior.

In reasoning with children, parents frequently provide them with examples of how they should or should not behave by referring to the actions of family members, acquaintances, friends, historical figures, and the fictitious characters of story books, movies, and TV shows. The parent expresses approval or disapproval for the model's behavior and cites its favorable or adverse consequences. There is a great deal of research (Walters and Parke, 1966; Bandura and

Walters, 1963) which indicates that a model punished for undesired behavior reduces the probability of the observers engaging in similar behavior. In other words, students observing one of their peers getting punished for disrupting the classroom usually will be less likely to engage in disruptive behavior.

The suppressive effect of punishment is usually only of value if alternative, socially desired behaviors are elicited and strengthened while the undesirable behavior is held in check (Bandura and Walters 1963; Walters and Parke, 1966). Bandura (1962) states that a learning theory of behavior modification would focus, however, upon positive reinforcement rather than punishing in bringing about desired behavioral changes. Instead of punishment, positive reinforcement of the desired behavior and removal of positive reinforcers supporting the disruptive behavior should be used. Whereas nonreward usually results in the extinction of responses, punishment merely suppresses rather than eliminates them. The most effective method for eliminating undesirable behavior while at the same time promoting the desired behavior involves the active reinforcement of behavior incompatible with the undesirable behavior.

There is some research on the use of punitive methods for classroom control. Kounin and Gump (1958) found that classroom control techniques high in roughness (anger, physical handling) were least successful of the techniques they studied in reducing undesirable behavior and tended to be followed by behavior disruption such as less involvement in school work and overt signs of anxiety on the part of the students observing the punishment. In a later study (Kounin and Gump, 1961) they found that punitive teachers "create or activate more aggression-tension than nonpunitive teachers." In responding to the question, "What is the worst thing a child can do at school?" first-grade children with punitive teachers manifest more aggression in their answers, seem to be more unsettled about misconduct in school, and are less concerned with learning and school values than their peers in nonpunitive classrooms. These findings are consistent with research on parental discipline. Hoffman (1960) found that parents relying primarily on physical punishment tend to have children who display a good deal of overt hostility in their school groups and Allinsmith (1960) found that children of parents who use physical punishment as their primary means of discipline show relatively weak inhibitions against aggression in projective-test stories. It should be remembered, however, that the above evidence is correlational and, therefore, does not show a causal relationship between the variables involved. It could be, for instance, that aggressive children cause the teacher to be punitive or that a third factor, such as social class, influences both the use of punitive methods and aggressiveness in the students. The bulk of the research, however, supports the notion that punishment results in counteraggression by the student.

Other Sources of Teacher Power

In addition to legitimate power obtained through the authority structure of the school and the ancillary system of rewards and punishments, French and Raven (1959) have specified two other bases of power which the teacher often uses: *expert* power based upon the possession of knowledge that another wishes to use to satisfy his needs, and *referent* power based upon the desire of others to be like or identify with the powerful person. There is some evidence that expert power may be used successfully in the classroom. Anderson (1950), for example, found that student performance is correlated with a teacher's competence in a given area.

The higher status of the teacher, when combined with positive regard, facilitates identification with him by the students (Backman and Secord, 1968). In addition, the more one perceives another as similar to himself, the more he is apt to identify with that person. There is some evidence that reward power can be translated into referent power, as individuals identify with those who reward them (Bandura and Huston, 1961). To the degree that identification results in the students adopting the teacher's norms, the teacher's legitimate power is also increased. The more the teacher rewards the students, the more similar the teacher is perceived to be, the more warmly regarded the teacher is, the higher the teacher's referent power. Since students often imitate those individuals with whom they identify, referent power is closely related to the teacher representing a model for the students.

Susceptibility to Social Influence

Individuals differ in their susceptibility to social influence (Walters and Parke, 1964). Susceptibility to social influence is defined as the extent to which individuals modify their behavior following exposure to social models or as a result of the presentation of reinforcers, both positive and negative. Walters and Parke believe that the development of habits of orienting and attending to others may facilitate the social influence process. They give two reasons for this. First, to imitate a model the individual must focus upon what the model is doing; the more precise the imitation the more the observer needs to focus carefully upon the model. Second, attending to others ensures that one will be aware of social reinforcers and their contingencies on his behavior.

A teacher, therefore, who wants to increase the susceptibility of his students to the teacher's influence would elicit the attending behavior and then reinforce it. A teacher might say, for example, "Johnny, pay close attention to what I am doing." The teacher would then reinforce Johnny for his attending response. There is research which demonstrates the efficacy of such an approach. Cairns (1963) successfully induced attending responses in six-year-old children by rewarding them with toys for attending to a female experimenter. The children were then rewarded by the approval of a second female experimenter for responding correctly to a discrimination task. This group was compared with children who were not rewarded and children whose rewards were not contingent upon attending to the experimenter. Only the children reinforced for attending responses showed any substantial amount of subsequent discrimination learning.

There is also evidence that increased emotional arousal may foster greater attentiveness to the behavior of an adult model. Several studies have found that emotional arousal increases performance in a task in which reinforcement is given for correct responses (Walters and Parke, 1964).

Teacher Power, Student Power, and Student Achievement

The higher the influence of the teacher upon the students the more one would expect the students to be achieving up to their capacity, given a competent teacher. Performance in the classroom, however, is affected by high-power peers as well as by teachers. Students as well as teachers reward and punish the behavior of other students. The classroom climate will favor achievement largely to the extent that high-power students within the classroom support it.

Since peers are favored as models for identification on the basis of their similarity as well as their mediation of important rewards, they are particularly potent sources of influence (Backman and Secord, 1968). Thus, the relationship between the teacher and the high-power students within the classroom is of crucial importance. Teacher coalitions with influential students are conducive to good classroom control and student achievement. Polansky (1954), for example, found that teachers who support the status structure among students in their classrooms have classrooms with better social climates. It is important, however, that the status of student leaders is not threatened by poor performance in academic areas; Short (1960) found evidence to suggest that where the status of high-power students is threatened by poor performance in one area, they are likely to encourage a shift into another area.

As discussed in Chapter 2, in most organizations there is both a formal authority structure and an informal influence structure affecting performance. In an organization such as a school, where membership is forced and the activities are based upon the preparation of the students for future adult roles, many of the students' needs are not met by the classroom activities; in addition to formal learning requirements, students are motivated to satisfy such needs as being liked and admired by others and to have others confirm one's attitudes and values concerning oneself and the world. Under such conditions the students form status systems and informal power structures based more upon their immediate concerns than the official concerns of the school. As discussed in the next chapter, these informal structures may be used productively by the teacher or may stand as major obstacles to the accomplishment of the school's objectives.

Implications of the Research on Reward and Punishment for the Teacher

What, then, are the practical implications of the research on reward and punishment? The following are some general guidelines for teachers.

1. In order to optimize the effectiveness of rewards and punishment, develop a warm, affectionate relationship with the students.
2. Make rules about student behavior for each period as explicit and clear as possible.
3. Reward (through such things as praise and attention as well as through grades) constructive student behaviors that facilitate learning and good class behavior.
4. Ignore student behaviors that interfere with teaching or learning, unless someone is likely to get hurt.
5. Whenever possible, reward student behaviors that are incompatible with those you wish to decrease.
6. Use punishment only if alternative, socially desirable behaviors are elicited and rewarded while the undesirable behavior is held in check.
7. If punishment is used, make sure it is consistent, immediate, and of appropriate intensity. Reasoning with the student often increases the effectiveness of punishment.
8. If a student does not engage in constructive behavior that can be rewarded, call his attention to other students engaging in the desired behavior and reward him for imitating those students.
9. Ensure that the student is paying close enough attention to the teacher and to his own behavior to be aware (a) that he is being rewarded and (b) what behavior he is being rewarded for.
10. To obtain optimal influence through the use of rewards and punishment, institute the proper norms and values within the classroom to obtain student support for student achievement and other constructive student behaviors.

SUMMARY

From the point of view of an ideal formal organization, the teacher has authority over students. Authority is legitimate power; that is, power that is vested in the position of teacher, and power that the students accept as the teacher's right to exert over them. But, since schools are organizations in which student membership is involuntary, the legitimacy of the authority structure may not be recognized by this subgroup. Consequently, a major part of the student's socialization into the school deals with the establishment of the legitimacy of the school's goals and authority structure.

Within an authority structure, there is an ancillary system of rewards and punishments. The basic rewards within the classroom include both the primary rewards of grades and promotions and secondary rewards such as praise from the teacher. Reward power can be considered to reside in the student's belief that a teacher has the ability to mediate rewards for him. As such, the teacher can make the attainment of these valued resources contingent upon the student's conformity to his standards of classroom behavior and thus control his behavior.

Bandura and Walters discuss three complementary methods of using reward power that are effective in increasing the probability that desirable behavior will be repeated. The first method is simply giving a positive reinforcement for the desired behavior. The second is withholding reinforcements when a student engages in undesirable behavior. The third, and most effective method, for eliminating deviant behavior while at the same time promoting desirable changes involves the active reinforcement of incompatible behaviors. An example of the latter would be the strategy of reinforcing a child for sitting quietly in his seat in order to keep him from wandering around the room.

The teacher can also control student behavior by administering punishments. A teacher's coercive power can be defined as the student's belief that the teacher can mediate punishments. The following four reasons were presented as to why punishment may be relatively ineffective: (1) The emotional reactions accompanying punishment give rise to patterns of behavior that are more socially undesirable than ones that punishment was intended to suppress. (2) Punishment is very likely to condition avoidance of the teacher. (3) Teacher use of physical punishment provides the student with an aggresive model to imitate. (4) There is the possibility that punishment will increase the frequency and amplitude of aggressive behavior on the part of the student. There is some evidence, however, that if punishment is consistent, immediate, sufficiently intense, and is combined with reasoning, it will be effective in suppressing, but not in eliminating undesirable behavior.

In addition to legitimate power and reward power, a teacher may have expert power based upon the possession of knowledge needed by students, and referent power based upon the desire of students to be like or identify with the teacher. With respect to the latter, reward power can be translated into referent power as individuals identify with those who reward them; and to the degree that identification results in the student's internalizing the teacher's norms, the teacher's legitimate power is also increased.

The chapter concluded with two final points. First, a student will be more susceptible to social influence if he pays attention to the teacher and to his own behavior so as to be aware that he is being rewarded and for what behavior he is being rewarded. Second, since certain students have a great deal of influence over their peers, teacher coalitions with these students are conducive to good classroom control and student achievement.

CHAPTER 12

GROUP NORMS AND SOCIAL CONTROL IN THE CLASSROOM

Introduction

In the previous chapter we discussed the relationship between the teacher's use of his authority and its ancillary system of rewards and punishments to accomplish the schools objectives. Within the classroom there are powerful group forces which the teacher can use productively to motivate his students. In the United States, however, these group forces often are not systematically utilized and often mitigate the teacher's influence upon the students and the accomplishment of the educational goals of the classroom.

The accomplishment of any systematic activity depends upon the coordinated behavior and attitudes of the individuals involved. Societies can not be sustained, social systems can not achieve their goals, without the coordination of behavior and attitudes resulting from conformity to group norms. As group norms specify appropriate behavior within the group they, perhaps more than any other factor, determine the motivation of the students to achieve the educational goals of the classroom and cooperate with the teacher. In the literature on discipline and classroom control, however, they have been markedly ignored. In this chapter we will discuss the nature and functions of group norms, the power of group norms over student behavior, and the teacher's use of group norms for classroom control and the achievement of the school's objectives.

Definition of Group Norms

Norms refer to the common beliefs of an evaluative type that make explicit the forms of behavior appropriate for members of the social system. Most schools, for example, have norms about the appropriateness of running in the halls, arriving late, and being absent. Some of these norms specify the behavior expected of all group members, whereas others apply only to individuals in specific roles; the norms within a school governing teachers' behaviors are usually different from the norms governing students' behavior. Since norms refer to the expected behavior sanctioned by the social system they have a specific "ought" or "must" quality; students *should not* run in the halls, *should not* arrive late to class, and *should not* be absent.

The norms of any social system vary in importance. Those that are less relevant to the objectives and values of the system usually allow for a greater range of behavior and bring less intense pressures for individuals to conform, than do norms which are highly relevant for the functioning of the system.

A norm exists where there is agreement or consensus about the behaviors which system members should or should not engage in and when there are social processes to produce adherence to these agreements. An existing norm will manifest itself to an outside observer in three ways: there will be regularity in behavior; in the event of disruption of this regularity the group will attempt to restore it by appealing to the norm and by exercising its power as an enforcer of the norm; and the person disrupting the regularity will be likely to feel some obligation to adhere to the norm and might even exhibit some conflict or guilt about deviating from it (Thibaut and Kelley, 1959).

In order for a norm to influence the behavior of an individual, the individual must recognize the existence of the rule for behavior, per-

211

ceive that other members of the organization or group accept and follow the rule, and accept and follow the rule himself. At first, individuals may conform to group norms because the group typically rewards normative behavior and punishes deviance. Later, the individual may internalize the norm and conform to it even when there are no other group members present. In the above examples, the organizational rule that students should not be late to class becomes a norm only to the extent that the individual student accepts the rule, perceives his classmates as accepting the rule, and the students in the classroom enforce the rule among themselves.

Functions of Group Norms

Norms have the general function of tying people into the social system so that they remain within the system and carry out their role assignments. Thus, within the classroom, the roles of teacher and student are integrated by the school norms that make explicit the forms of behavior appropriate for them. Teachers, for example, "ought" to teach as competently and effectively as possible; students "ought" to want to learn, to get good grades, and to be promoted. As stated above, these "oughts" become norms as the individual perceives their existence, accepts them, and perceives that his peers within the organization accept them. Norms develop around and derive their support from the dominant ongoing functions of the social system; they give cognitive support and structure to the behavior in which system members are engaged. Within the classroom the school's norms are concerned with the educational process, the teacher-student and student-student interactions that lead to learning. Productive norms derive their support from improving the educational process; for example, a norm that states that only one student should speak at a time ensures, among other things, that the teacher can deal adequately with every question that arises and that all the students will hear and understand the answer.

The acceptance of the social system's norms provides a common frame of reference from which behavior within the system is evaluated (Sherif, 1936; Festinger, 1950). This frame of reference produces homogeneity of values among members of the social system.

Norms serve as substitutes for informal or short-term influence

(Thibaut and Kelley, 1959). A teacher, through the use of his superior power, can force a student to sit still and pay attention in class. Such moment-to-moment use of power can be obviated by establishing relevant norms. Such norms produce more economically and efficiently certain consequences otherwise dependent upon influence processes. Both the weaker and the stronger parties stand to gain from the introduction of mutually acceptable norms that introduce regularity and control into the relationship without recourse to the direct interpersonal application of power. The teacher avoids the resistances and lack of whole-hearted cooperation that often results from applying power in coercive ways; the students gain increased ability to influence the teacher through the norms that specify the teachers role requirements and the limits of the teacher's authority, and, thereby protect students from having teachers use their power in capricious ways.

Power accrues, therefore, to norms because the people involved give up some of their individual power to the norms. Individuals allow themselves to be influenced by norms in ways in which they would never allow themselves to be influenced by other people, as norms often assume the characteristics of moral obligatons. At the very least, conformity to the social system's norms is a requirement for continued membership in the system.

The stability of behavior resulting from conformity to norms reduces the necessity of high-power individuals constantly surveying the behavior of low-power people to ensure that they are conforming.

The Power of Group Norms over Member Behavior

Group norms have a powerful influence upon the behavior of members of a group. In a classic experiment utilizing the autokinetic effect, Sherif (1936) demonstrated the effects of a group norm upon judgments about an ambiguous stimulus. The autokinetic effect is a phenomenon where a stationary pinpoint of light seen in a completely dark room appears to move. Subjects were placed in a dark room, exposed to the stationary point of light, and asked to judge how far the light moved. Under these conditions each subject developed a range in which he made his estimates; for one subject the range was an inch, for another it was several inches. When subjects were placed together in groups of two or three their judgments converged, forming a group norm. Sherif found that the group norm persisted for each group member even when he faced the same stimulus alone at a later time.

In a later experiment, Asch (1952) demonstrated that there is a tendency for individuals to conform to the group's judgment even when that judgment is obviously contrary to fact. In the experiment a "naive" subject was placed in a group of confederates of the experimenter who were instructed to give incorrect judgments on twelve of eighteen trials. The naive subject was seated at the end (sometimes next to the end) of the line of participants. The participants were instructed to choose which of three lines came closest in length to a line they had just seen; the correct answer was quite easily recognized (that is, a control group invariably was correct in their judgments). One by one the participants stated their opinion as to which line was the same length as the line they had just seen. On the trials where the unanimous judgment of the other group members was obviously wrong the subject faced a conflict between going along with the group or accepting the evidence of his own eyes. Sixty-eight percent of the naive subjects' estimates remained independent of the group's judgment and 32 percent were deflected part or all of the way to the unanimous judgment of the confederates. Seventy-five percent of the subjects showed some errors in their judgments in the direction of the erroneous group judgments, one third conformed in half or more of the trials. It made little difference whether the majority consisted, in absolute size, of three or fifteen members, so long as it was unanimous. When one other group member agreed with the naive subject (going against the rest of the group's judgments), the tendency to conform to the majority judgment dropped from 32 to 10 percent.

Sherif's (1936) experiment demonstrated that group norms exist and influence behavior in ambiguous situations, even when the group is not physically present. Asch's (1952) experiments demonstrated that even on matters of unambiguous fact many people will conform to an erroneous group judgment. In both studies the subjects simply made their judgments in the presence of strangers without any direct interaction taking place. Relatively speaking, there were no explicitly defined relationships among the participants nor were they pursuing a group objective. The findings of these studies, therefore, may be taken to be conservative demonstrations of the power of group norms.

Newcomb (1952), in a study of student attitudes at Bennington College, demonstrated that membership in a group does not invariably lead one to accept the norms and standards of that group. The acquisition of group norms is more a function of the individual's use of the group as a positive or negative referent for particular attitudes and behavior. In order to discuss the effects of group norms upon an individual's behavior, therefore, it is important to make the distinction between membership groups and reference groups (Seigel and Seigel, 1957). Membership groups are groups in which the person is currently a member; reference groups (Kelley, 1952) are (1) groups whose norms and values the person utilizes to evaluate his own behavior and attitudes or (2) groups that a person uses as a standard of comparison. A reference group may be a group to which an individual belongs or it may be one to which he aspires or, as in the case of a negative reference group, one which he rejects. Membership groups often, but not always, function as reference groups for their members. Thus, one of the factors influencing the effect of the norms of a classroom group on the behavior of a student is the extent to which the group serves as a referent for the student.

It is evident that the values and norms that develop in student groups may help or hinder the educational process. Currently in the United States, classroom norms usually give far less support to academic achievement than is desired. Coleman (1961), for instance, found in a survey of ten midwestern high schools that the student norms valued athletic achievement over academic success. In the schools where these norms were most powerful, the students who endorsed academic values were not the most intelligent but were the ones most willing to work hard at an activity which was relatively unrewarded by their peers. In a study of a similar situation at the Harvard Graduate School of Business, Orth (1963) found that the greatest number of overachievers were in a student subgroup that endorsed academic values, while the greatest number of underachievers were in a student subgroup that was nonacademically oriented. Other studies, in both educational (Hughes, Becker, and Geer, 1962) and industrial (Roethlisberger and Dickson, 1939) settings suggest that informal norms can specify a lower output than is desired by the social system. It is not uncommon for classroom norms to explicitly

215

express disapproval toward those who achieve too high or overexert themselves for grades (gentlemen should get "C's"; people who get high grades are "curve-breakers").

The Use of Group Norms for Behavioral Change

Schools in the United States, instead of deliberately attempting to use student subcultures in ways that will improve learning, have largely chosen to ignore or fight peer-group interpersonal forces. Consequently, the subcultures that eventually develop may adhere to norms that hinder the academic effort. Other countries such as the Soviet Union, however, have attempted to systematically develop and use the norms of student groups (Bronfenbrenner, 1962). In order to accomplish this, the schools begin to develop intragroup co-operation and intergroup competition in the classroom in the first grade (and in some cases in preschool programs). First, groups within the classroom are arbitrarily formed. These groups, under the teacher's leadership, rival and soon surpass the family as the principal agent of socialization. The classroom groups compete with each other for awards given to the highest-achieving and best-behaved group. Since the rewards and punishments are given on a group basis the entire group benefits or suffers as a consequence of the conduct of individual members. The group, furthermore, is made responsible for the behavior and achievement of each member. As soon as possible, the tasks of evaluating the behavior of group members and of dispensing classroom rewards and punishments is delegated to the group. The principal methods of social control are public recognition and public criticism.

Suppose, for example, that a class is given the task of working several math problems. A group member appointed by the teacher as the group monitor surveys how well each member of his group is doing. Those students who work quietly and do the problems correctly are publicly commended by the group monitor; those students who work the problems incorrectly or disturb the other group members are publicly criticized. The best group within the classroom is rewarded, perhaps through a special privilege such as being able to leave the classroom first. Since it is the responsibility of each group to improve its performance, the losing groups may decide to assign a superior math student to tutor another group member who did not do the problems correctly and a well-behaved student may be assigned to a noisy group member to ensure that he will be quiet in future classroom activities.

The students receive explicit training and practice in helping one another in academic areas and in sanctioning disruptive members. Furthermore, during periods of public criticism, group members are encouraged to "help" the group by reporting other members who are deviating from the group's norms. The teacher seeks to create group unity, a feeling of common responsibility for the group's achievement, and norms of mutual aid within the group.

Similar group methods have been used in the United States to resocialize delinquents (Pilnick, et al., 1966; Empey and Rabor, 1961; McCorkle, Elias, and Bixby, 1958), drug addicts (Yablonsky, 1962), and alcoholics. Pilnick and his associates began with the following assumptions: (1) much of the behavior that society terms "delinquent" and antisocial is of a group nature and is socially prescribed by the delinquent's peer group and community; (2) adolescents especially have a need to conform to peer-group norms and values; and (3) where middle-class channels for achievement are blocked, delinquent subcultures will form that contain the opportunity for status and masculine identification, which are denied its members by society. If delinquency is based upon conformity to peer-group norms, it follows that a way to rehabilitate delinquents is to resocialize them into a new peer group with norms that are acceptable to society and antithetical to the delinquent "street" norms. Socialization into a nondelinquent peer group is accomplished through the use of "guided-group interaction."

Guided-group interaction generally consists of the following steps. First, the delinquent must tell his entire delinquent history to the group (which usually consists of ten to twelve members). During this procedure, group norms of honesty and truthfulness are stressed; if the group is going to help the member, the member must be completely honest with the group. After hearing the member's history, the group assigns him his problems to work on (for example, stealing, fighting, or failure to control one's temper).

In order to achieve acceptance in the group, and to gain status, the member devotes himself to overcoming his problems by utilizing the aid, suggestions, and insights of his peers and the staff. Emphasis is placed upon revealing one's true feelings to the group at all times; otherwise the group will not be convinced that the member has really been helped. Correspondingly, he must try to help the other group members solve their problems. The assumption is that if a delinquent seriously attempts to reform others he must automatically accept the common purpose of the reformation process, identify himself closely with others engaged in it, and award prestige to those who succeed in it (Empey and Rabor, 1961). This establishes a group norm: a group member has to care about what happens to the other group members and they in turn have to care about what happens to him. In helping the other members of the group, the street maxim, "Thou shall not squeal," basic to the existence of the usual criminal culture, is reversed: helping a fellow member includes exposing his violations to the group so that he may be punished and helped not to commit the same violation again. Not reporting a violation is taken as a sign that one does not care whether the violator is "helped" to overcome his problems.

Commiting a serious offense against the group's norms, such as failing to report a fellow member who has engaged in undersirable behavior, is punished by the group. The group, as well as the staff, has the power to send the delinquent back to court for sentencing to another institution. Furthermore, the group decides when a boy has overcome his problems and can be released from the program. In other words, until each member convinces his group (and the staff) that he can be trusted not to engage in delinquent behavior, he is not released from the program.

Finally, in such groups there is a strong norm against physical violence, which reverses the status system of the "street" that emphasizes physical prowess, and hard work is valued, which reverses the street norm that work is for "squares."

Guided-group interaction has had unusual success in rehabilitating delinquent boys. Pilnick and his associates (1966) report that in four years, of the 246 boys admitted to the Essexfields program, 196 successfully completed the program (50 boys were returned to the Juvenile Court). Of those 196 boys, only 24 (12 percent) were committed to correctional institutions after their release from Essexfields. They state that this is a remarkable figure, as the usual recidivism rate for delinquents ranges between 50 and 75 percent.

Yablonsky (1962) gives several reasons why group approaches have been successful in resocializing delinquents and drug addicts.

First, the other group members are one's peers who have had similar experiences and are not taken in by one's manipulative behavior. Many delinquents learn various ways to manipulate the middle-class adults they have to deal with, such as social workers, teachers, and parole officers: their peers, however, are not easily manipulated. Second, the group represents an achievable status system that provides the person with the possibility of legitimate achievement and prestige. Third, through the work programs connected with guided-group interaction the member learns a new social role. Fourth, through the group programs he learns to relate, communicate, and work with others. Finally, through the constant self-assessment required by the group, self-identity and empathy with others is developed.

An example of successful use of group methods of classroom control is reported by Lippitt (1964). After having serious control problems, a fifth-grade teacher collected data on her class that indicated that four of the five most influential members of her class were the most antischool in their attitudes. Subsequently, the teacher formed a rotating student steering committee that (1) examined the problems of being a steering committee, (2) observed classroom behavior at different points in time, (3) classified behavior as either demonstrating that they were having a good or bad day in class, and (4) made recommendations to the class about improving classroom conditions. In time, the class began to handle classroom control as a group, the attitudes of the antischool students and their position in the class-status hierarchy changed, the problems of control eased, and the class functioned more adequately.

The examples discussed in this section suggest that schools can systematically develop classroom norms that support educational goals and facilitate their accomplishment. Since individual behavior and attitudes are determined primarily by the norms of one's reference groups, classroom norms can be powerful forces in classroom motivation and control. The essential elements of the examples discussed seem to be that although the group norms and goals were initiated by adults from outside the group, the groups were given the responsibility of enforcing the norms in ways that resulted in the internalizing of the norms and goals by the group members. In order to have the group enforce the norms, the group was given the power to reward conformity to the norms and to punish violations. Thus the pressures to behave in socially desirable ways came from one's peers and were enforced by one's peers. Such a situation within the classroom avoids all problems connected with authority and adult-centered control.

Conformity to Norms

One of the most frequently researched areas in social psychology is conformity to group pressure. Recent formulations of conformity (Willis, 1963; Allen, 1965; Hollander and Willis, 1967) have stated that in discussing conformity it is necessary to posit at least two dimensions: conformity-anticonformity and independence-dependence. The conformers and anticonformers both react to the group norm and base their behavior upon it, the conformers to agree with the norm and the anticonformers to disagree with the norm. An independent person, on the other hand, does not give much weight to the group norm in making his judgment. Most of the research on conformity deals with conformity to majority opinion in the group and has little to do with the "ought" quality of group norms.

In our society conformity has acquired a general negative connotation. Conformity to organizational norms is often seen as selling out one's individuality in order to get ahead or as violating one's principles in order to obtain group acceptance. Much of the research on conformity is based upon negative behaviors such as lying about one's perceptions or beliefs. Conforming to group norms, however, frequently improves the functioning of a group at no expense to the person's principles or beliefs. Conformity to a classroom norm that one should not molest others who are trying to study, for example, is beneficial for the group and the individuals involved. One experiment (Milgram, 1965) found that conforming to group norms enables the individual to resist the demands of a malevolent authority. In some situations, therefore, conformity to group norms is constructive and appropriate, in other situations, it is not.

Not all behavior is covered by group norms. The norms for classroom behavior, for example, do not usually state that the students should like green vegetables better than yellow vegetables, coke better than orange drink, or movies better than television. Group norms deal primarily with the behaviors affecting the accomplishment of the group's task and the ability of the group to maintain itself over time. Within the classroom the behaviors usually regulated by group norms are those affecting the quality and quantity of learning (task behaviors) and the harmony and friendliness of relationships within the classroom (maintenance behaviors). In general, the more relevant the individual's behavior is to the accomplishment of the group's task and the maintenance of the group, the more the pressures toward conformity. Schachter (1951), Emerson (1954), and Schachter et al. (1954), for example, have found in their studies of deviation from group norms that the more the deviation was relevant to the purposes of the group, the greater was the rejection of the deviant by the group. Cartwright and Zander (1968) state that the more the group values its goals and the more it sees these goals as obtainable the greater will be the pressures to conform to task-related norms. Raven and Rietsema (1957) found that the clearer the group goal and the path to the group goal are to the group members, the stronger will be the pressures toward uniformity in task behavior. Finally, Festinger (1950) and Allen (1965) state that there will be greater pressures to conform to task-related norms where the goal obtainment of group members is interdependent, that is, in order to obtain their goals the members of the group must coordinate their behavior.

Not everyone in the group is expected to conform to group norms to the same degree. Usually as part of their initiation into the group, new members are expected to conform closely to group norms. According to Hollander and Willis (1967) there is greater group tolerance of nonconformity in some directions for the high-status person and greater restrictions in others. This is due to the fact that leaders are often "keepers of the group's traditions" while at the same time they are expected to innovate and initiate change within the group. In general, nonconforming behaviors that are seen by the group as potentially leading to improvements in the group's ability to accomplish its task and maintain itself are accepted; nonconforming behaviors that interfere with group maintenance and task accomplishment are not accepted.

At any one time numerous social influences encroach simultaneously upon the individual. Some of these influences come from face-to-face groups within which the individual is interacting, other influences derive from reference groups and individuals who are not physically present. Whatever action the individual takes, it is a result of the balance of the various influences acting upon him at the time. The normative expectations of the influences upon the individual can be congruent or incongruent. For instance, the normative expectations of the school class, the family, and the peer group are for the most part congruent for most middle-class children. For lower-class children, however, the normative expectations of the school class, the family, and the peer group are often discrepant. When social influences prescribe conflicting behavior the individual is faced with a norm conflict, that is, he has to decide which group's norms he is going to conform to. Conformity to classroom norms, therefore, is dependent upon the degree of the individual's norm conflict.

Several factors affect the intensity of the individual's norm conflicts. One is the number of the individual's reference groups. Festinger, Schachter, and Back (1962), for example, found that in a housing project the occupants showing least conformity to the project's norms had more affiliations with outside groups. Second, as not all membership groups are reference groups, the individual's conformity to group norms depends upon the extent to which the group serves as a reference group for him. Usually, the greater the similarity of the group to the person, the greater the likelihood that the group will be an acceptable reference group (Allen, 1965).

Perhaps the greatest influence upon conformity to reference-group norms, however, is the saliency of the group to the situation the individual is experiencing. Kelley (1955), for example, found that when counterpressures were applied to attitudes related to Catholic doctrine, the resistance to change in the participants' attitudes was greater the more that participants had had their belonging to the Catholic Church made salient before being exposed to the counterpressures. In the study by Charters and Newcomb (1952), the religious affiliation of one group of Catholic students was made salient by a discussion of the assumptions underlying the opinions of Catholics. A similar group of Catholic students did not engage in such a discussion. An attitude scale which included items relevant to Catholic doctrine (for example, "Birth control information should be provided to all married individuals who desire it") was administered to both groups. Differences between the two groups appeared only on the items relevant to the Catholic Church. The experimental group, who had engaged in the discussion of the assumptions underlying the opinions of Catholics, tended to adhere to the norms of the Catholic Church. The control group, who had not engaged in the discussion, tended to adhere to the general college norms. Increasing the saliency of the religious norms, therefore, led to increased conformity to those norms even though replies to the attitude scale were anonymous. In other words, the greater the saliency of a group, the greater will be the conformity to its norms (Cartwright and Zander, 1968).

A number of investigators have reviewed the literature on conformity to group norms and specified the conditions under which conformity will occur (Thibaut and Kelley, 1959; Cartwright and Zander, 1968; Hare, 1962; Allen, 1965; Deutsch, in press). The bulk of the research that has been conducted supports the following principles. First, in order to conform to a norm an individual must be clearly aware of the norm's existence. The greater the ambiguity of the group norm or the greater the individual's unawareness of the norm, the less will be the conformity. Second, the group must be able to ascertain whether or not the individual is conforming. The greater the group's surveillance of the individual's behavior, the greater will be the conformity. In addition, the group must be able to apply strong sanctions for the individual's behavior. The greater the rewards for conformity and the greater the punishment for deviation the greater the conformity will be. The cohesion of the group or the attraction of the individual to the group will also affect his conformity to the group's norms. The greater the individual's attraction to the group the greater his conformity to the group's norms. Allen notes, however, that conformity must be instrumental to being liked by others before high attraction will lead to conformity; even if he is attracted to the group a person will not conform to the group's norms if he knows that the group will still reject him.

The individual's personality characteristics will affect his conformity to group norms (Cartwright and Zander, 1968; Hare, 1962; Allen 1965; Deutsch, in press). There is general agreement that the lower the self-confidence, the greater will be the conformity. Hare discusses research studies which have indicated that (1) individuals who are high on the F-Scale (authoritarianism) conform more than those low on the F-Scale, (2) individuals who are rated as submissive or dependent or who describe themselves as submissive are found to submit more frequently to majority opinion, and (3) a high need for approval of others is positively related to conformity. In a series of studies on the Asch-phenomena, Crutchfield (1955) found that conforming individuals tend to be defensive, rigid, moralistic, intolerant of ambiguity, highly respectful of authority, low in self-understanding, and insecure. Individuals who were markedly independent of group influence were more confident, open, secure, expressive, nondefensive, unaffected, and spontaneous. The above findings, however, apply

223

basically to situations such as the Asch experiment where individuals had to lie about their perceptions in order to conform to group opinion and, therefore, it is unclear how applicable the results are to other types of situations. As stated earlier, conformity to group norms is usually a constructive act facilitating the accomplishment of the group's task and maintaining the group; the above findings do not necessarily apply to such a situation.

Finally, Hare and Allen both emphasize the effect upon conforming support for deviation. They state that conformity to group norms will be less where the group accepts deviant behavior and where several members of the group deviate from the group's norms.

In summary, conformity to group norms will be high when the group norm is clear, the group keeps its members under constant surveillance, the group's sanctions are strong, the group is highly cohesive, and the social support for conforming is high. A teacher, therefore, who is trying to increase the conformity of a class to appropriate learning norms should make the norms clear, specify behavior which the group can survey, increase the ability of the group to apply sanctions, increase the cohesion of the group, and increase the social support for conforming to group norms. The following section illustrates some of the ways in which a teacher can effect these often elusive goals.

Initiating Group Norms

There are several ways norms can be initiated in a group. Norms are very commonly initiated into a classroom by the teacher directly stating the norm and instructing the class to accept it. In many classrooms, for example, a list of prescribed norms is displayed—"We work quietly; we do our own work; we stay in our seats." Such an approach can be successful. Deutsch (1962), for instance, instructed subjects in an experiment to follow a cooperative, competitive, or individualistic norm. Under the conditions of the experimental situation, such norms were accepted and abided by. There are, however, many limitations to such an approach. An uncooperative class, for example, may delight in rejecting and even flouting teacher-imposed norms. Especially when the teacher is perceived as an illegitimate or malevolent authority figure, direct statements of norms will be ineffective.

Norms can be initiated through *modeling*. Individuals do learn to conform to group norms by watching others conform. Numerous experiments demonstrate the effectiveness of modeling in eliciting desired behavior (Bandura and Walters, 1963), especially when an opportunity for both observation and rehearsal of the desired behavior is given (Rosenhan and White, 1967). A teacher wishing to initiate a group norm that one should not talk when someone else is talking can model appropriate behavior by avoiding interrupting anyone in the classroom and he can point out conforming students to serve as models for the rest of the students.

Thibaut and Kelley (1959) point out that norms from other relationships can be imported into a group. Most children learn naturally the cultural norms of social responsibility (you should help someone who is in need of help), fair-play (don't kick someone when he's down), reciprocity (if someone does you a favor you should do a favor in return), and sex role (boys don't hit girls, but girls can bite boys); but a teacher can reinforce and add to these *cultural* norms in the classroom. Also, a teacher who is aware of the norms the students adhere to outside of the classroom can productively initiate such norms within the classroom in ways which facilitate the accomplishment of the educational goals of the school.

Perhaps the most effective way to initiate group norms is through group discussion. Research on group decision making indicates that members will probably become more committed to norms developed through group discussion than to norms directly stated by a speaker or superior. During World War II, for example, Lewin (1947) attempted to persuade housewives to increase their consumption of kidneys, sweetbreads, and beef hearts, which were not generally preferred. Some groups heard lectures on the attractiveness, tastes, and preparation of these foods; other groups discussed the same topics with the help of a nutrition expert. At the end of the discussion period, the housewives were asked to indicate by a show of hands whether they intended to serve the meats. A follow-up found that 32 percent of those in the discussion groups and 3 percent of those who had heard a lecture had served one of the three meats. A second study by Lewin (1947) and a study by Levine and Butler (1952) confirmed the finding that group discussion is superior to lectures in initiating conformity to new group norms. Kostick (1957), in addition, found that group discussion could be used to induce a college class to set higher achievement goals.

Pelz (1958), Bennett (1955), and Pennington et al. (1958) dem-

onstrated that public commitment to a group norm and the perceived consensus of the group about the norm influence conformity
to group norms. A teacher initiating a norm should attempt to get
public commitment by the class to adhere to the norm and a consensus of the class that such a norm is desirable. McKeachie
(1954) found that group discussion followed by a group decision resulted in group members shifting their attitudes in the direction that
they thought the class was moving. When new norms for behavior
were decided upon by this procedure, they were internalized more
than norms set up by the teacher.

Finally Coch and French (1948) tested the effectiveness of different methods of making decisions in reducing resistance to changes
made in an industrial factory. In general, groups of workers who
participated in making decisions about how the changes were to be
carried out were compared with other groups who were simply noti-
fied that such changes would occur. Those workers who participated
in the discussions of the changes not only showed a rapid rate of re-
covery in their production levels immediately following the change, but
in many instances increased their production over what it had been
before the change. The uninvolved groups showed a sharp decline in
their production rate after the change and within the period in which
they were studied they never returned to their original level of output.
A follow-up study in Norway found that the perceived legitimacy of
their involvement by the workers mediated such results; if the workers do not think they should participate in the decision, participation
will not produce such marked effects.

In a study of establishing norms in an urban elementary classroom, Smith and Geoffrey (1968) distinguished between a belief
about classroom rules (a generalized perception of what exists) and
a classroom norm (a generalized or group expectation of what *ought*
to exist). On the basis of intensive observation of a successful teacher
they formulated a four-step procedure for establishing classroom
norms. First, the teacher establishes a belief about teacher authority
in the classroom: "The teacher gives directions and the students follow them." Specifically, during the first few days of class the teacher
observed gave literally dozens of orders to both individual students
and to the entire class that involved a number of trivial items such as
distributing books and asking permission. As the number of situations in which the teacher gave orders and obtained compliance in a
variety of mundane and critical situations accumulated, the students
developed a belief system (the way things are done in this class is

that the teacher gives direction and the students follow them) and ultimately a normative system (in this class the teacher should give direction and the students should follow them). Second, the teacher convinced the students that "he really meant what he was saying." Disobedience was never tolerated. Students who disobeyed the teacher were warned that their behavior would not be accepted by the teacher. Third, the teacher followed through on any statement of intent or warning he made. If the teacher had warned a student that he would be punished next time he did not follow the teacher's directions, the student was punished for his next instance of disobedience. Finally, the teacher softened the tone of the classroom management through humor and by overdramatizing situations. In this way he made conformity to the rules less a matter of personal power and more a matter of obeying classroom regulations. An example of the teacher's humor when making an announcement to his class is as follows:

> Stop work and listen. Know what I have done on occasions with someone who wouldn't stop working? Don't guess. Ask someone who knows me. (p. 71)

Thus, through his humor the teacher established a warm, nonpunitive relationship with his class while at the same time making classroom regulations clear, warning students that no divergence from the rules would be accepted, and constantly following through on his warnings. During all four steps the teacher continually made the classroom regulations clear to the students. The observed teacher was very successful in establishing the classroom regulations as norms.

Implications for the Teacher

The following are some general guidelines for establishing classroom norms:

1. In order for students to accept classroom regulations as group norms they must: (a) recognize the existence of the regulation, (b) perceive that the other students accept and follow the regulation, and (c) feel some internal commitment to following the regulation. The teacher, therefore, in initiating classroom regulations as norms should ensure that everyone to which the regulation applies clearly understands the regulation, clearly perceives the situations in which it applies to their be-

havior, and knows the extent to which other students accept and abide by the regulation.

2. Students will accept and internalize norms to the extent to which they see the norms as facilitating the accomplishment of goals and tasks to which they are committed. The teacher, therefore, should constantly clarify the ways in which conformity to classroom regulations facilitates the accomplishment of the students' goals.

3. Students will accept and internalize norms for which they feel a sense of ownership. Generally, students will support and accept norms which they have helped formulate. Teachers, therefore, should ensure that the setting of classroom norms is conducted in as democratic a manner as possible.

4. As soon as possible the students should enforce the norms themselves. When the teacher enforces the norms, however, he should be as consistent as possible and always carry through on any warnings about misbehavior he makes. The teacher should remember, furthermore, that any norm he or the class enforces exists only to facilitate goal accomplishment. Too many norms strictly enforced leads to an overrestrictive classroom in which creativity, spontaneous learning activities, and a climate for self-generated growth and development is stifled.

5. The teacher should point out appropriate models for conforming to norms and provide opportunities for the students to practice appropriate behavior.

6. The teacher should import the cultural norms of the students which facilitate classroom goal accomplishment into the classroom.

7. The teacher should not make conformity to norms a matter of direct influence between himself and the student; a student conforming to a classroom norm is not being directly influenced by the teacher, he is being directly influenced by the norm.

8. A warm, cooperative, trusting classroom climate will facilitate conformity to classroom norms.

9. It is important to remember that since norms exist only to facilitate goal accomplishment they should be flexible so that at any time a more appropriate norm can be substituted. Many norms should be under constant negotiation within the classroom until the most facilitative are agreed upon by the majority of the students.

SUMMARY

In order to prepare students for adult roles by teaching them the required knowledge and values, the behavior of the students in the classroom must be coordinated and ordered. Group norms provide the needed structure by (1) tying students into the school so that they remain within the school and carry out their student role assignments, (2) providing a common frame of reference for the students and staff within the school, and (3) serving as substitutes for informal influence within the school and the classroom.

Group norms have powerful influences upon the behavior of the members of a group. Membership in a group, however, does not invariably lead one to accept and conform to the norms of that group. The acquisition of group norms is more a function of the individual's use of the group as a positive or negative referent for particular attitudes and behavior. Students, therefore, have to be socialized into the school in such a way that they will accept their class as a referent for attitudes and behavior.

Peer-group norms can be used successfully to further educational goals and to cause marked behavioral changes in disruptive students. The ability of the teacher to establish the appropriate classroom norms and ensure student conformity to the norms is a major factor in the successful accomplishment of the educational objectives of the school.

The teacher can initiate group norms by directly stating the norms by modeling the norms, through importing norms from other groups, and through group discussion techniques.

Conformity to group norms is most likely to occur when (1) the norm is clearly stated, (2) the person's conformity is under group surveillance, (3) the group has strong sanctions to apply for conformity or nonconformity, (4) the group is highly cohesive (that is, the person is attracted to the group), (5) there is little support for deviation from the norms, and (6) the person's conformity or nonconformity affects the task accomplishment or the maintenance of the group. Once a classroom norm is established, the teacher can reward or punish conforming and nonconforming behavior.

CHAPTER 13

SCHOOL
AND CLASSROOM
CLIMATE

Introduction

At the college level it has long been noted that educational institutions show marked differences in climate. Even a casual visitor can detect differences between the atmospheres of Antioch, Harvard, City College of New York, and the University of Minnesota. When visiting a suburban public school one is likely to find a warm, pleasant atmosphere where students visit independent-study resource centers, smile at teachers in the hall, and study in the library. When visiting an inner-city school one is likely to find a grim, hostile, prison-like atmosphere where policemen patrol the halls and guard the doorways, teachers and students exchange hostile glances in the hall, security checks are common, and students are contained in their "home" rooms. It is evident that such differences in climate can have serious effects on student attitudes toward school, student achievement, and the accomplishment of the school's objectives. For example, there have been studies that have demonstrated amazing differences in achievement among the students attending the various colleges in a single state (Learned and Wood, 1938) and in the country as a whole (Knapp and Greenbaum, 1953).

Each school has its own climate, which in turn is made up of a whole spectrum of more-or-less recognizable subcultures affecting student behavior and performance. The climate of an organization is a combination of all the organizational factors and of all the personality characteristics of the members of the organization. It is such a significant force that it affects almost every other topic in this book.

Most studies of organizational climates of schools have confined themselves to the college level, a few have investigated high schools, and practically none have dealt with elementary schools. With regard to colleges, it is possible for students to choose to attend colleges that have climates compatible with their personal needs. Most high-school and elementary students, however, have no choice in selecting what school they are to attend; in the great majority of cases they attend the school to which they have been assigned by virtue of location. The climates of the elementary and high schools therefore, may or may not be congruent with the needs of the students, and perhaps affect their behavior more than do the climates of colleges. The results of the studies on college and high-school climates have revealed wide differences in climates between schools, particularly on variables such as the emphasis on academic excellence, the intellectual, political, and social orientation of the students, and the students' educational and consequent occupational aspirations.

Conceptualization and Definition of Organizational Climate

In spite of the obvious differences between the climates of organizations performing similar functions, it is not easy to specify the dimensions of such differences or "how" different aspects of the organization and its members influence the climate. This has resulted in a variety of conceptualizations of the nature of organizational climate and how it influences student behavior.

Perhaps the most influential one is based on the personality theory of Murray (1938). Murray introduced a taxonomy for classifying both the environmental pressures and the characteristic ways in which an individual strives to structure the environment for himself. He called the external pressures "press" and their internal counterparts "needs." These two terms served a dual function in classifying self-directing personality trends (needs) and externally controlling situational pressures (press). Both needs and press are inferred from characteristic activities and events, the former from things that the individual typically does and the latter from things that are typically done to him in some particular setting. Pace and Stern (1958) applied Murray's personality theory to the climate of educational organizations. Thus, they conceptualized the climate of an educational organization as consisting of the personality characteristics and values (needs) of its members and the organizational pressures on the students, administration, and faculty (press).

In a later discussion of the organizational climate of schools Astin and Holland (1961) and Michael (1961) theorized that the major portion of environmental pressures is dependent on the nature of the people within the environment; organizational climate, therefore, was defined as the personal orientations and characteristics of the majority of the students within the organization. In a review of the literature on the effect of organizational climates on students' aspirations and behavior, Boyle (1965) conceptualized climates as consisting of both structural characteristics of the school and the characteristics of the students. He felt that the students' aspirations for attending college were jointly determined by the educational standards and practices of high schools and the scholastic abilities of the students on the one hand and the peer-group influences on short- and long-range values and attitudes on the other hand.

Backman and Secord (1968) contribute an additional variation. According to their theory, three factors define the climate: (1) the personality characteristics, abilities, motives, values, career and educational plans and past experiences of the entering students; (2) the norms, values, role requirements and other characteristics (such as the exercise of authority, size, availability of facilities, and nature of setting) of the school itself; (3) the values and norms of the informal organization within the school, that is, the traditions and collective feelings passed from one generation of students to another. Student characteristics, especially in heterogenous organizations such as large universities, can be quite disparate. In contrast, a public high school drawing from a homogeneous residential area, such as a middle-class

232

suburb, will have a much smaller variation. And finally, any school older than a few years will have developed traditions and attitudes, both on academic and social activities. New students rapidly accept the values of their older peers. These three factors, however, are not independent of each other, but interact to some extent. For example, the quality of the entering students is dependent on the characteristics of the organization if self-selection for students is possible, that is, intellectually oriented students enroll in colleges that have reputations of being intellectually oriented schools. The interactive process is complicated by the fact that incoming students react differently to the formal and informal aspects of the organization. The personal characteristics of the incoming students interact with the formal and informal aspects of the organization to influence the students' behavior. That is, unique characteristics make a student receptive to certain types of influences and resistant to others, and this receptivity will determine the extent to which he is influenced by the organizational characteristics of the school and the traditions and norms of the ongoing student body. Thus, the climate of a school does not affect all the students in a given school uniformly.

The three variables determining climate are not necessarily homogeneous. There are subcultures present in all three variables, within the organization, the student body, and the incoming students, which differentially influence the individual student. The structure of the school, furthermore, is usually heterogeneous, so that students differ with respect to their chances of encountering formal influences.

There is some evidence which indicates that the influences of the structural aspects of the school may be greater for new students than for individuals who have attended school for some time. Newcomb (1961), in a study of the acquaintance process, found that mutual attraction develops first among individuals in close proximity to each other (determined by the organization), but as contacts spread out, similarity of values becomes the most important determiner of friendships.

The Existence of Different Educational Climates

There is a large body of research using a variety of instruments that demonstrates that schools and colleges vary according to how they

233

are perceived by their members. Perhaps the most extensive study was conducted by Davis (1963) on the intellectual climates of 135 American colleges and universities. In this study Davis analyzed the responses of 33,982 graduating seniors of the class of 1960–1961. His measure of intellectual climate was based on the following question:

> Listed below are some purposes or results of college. Circle the one which is most important to you personally and also circle the one which you think is most important to the typical student here.
>
> A. Most important to you personally.
>   a. A basic general education and appreciation of ideas.
>   b. Having a good time while getting a degree.
>   c. Career training.
>   d. Developing the ability to get along with different kinds of people.
>
> B. Most important to the typical student here.
>   a. A basic general education and appreciation of ideas.
>   b. Having a good time while getting a degree.
>   c. Career training.
>   d. Developing the ability to get along with different kinds of people.

Davis defined the *"true" climate of intellectualism* of a school as the percent of seniors who circled "basic general education" as "most important to me personally." He defined the *perceived climate of intellectualism* as the percent of seniors circling the same item as "most important to the typical student here."

The results of Davis' study indicate that high quality, private, small institutions, have high proportions of seniors endorsing intellectual values, while lower quality, public, and larger institutions have lower proportions. Technological schools were quite low on intellectual values. In addition, while "perceived" value climates were directly related to "true" value climates, students' perceptions of value climates were distorted toward their own value positions, and students with high grades tended to give lower estimates of the intellectuality of their campuses than students with poorer grades.

Pace (1963), in a study of thirty-two colleges representing a wide assortment of sizes and locations, found that although there are some things that are true about all colleges (that is, student reports must be neat, most courses are well organized, classrooms are kept neat and tidy, and the like), colleges are vastly different from one another. He concludes that the differences between college climates, across a wide assortment of schools, fall into five fairly clear patterns. The first two are both predominantly intellectual, with one more strongly oriented toward humanism, valuing reflection and the study of ideas, and the other more strongly oriented toward science, emphasizing investigation and evaluation. The third emphasizes the practical and applied side of the humanities and sciences. This subculture is particularly concerned with its position in the organizational hierarchy. The fourth emphasizes individual responsibility, both to fellow students and to society as a whole. Finally, the fifth favors rebellion against the conservative, structured nature of the organization. Pace labels these patterns: intellectual-humanistic, intellectual-scientific, practical-status, group welfare, and rebellion.

In comparing Antioch College, a private, midwestern, coeducational, liberal-arts college, with Vassar College, a private, eastern, girls' liberal-arts school, Pace (1963) made the following conclusions:

> In both colleges the intellectual-humanistic-scientific clusters emerge as the strongest emphasis in the environment, with the practical, status-oriented cluster being correspondingly low. At Vassar the rebellion emphasis is about average. At Antioch the social welfare emphasis is about average. Rebellion is somewhat higher at Antioch and social welfare is somewhat lower at Vassar. Comparing the two schools, one finds Antioch having the stronger scientific press, and also being higher in rebellion and in social welfare.

Trow (1962) developed a similar categorization of four subcultures that he found to vary in prominence from college to college: collegiate, vocational, academic, and nonconformist. In the *collegiate* subculture, the school is important as a social object rather than an intellectual institution. The emphasis is upon sports, dating and other types of campus fun; intellectual achievement beyond that necessary to remain enrolled is not viewed as critical. In the *vocational* subculture the school is seen as a "student placement office." The main function of the school is typified by the solgan "to get a good job, get a good education." Students in the *academic* subculture identify with the academic atmosphere of the school, particularly as it is represented by the intellectual ideals of the faculty. The *nonconformist*

235

subculture views the college administration with a general hostility. These students often consider the values of both the organization and the faculty incompatible with their own. Although nearly every campus supports each of these subcultures, one or two will usually be the dominant determiners of the climate.

Differences in climate are also evident in high schools. Coleman (1961) asked high-school students to rank the alternatives to the following question from one to six:

What does it take to get to be important and looked up to by the other fellows (girls) here at school?

Boys	*Girls*
Coming from the right family.	Coming from the right family.
Leader in activities.	Leader in activities.
Having a nice car.	Having nice clothes.
High grades, honor roll.	High grades, honor roll.
Being an athletic star.	Being a cheerleader.
Being in the leading crowd.	Being in the leading crowd.

In the ten high schools he studied he found differences in the way in which the alternatives were ranked, indicating differences in the climate of the schools.

Mitchell (1968) administered the Stern High School Characteristics Index, which is the high-school-level edition of the College Characteristics Index (Stern, 1963), to 2819 seniors of eleven high schools in a large metropolitan area. Student aggression, defined by questions dealing with the damage of school property by students and frequent fist fights among students on school grounds, was the single most important variable serving to differentiate among the school climates. Differences in school spirit and opportunities to participate in school activities were also markedly apparent. The press for achievement within the school was not only differentiated between schools but was also highly correlated with the proportion of students within the school who expressed a desire for college training. Although there was a moderate correlation between the press for achievement and the school mean for socio-economic status (rank-difference correlation of 0.54), low press for achievement in the school was not an inevitable concomitant of low socio-economic stuatus within the student body. The lowest-ranking school in terms of socio-economic status, for example, was ranked in the middle in terms of press for achievement.

There are, finally, many other studies that have shown differences between climates of educational organizations (for example, Astin, 1962; Astin and Holland, 1961; Stern, 1963; Halpin and Croft, 1963). Since these studies do not add significantly to the basic point supported by the studies reviewed above, they are not discussed here.

Self-Selection of Students to Colleges

Several studies have demonstrated that there is a self-selection proc-ess by which students enter colleges with characteristics compatible with their personalities. Heist and his associates (1961), in a study of all the winners of the National Merit Scholarships and a 10 percent sample of those who received certificates of merit, found that students entering institutions of high scholastic standards were more scholarly and flexible and less authoritarian than the students entering institutions of low scholastic productivity. In other words, students of high ability attending highly productive institutions have a pattern of traits, values, and attitudes that is more closely related to serious intellectual pursuits than have students of high ability attending less productive institutions. Farwell, Warren, and McConnell (1962), in another study of National Merit Scholars, reported that students entering Ivy League universities were more strongly attracted to intellectual pursuits and more independent, original, and flexible than students attending public universities; men who entered Roman Catholic institutions were generally less intellectually oriented and more authoritarian than men who entered Protestant institutions. Webster, Freedman, and Heist (1962) stated that the students entering Bennington and Vassar were very similar in intellectual level and social-class background but were different in personality. They conclude that differing public images attract different students to the two colleges and that the differences persist despite developmental processes that lead students in both schools in the same direction, which is one of less conservatism, increased tolerance for individual differences, and more freedom to express impulses.

The Effect of the Overall
Organizational Climate on Achievement

Organizational climates do have marked consequences on the behavior of the members. Since the organizational climate is a cluster of variables including factors such as organizational norms and values, peer-group norms and values, organizational authority structure, and the like, all the research on the effects of power and norms upon behavior is applicable to the effect of organizational climate on behavior. In addition, there are several studies directly conducted on organizational climates that confirm their effects upon behavior in several areas.

In studying the exceptional productivity of a few small liberal-arts colleges in producing scientists and scholars, Knapp and Greenbaum (1953) discuss the colleges' "singular hospitality to intellectual values in general" and declare that "the *climate* of values sustained by the institutions elevated the scholar and intellectual to the position of the 'cultural hero.' " In an earlier study Learned and Wood (1938) documented amazing differences in achievement among the students attending the various colleges in a single state. Other studies, however, have noted that the small liberal-arts colleges that have a climate that encourages intellectual achievement attract a great number of very bright students, which might account for their exceptional productivity as organizations. It is difficult to separate the influence of college climate on achievement from the confounding effect of student self-selection, which matches intellectually oriented students with intellectually oriented schools.

Another factor complicating the issue is the fact that schools differ in the proportion of talented students they attract. Thistlethwaite (1959, 1960) conducted two studies which attempted to evaluate only the effects of the school on student Ph.D. aspirations. He attempted to separate the confounding effects of students who already had high aspirations by adjusting the number of students from each school intending to obtain a Ph.D. according to the proportion of talented students attending each school. In his second study, only students whose graduate school plans changed *after* entering college were considered. Any students whose aspirations were neither raised nor lowered were omitted from the sample. In general, he found that certain characteristics of the school climate resulted in a high proportion of Ph.D.-oriented graduates in all fields. Different types of college climate, furthermore, were associated with high productivity of graduates who later received doctorates in the natural sciences and the arts, humanities, and social sciences. In addition, in his second study he concluded that National Merit students are influenced by the student climate much less than the average college student and are more likely to be influenced by the pressures from faculty.

Boyle (1965), in a review of four major studies of the effects of high-school climate on student behavior (Wilson, 1959; Ramsøy, 1961; Coleman, 1961; Turner, 1964), states that adolescents in high school encounter experiences that have an important influence on their aspirations for further education. When high schools are classified according to the *average* socio-economic status of the student body, the aspirations of the individual students are influenced in the direction of the majority. Thus, working-class students attending predominantly middle-class high schools plan to attend college much more frequently than those attending predominantly working-class high schools. The reverse process is evident among middle-class students attending working-class high schools. He goes on to discuss the importance of the effect of family background. He concludes that of the three variables—ability, social-class background, and organizational climate—ability and social-class background are probably the most important, but they are significantly affected by the climate of the school. In those high schools with a climate supporting college attendance, ability was the most important predictor of educational aspirations, although social background also influenced a senior's decision. In the least favorable climate, social class was the more important variable.

Jacob (1957) assembled an impressive array of evidence which indicates that only the small liberal-arts colleges exert much lasting influence on students. He states that the chief result of college is that students become more like one another; they accept a body of standards and values characteristic of men and women who have graduated from college. In a more recent review of the literature, Freedman (1967) concludes that the evidence seems to be that the college experience does not exert a profound influence on the great majority of students. He notes, however, that the accumulative effect of influencing a large number of people to a small degree in the same direction is potentially great, since large-scale social movements are often based on slight shifts of attitude or opinion in individuals. How-

239

ever, the evidence on long-term effects of an educational organization does not diminish the significant influence it does exert on a student's behavior while he is actually attending school.

Finally, Walberg and Anderson (1968) studied 2100 high school juniors and seniors in seventy-six physics classrooms throughout the United States to see if student perception of classroom climate affects their learning. They conceptualized classroom climate as consisting of both structural and affective dimensions. The structural dimension refers to the role expectations for the student of the teachers and other school personnel. The affective dimension pertains to the idiosyncratic personal dispositions of the students to act in given ways to satisfy their individual personality needs, such as felt satisfaction, intimacy, and friction in the class. Student perceptions of the structural and affective aspects of classroom climate are highly correlated. The investigators found that different perceptions of classroom climates were associated with different kinds of cognitive and affective growth. Students who perceived their classes as socially homogeneous and as being an intimate group working on one goal, for example, gained the most on the Physics Achievement Test, while the students who grew more in science understanding perceived their classes as being well organized with little friction between their fellow students. In addition, there is evidence that (1) the tendency for class members to be treated equally and the efficient direction of classroom activity and (2) the perception of the class as being personally gratifying and without hostilities among the students, are associated with learning.

Press Variables and Their Effects
on Student Achievement

The climate of an organization such as a school is the result of a cluster of variables which, taken together, result in a certain atmosphere or environmental press within the school. In this section these variables—facilities, size of school, teacher competence and morale, the norms and values of the informal organization of the students, and the cohesion of the organization—and their effects on student achievement will be discussed.

School Facilities

There is little evidence that the facilities of the school, such as the quality of library facilities, has much effect on the climate of the school. Coleman and his associates (1966) found that such characteristics as well-equipped laboratories and libraries were relatively ineffective in improving student achievement. The socio-economic background of the students produced most of the differences in achievement in the schools. School facilities did have more effect on the achievement of minority-group students, however, than on that of white students. Coleman concluded, therefore, that improvement of student facilities will increase the achievement of minority-group children more than it will that of white children. Coleman's findings, however, are suspect, since the investigators had to compare schools that differed only slightly in facilities in order to control for the socio-economic backgrounds of the students. This was necessary because well-equipped schools are generally attended by students from the higher socio-economic strata, and vice versa.

Pace (1963) correlated the College Characteristics Index with relatively enduring characteristics of colleges, such as the quality of library facilities, the characteristics of entering students, and the percentage of Ph.D.'s on the faculty. He found that those schools having substantial libraries, a high percentage of Ph.D.'s on the faculty, and a large number of seniors in liberal-arts courses tended to have climates emphasizing humanism and intellectualism. This would indicate that in combination with other forces for intellectual pursuit, facilities can have some effect on the climate of the school. In general, however, facilities do not seem to have much effect on the climate of the school or the achievement of its students.

Size of School

There have been mixed findings on the effect of school size on students. A study of high-school size in Kentucky found that pupils from larger schools score higher on standardized achievement tests than those from smaller schools (Street et al., 1962). Altman (1959) in a study of the academic achievement of students reported no difference between students from small and large high schools. Jacob

(1957) in a study of the effect of colleges on students found that only the small, private liberal-arts colleges exert very much influence on students. Studies in cooperation and competition found that students at larger universities tend to be more competitive in bargaining games than do the students at smaller colleges. Students at large universities tend to participate more in social action projects than do the students of smaller colleges. Perhaps the most conclusive evidence on the size of school is a study conducted by Barker and Gump (1964) on thirteen high schools of varying size. They found that students from smaller schools participated more actively in a variety of extracurricular activities. There were also more opportunities for student exercise of leadership. Overall, the evidence seems to be that the smaller the school, the more influence the climate exerts on students.

Teacher Competence

Coleman and his associates (1966) measured the effect of teacher competence on student achievement. Teacher competence was based on a self-rating, plus educational background of the teacher and his family. They found that teacher quality as they defined it had a much greater effect on pupil achievement than school facilities, particularly among pupils in the upper grades. Teacher quality seemed to be more important for minority-pupil achievement than for the achievement of the majority of white students.

Student Peer Influence

Within an organization formal and informal norms and values can be distinguished. The formal regulations and values refer to the organizational pattern designed by the management; examples are the blueprint of division of labor, the rules and regulations of the organization, the nature of the authority hierarchy. The informal norms and values refer to those that develop among the staff or workers or, in the case of schools, the students. Freedman (1967), after an extensive review of the literature, states that students are swayed more by fellow students than by any other school influence and that the scholastic and academic goals and processes of colleges are in large measure transmitted to incoming students or mediated for them by the predominant student culture. In studies by Wilson (1959), Ramsoy (1961), Coleman (1961), and Turner (1964) discussed in depth earlier in the chapter, the socio-economic background of the majority of the students in a school had a large influence on the educational aspirations of individual students.

The equality of opportunity survey (Coleman et al., 1966) shows that the educational background and aspirations of the majority of students in a school is the most important factor in improving achievement patterns of disadvantaged minority pupils. A disadvantaged child will probably not improve if he attends school with similarly disadvantaged peers. However, if the other pupils have better backgrounds and higher aspirations, he is likely to improve significantly. In contrast, white pupils from homes that value education highly who attend a school with a majority of lower-ability pupils do as well as they would with peers sharing their aspirations. These results confirm the important influence of a family background supportive of educational achievement. When this is lacking, attending a school where one's peers are academically oriented may be an adequate substitute.

The influence of the peer group on academic performance can be supportive of or antithetical to the formal organizational norms concerning the importance of academic achievement and the internalization of the values and habits promoted by the school. The more cohesive the peer group, the greater the influence on its members. Seashore (1954) demonstrated that cohesive work groups in industry with low-production informal norms work very inefficiently compared to cohesive groups with high-production informal norms. If students in a cohesive peer group agree about the undesirability of academic achievement, they will not perform at a high level; if they agree about the importance of academic achievement, however, there will be strong pressures toward achieving at the highest possible level.

Schmuck (1966) studied 727 students drawn from twenty-seven public school classrooms and differing markedly in age and background. He identified two types of classroom peer-group structures, diffuse and structured. In the diffuse type almost every student was chosen as most liked or least liked and as most influential or least influential by some other student. There were no distinct subgroups or cliques whose members received a large proportion of the choices and there were few, if any, neglected members. In this type

243

of peer-group structure there was a fairly equalized distribution of positive and negative sociometric choices. In the structured type, however, there were hierarchical relations where a few students were identified as being the least liked or least influential by the majority of their classmates. The rest fell somewhere in between. Pupils in peer groups with diffuse liking structures, compared to those in hierarchically structured groups, showed more positive attitudes toward classroom peers, school life, and themselves as pupils. They also shared a more supportive perception of the teacher and of academic work.

Need Variables in Organizational Climates

The needs of the members of an organization consist of such variables as their personality characteristics, abilities, motives, values, career and educational plans, and past experiences.

There is now substantial research which indicates that differences in performance between "advantaged" and "disadvantaged" students are not due to differences in aspirations, but are partially due to the differences in expectations of realizing these aspirations. In other words, a middle-class child may aspire to be a medical doctor and see such an aspiration as being reasonable. A lower-class child, on the other hand, may aspire to be a medical doctor and see such an aspiration as being beyond the possibilities of reality. Battle and Rotter (1963) found that lower-class children see themselves as more externally controlled and less capable of determining what will happen to them than middle-class children. Haggstrom (1964) and Clark (1965) state that poverty and minority-group status may produce a feeling of powerlessness, of a lack of control over one's fate. If a student believes that he is a pawn with no ability to change his circumstances, he is apt to feel that it is useless to do anything about it. In the United States minority groups actually do have less control over their future than members of the white majority and, therefore, the perception of control of one's fate may be an important variable in their achievement in school.

Coleman and his associates (1966) measured fate control by the following questions:

1. Agree or disagree: Good luck is more important than hard work for success.

2. Agree or disagree: Everytime I try to get ahead, something or somebody stops me.
3. Agree or disagree: People like me don't have much of a chance to be successful in life. (p. 288)

The answers of Negro and other minority-group children on all three items portrayed a sense of powerlessness against a neutral, if not hostile, environment. Such an orientation toward life, while an accurate assessment of reality in the United States, constitutes a handicap for both the individual student and for the school in its attempt to socialize minority-group students into its formal goals and values. The school, to a large extent, needs a belief in the future payoff of being an "ideal" student on the part of students in order to run a successful educational program. With minority-group students this often means convincing them that there really is "pie in the sky when you die," even though the reality of the society clearly indicates to them that this is not true. Coleman and his associates did, however, find that minority-group students in integrated schools were somewhat more likely to feel that they could control their destinies than did minority-group students in segregated schools. It may be possible, therefore, to increase the internalization of formal school norms and values in minority-group students by integrating schools.

There is a great deal of evidence that informal preschool training in the home is important in determining the start a child gets in the first grade, and that the kind of start he makes may have a lasting effect on his performance (Backman and Secord, 1968). In other words, the pattern of academic achievement is set early and few children improve once they make a poor start. Effectively run preschool programs and increased efforts on the part of schools to concentrate on increasing the learning skills of students who make poor starts in school may decrease this effect.

Poor motivation produces poor performance in the school and increases the probability of the student dropping out altogether. Motivation is largely determined by family background. Furthermore, for most disadvantaged students, this lack of adequate motivation is reinforced by peers with similarly deficient motivation. The influence of the family background can be changed by involving parents in the problems of the school and enlisting their aid in increasing the motivation of their children. By properly mixing the middle-class and lower-class students within the classroom it is possible to increase motivation of the lower-class children. And perhaps as teachers become more enlightened about the effects of social psychological variables upon achievement they will not be so rejecting of students who do not cooperate with the teacher and the school.

Finally, students' self-attitudes will, under certain conditions, affect their performance in school (see Chapter 5). Both experimental and field studies have found that individuals tend to like and associate with others who see them as they see themselves, who allow them to behave in a manner consistent with their self-attitudes, and who have similar values and attitudes (Secord and Backman, 1964; Newcomb, 1961). These tendencies serve to maintain stability in self-attitudes and discourage change. When self-attitudes retard academic achievement, it is necessary to change self-attitudes and attitudes toward school achievement.

Conditions Affecting Influence of Organizational Climate

There are a variety of forces toward homogeneity of background and personal characteristics of students in schools that mitigate the influence of school climate. Because of the homogeneity of school districts, students usually attend school with students from similar backgrounds. Even when there is a heterogeneous student body, ability grouping and a differentiated curriculum minimize exposure to students different in background, values, and attitudes. In addition, there is a tendency for persons to choose as friends those with similar interests, abilities, and social-background characteristics (Newcomb, 1961; Backman and Secord, 1968). In other words, within the school there are formal and informal pressures toward association only with students from similar backgrounds, attitudes, and values. Under these conditions, the overall climate of the school will not be very influential.

Because the major influence on the value structure of the informal organization of the school is the values of the entering students, one method of affecting the value climate of the school is to control the mix of input characteristics. There is evidence that this can be done in ways to increase the influence of the school climate on lower-class students without interfering with the education of the middle-class students. Coleman and his associates (1966) found that although the disadvantaged child benefits from contact with peers from families supporting academic achievement, a student with strong family pressures for advancement appears relatively unaffected by the attitudes of peers who come from disadvantaged backgrounds. As discussed in the chapter on group norms, furthermore, when one cannot control the mix of student-input characteristics, socialization into the formal school norms and values can be accomplished through the use of in-group cooperation and outgroup competition to motivate students.

Because of differences in social background and personality traits, individuals will accept some school values to a greater extent than others. It is the norms and values of the subcultures the individual belongs to within the organization, however, which will most markedly affect his behavior. In addition, the pressures a student is exposed to vary with the position he occupies in the school. Thistlethwaite and Wheeler (1966) followed 1772 students from the beginning to the end of their college training and found that pressures from the faculty and the students were quite different for upperclassmen than for lowerclassmen. Lowerclassmen perceived intense competition from other students for high achievement while upperclassmen did not; upperclassmen perceived strong pressures from the faculty toward high academic performance and independent thinking while lowerclassmen did not.

Finally, Pace (1963) states that to the extent that a college environment is an unrelated assortment of policies and practices and events and features, its influence upon the student is probably small. To the extent that a college environment is a culture, that is, the different forces on a campus are related, coordinated, and reinforce each other, the influence of the organizational climate is probably large. Since the climate of small liberal-arts colleges is probably more uniform in the direction of its pressures than larger, more diverse universities, one would expect it to have more influence on the students. In order to increase the influence of the climate of a school on the students, therefore, one would ensure that the organizational demands and pressures are related, coordinated, and reinforcing each other.

SUMMARY

All organizations have a certain type of social climate. A school's organizational climate can be seen as consisting of (1) the personality characteristics, the abilities, motives, values and career plans of the entering students; (2) the norms, values, role requirements, and other characteristics of the formal organization; and (3) the norms and values of the informal organization. The personality characteristics of the incoming students interact with the formal and informal aspects of the organization to influence the students' behavior. There is a large body of research that demonstrates that schools and colleges vary according to how they are perceived by their members. Analyzing responses to a variety of measuring instruments, investigators have found that differences between the social climates of educational institutions fall along such dimensions as serious intellectual concerns, emphasis on social life, and practical-vocational emphasis. Several studies have also shown that there is a self-selection process by which students enter colleges with characteristics compatible with their personalities.

Other studies in this area have shown a complex relationship between the organizational climate, an individual's personality traits, and academic pursuit. Controlling the academic aspirations of incoming students, two studies found that different types of college climates were associated with high productivity of graduates who later received doctorates. Other evidence, however, has shown that only the social climate of small liberal-arts colleges has very much lasting influence on students. Considering social climate as a conditional variable, one review of the literature concluded that in those high schools having a climate most favorable to college attendence, ability was more predictive of educational aspirations than was socio-economic background, whereas in the least favorable climates, social class was the better predictor.

Other research has pointed out the conditions under which the school climate will be most influential. These conditions are: (1) the character and the climate of the school are markedly different from the student characteristics and family background, (2) the students' attitudes, values, and self-attitudes are inadequately anchored in nonschool groups, (3) there is a cooperative relationship between the students and the school, and (4) the different press variables of the school environment are related, coordinated, and reinforce each other.

The effects of specific environmental-press variables have also been investigated. One comprehensive study found that teacher competence effects pupil achievement, having an appreciably greater effect on minority-pupil achievement than on the achievement of white students. There is evidence that in both high schools and colleges the most important and powerful influences upon student values and behavior are the norms and values of fellow students. A number of studies have shown that a student's peer group has a great influence on his academic motivation and performance; this most likely being the case when the peer group is cohesive. In a final study it was demonstrated that Negro children have a much lower sense of control over their environment than whites, but if Negroes are integrated with white students within a classroom, their feeling of control over their destiny increases and thus they become more academically motivated.

CHAPTER 14

ORGANIZATIONAL DEVELOPMENT AND INNOVATION IN EDUCATION

Organizational Effectiveness and Health

What makes a school effective as an organization? How can you tell when a school is a healthy organization? Some assistance in specifying what constitutes an effective school can be obtained from discussions of effectiveness of economic organizations. Katz and Kahn (1966) state that organizational effectiveness is determined by the efficiency of the organizational design for enhancing the smooth functioning of the organization, the members' motivation to increase their own and the organization's effectiveness, and the ability of the organization to negotiate from the environment less expensive and higher quality inputs and better markets for the product. For schools, therefore, organizational effectiveness can be defined by such measures as: (1) the total cost of educating each student to a certain level of competence and socialization, (2) the motivation or morale of the school personnel and the students, and (3) the ability of the school to obtain good personnel, facilities, materials, and students from the environment and to place graduates in good colleges or good jobs. Argyris (1964a) states that an organization has three core activities: achieving its objectives, maintaining itself internally, and adapting to its external environment. An organization's effectiveness is indicated by the organization's ability to accomplish these core activities at a constant or increasing quantity or quality of outputs with the same or decreasing increments of inputs. In other words, an organization increases in effectiveness as it obtains (1) increasing quantity or quality of outputs with constant or decreasing inputs, or (2) constant quantity or quality of outputs with decreasing inputs, and (3) is able to accomplish this in such a way that it can continue to do so. For a school, effectiveness would then be defined as its ability to increase the number or quality of graduates with the same or decreasing increments of teachers, materials, buildings, services, and other inputs, in such a way that it can continue to do so.

In a recent study Woodhall and Blaug (1968) evaluated the effectiveness of English schools. They state that in order to see whether schools are effective, one needs to measure their success in achieving their objectives in relation to their available inputs. This must be done in a way that accounts for changes in educational standards and in the quality of instruction over time. Productivity of the schools is defined as the ratio of some specified output to the inputs of resources required to produce it. To measure productivity means simply to specify how costly it is, in terms of money, time, effort, or any other input, to achieve given objectives. It is their position that the effects of school must be measured in terms of changes in the children who pass through the school. Some of these changes can be measured while the child is at school. For instance, the school's effectiveness in teaching certain skills (reading, math, and so forth) can be measured by the pupils' performance on standardized examinations. The school, however, is also concerned with many long-term effects of education that appear after a student has been graduated, such as his success in adopting adult roles, which may be indicated by achievement in subsequent careers. The evaluation of a school's effectiveness should include both "in-school" and "post-school" measures of student performance.

Woodhall and Blaug (1968) used as measures of output: (1) the earnings the graduate can command in the labor market to indicate occupational status and success, (2) the length of time the graduate spent in further education, and (3) the number of graduates who are qualified to enter the next level of education. Comparing these outputs to such inputs as the value of the teachers' and students' time, the investment in buildings and equipment, and the cost of other materials such as electricity, stationery, and so on needed to run a school, they found that the British schools have declined in productivity between 1950 and 1963. That is, unless the quality of the students who graduate has increased in a way that no one has yet been able to measure, even after such factors as inflation have been taken into account, it takes more resources in 1963 to produce a standard secondary-school graduate than it did in 1950.

The continual effectiveness of an organization depends upon such factors as the "health" of the organization and its ability to change in a planned, deliberate manner as the conditions of the environment and internal factors change. Organizational health can be defined as the ability to grow, develop, and change in productive ways continuously over a period of years. Miles and his associates (Benedict et al., 1967), following Agryris (1964a), Bennis (1966), and Parsons (1955) divide organizational health into three broad areas: task accomplishment, internal integration, and mutual adaptation of the organization and its environment. In the *task-accomplishment area* a healthy organization is one with (1) reasonably clear, accepted, achievable, and appropriate goals, (2) relatively undistorted communication flow horizontally, vertically, and to and from the environment, and (3) optimal power equalization, with the style of influence being essentially collaborative, based on competence and problem-solving needs, rather than upon organizational position. In the *internal-integration area* a healthy organization is one with (1) full utilization of its resources, which includes a relatively good fit between the personal dispositions of its members and the role demands of their positions (thus, teachers in a relatively healthy school environment would have an accompanying sense of self-actualization in terms of their own goals and personalities), (2) an organizational identity clear and attractive enough so that members feel actively connected with the organization, and (3) high member morale, which involves feelings of well-being, satisfaction, and pleasure at belonging to the organization, as opposed to feelings of discomfort, dissatisfaction, and anxiety.

Finally, four dimensions of organizational health deal with *growth and change.* They are: (1) innovativeness; a tendency to grow, develop, change, diversify over time, (2) autonomy; the ability to act from internal strength rather than being a passive tool of the environment, (3) adaptation; the simultaneous changes in organization and environment that occur continuously during organizational-environmental contact processes, and (4) problem-solving adequacy; the organization's ability to detect the problems which inevitably arise, to invent possible solutions, decide on certain solutions to adopt, carry them out, and evaluate their effectiveness.

The dimensions of organizational health can be used to diagnose the state of health of a classroom or school. A school would be considered unhealthy in the task-accomplishment area if it had unclear, inappropriate goals, distorted communication within the school and between the school and the environment, and an authoritarian orientation in which power was based upon position. It would be unhealthy in the internal-integration area if it did not use everyone's resources in ways which led to feelings of self-actualization and growth on the part of the members, if the members did not want to be identified with the school, and if the morale of the personnel or students was low. Finally, it would be unhealthy in the organizational growth and change area if it had a low level of innovation, poor adaptation to changes within the environment, low autonomy from the community, and poor problem-solving adequacy. Such a diagnostic scheme can be very useful for consultation with a school in facilitating the analysis of the problems of the school's functioning.

Planned Organizational Change

As noted in the previous section, in order to function effectively an organization must be "healthy," that is, have the capacity to continuously grow, develop, and change in productive ways. Planned organizational change is commonly defined as the attempt to bring about organizational change in a conscious, deliberate, and intended manner through the utilization and application of behavioral science knowledge. Typically, planned change involves a collaborative relationship between a client system (that is, an organization for which change is planned) and a change agent (that is, a person or group which works toward bringing about change). The change agent, through the utilization and application of behavioral science knowledge, has a conceptual framework from which to approach the problems of aiding the client system to change and a foundation of knowledge from which to control and affect the processes of change. A collaborative relationship is defined as a relationship that involves a joint effort with mutual determination of goals in which the client system and the change agent have approximately equal opportunities to influence each other. A collaborative relationship is considered necessary because (1) it generates the necessary trust that facilitates the collection and interpretation of meaningful data and (2) the positive aspects of the relationship are vitally necessary in order to overcome some of the strong fears of and resistance to change in the client system.

Fallacies in Approaches to Planned Change

There are three common fallacies in attempts to change organizations that should be noted before discussing methods of planned change. First, a common error in attempting to change the behavior of members of an organization is to disregard the systemic properties of the organization and concentrate only upon the individuals involved (Katz and Kahn, 1966). Taking members out of the organization, giving them special training, and then returning them to the organization is a poor strategy for changing their role behavior, as it ignores the power of role expectations and other organizational variables in determining organizational behavior. The essential weakness of the individual approach is the *psychological fallacy* of concentrating upon individuals without regard to the role relationships and organizational norms and values which constitute the social system of which they are a part.

The *sociological fallacy*, on the other hand, is the belief that any change in the organizational structure will result in changed behavior of the members of the organization in the desired direction. With this fallacy, the essential weakness is the assumption that one can change an organization without regard to the attitudes, values, and behavior of the individuals occupying the organizational roles. One of the major findings of the research of the 1940s on organizations, for example, was that changing the production process would not result in increased production in and of itself (Coch and French, 1948).

Finally, the *rationalistic fallacy* is the assumption that telling people about the desirability of change will result in change. Providing school personnel with the relevant information that builds a strong case for the desirability of change is not sufficient to motivate them to change their behavior in the desired way. This fallacy ignores both the structural constraints on role behavior in organizations and the research on attitude change which indicates that information will change attitudes only under certain limited conditions (see Hovland et al., 1953, for example).

There are, therefore, no simple answers to the question of how one changes an organization. The behavior of members of an organization will not necessarily change when their attitudes change, when their roles are redefined, or when they are presented with information about the desirability of new behavior. The following section discusses the methods and targets of organizational change.

Target for Change

There are two separate aspects of organizational change: the methods employed to bring about change and the target at which such methods are directed (Katz and Kahn, 1966). Some methods of change are specific to certain targets, other methods of change can be applied to several different targets. The primary targets for organizational change are: (1) the personalities, skills, and attitudes of the individual members; (2) the roles, norms, communication patterns, interpersonal relationships, power relationships and influence structure, and the problem-solving effectiveness of the *work team*, (3) the roles, norms, communication patterns, influence structure, and problem-solving effectiveness of the organization as a whole; (4) the technology of the organization which, in regard to schools, includes such things as the curriculum, the methods of classroom grouping, team teaching, modular scheduling, programmed-learning devices, computers, and the like; and (5) the task objectives of the organization.

The difficulty with many attempts at organizational change is that the change agents have not clearly distinguished their targets for change and have assumed that the individual or the group-level target was the same as the social-structure of the organization target (Katz and Kahn, 1966). In an attempt at organizational change, therefore, it is important to diagnose the organization carefully in order to specify clearly the desired target of change. Perhaps a major reason for failure in attempts at organizational change is that the change agents have accepted inappropriate targets for change; for example, they may have changed the attitudes of individuals when they should have changed the structure of the organization.

Targets for change are identified by diagnosing the functioning of the organization through such methods as interviews, questionnaires, and observing subunits of the organization in action. Working out the objectives of the change program often implies specific targets. Once a target for change has been identified, it may be conceptualized for diagnostic purposes as a "quasi-stationary equilibrium." That is, the present state of the target can be viewed as a balance between forces working in opposite directions, facilitating forces and restraining forces. A diagramming of the forces acting for and against the proposed change is called a force-field analysis and is a significant aid in analyzing the dynamics of the change situation.

Methods of Change

After the target for change has been specified, the appropriate method or combination of methods should be chosen for enacting the change. The most commonly used methods for organizational change are: (1) decree by a high authority, (2) replacement of personnel, (3) presentation of information, (4) skill training, (5) individual counseling and therapy, (6) sensitivity-group training, (7) survey feedback, (8) the clinical-experimental approach, and (9) the direct manipulation of the role structure and the systemic variables of the organization.

It should be noted that while these methods will be discussed in isolation from each other, they may be most profitably used in combination. To institute team teaching within a school, for example, one might use decree by a high authority to change the role structure of the school, sensitivity-group training to change the norms and patterns of interaction among the teachers, survey feedback to facilitate the development of productive team functioning, and skill training to develop the necessary skills.

Decree by a High Authority

Perhaps the most common approach to organizational change and innovation is by decree of a high authority, such as the superintendent, the school board, or the principal (Greiner, 1967a). This approach is essentially a one-way announcement that is directed downward to the lower levels of the organization with the expectation that the members of the organization will comply in their outward behavior and that this compliance will lead to more effective organizational functioning. This approach is impersonal, formal, and task-oriented. It expects people to comply with directives from their superiors. It assumes that individuals are best motivated by authoritative directions. To initiate team teaching in a school, for example, the decree approach would specify that the principal inform the teachers that on a certain date the school will adopt team teaching and which teachers will be in what team. The expectation would be that the teachers would comply to this directive with little or no resistance. There is research that indicates that authoritative legal, military, and housing rulings modify white prejudice against Negroes (Berelson and Steiner, 1964), a finding which supports the effectiveness of the decree approach to change; but most of the literature in the area indicates that the decree approach will result in lack of commitment to and involvement in the change and, in many cases, active resistance (Lewin, Lippit, and White, 1939; Coch and French, 1948; Argyris, 1964a).

Replacement of Personnel

Based upon the assumption that organizational problems tend to reside in a few strategically located individuals, this approach replaces personnel to bring about organizational change (Greiner, 1967a). Containing much of the formality and explicit concern for task accomplishment that is common to the decree approach, this approach is also initiated at the top and directed downward by a high authority figure. It assumes that individuals cannot change their own behavior and, therefore, they need to be replaced when changes are desired. The targets for change are key personnel.

For example, use of the replacement approach to initiate team teaching would involve the superintendent's replacing the principal of a school with a new person who favored, and was experienced with, team teaching. Or, perhaps the principal would replace his department heads with individuals who were experienced with, and in favor of, team teaching. The new personnel would then initiate the change by decree or some other method. Taken to its logical conclusion, this approach would change the role occupant every time a role definition was changed.

Presentation of Information

The presentation of information approach to organizational change assumes that all men are rational and will follow their rational self-interest once this is revealed to them (Chin and Benne, 1969). Once an innovation or change is shown to be rationally justified and to be in the client's self-interest, it is taken for granted that the client will automatically adopt it. This approach, although quite commonly used, has real, but limited value. Information about an innovation can support other methods of organizational change, give the rationale for proposed changes, explain what will be expected of the individuals involved, but it is not in and of itself a source of motivation for change (Katz and Kahn, 1966). Other methods are required to provide the necessary motivation for change.

Under certain conditions, however, the presentation of information may be an adequate method of changing organizations. Research in attitude change has demonstrated that rational arguments do sway opinions, particularly among the doubtful or the uncommitted (Hovland et al., 1953). Katz and Kahn state that techniques relying primarily upon information-giving are effective in ambiguous situations, where lack of information is the obstacle to appropriate performance. Such situations, however, are rare within organizations. Finally, Chin and Benne (1969) state that when there is almost universal readiness for accepting the change, information campaigns do work well, but when such readiness is not present, they are ineffective.

Watson (1967) notes that when presentation of information is used to change an organization it is assumed that the information will be viewed objectively, that is, it will not be distorted. Research demonstrates, however, that information often is distorted to fit in with previous views and prejudices. Allport and Postman (1945), for example, demonstrated that a common stereotype (associating Negroes with carrying razors) led observers of a cartoon to think they had seen the razor in the hand of the Negro rather than the white man when presented with a picture in which a white man was threatening a Negro with a razor. Watson and Hartmann (1939) and Levine and Murphy (1943) demonstrated in experiments with materials designed to bring about changes in attitude that subjects did not hear clearly, nor remember well, communications with which they disagreed. It is a common observation, furthermore, that people usually prefer news sources, whether in print or broadcast, with which they are already in agreement (Klapper, 1960). By reading or listening to what agrees with present views, by misunderstanding communications that, if correctly received, would not be consonant with pre-established attitudes, and by conveniently forgetting any material that would lead to uncongenial conclusions, people successfully resist the possible impact of new evidence and information upon their earlier views (Watson, 1967). There are relatively few instances, for example, in which old prejudices have been changed by better information or persuasive arguments.

The target of information campaigns is necessarily the individual and not the organization as a whole. This approach is aimed at changing the cognitions of the individuals within the organization, not at changing the actual structure or roles of the organization. This approach would institute team teaching within a school by providing the personnel with information about the effectiveness of team teaching and a rationale for why they should adopt it. It assumes that the introduction of such information would be sufficient for initiating change within the school. Most of the available research, however, indicates that information by itself does not generate the necessary motivation for organizational change.

Skill Training

The skill-training approach to organizational change assumes that once members of the organization are given the appropriate skills,

259

their performance and the effectiveness of the organization will change. Inservice-training programs and management-training programs are examples of this approach. The target for change is the skill level of individual members of the organization.

For example, team teaching would be instituted with this approach by giving the teachers training in how to operate effectively within a teaching team. Once these skills were learned, it is assumed that the school would adopt team teaching. With this example, it is apparent that skill training in and of itself will not bring changes in organizational role behavior, but used in conjunction with other methods it may increase the effectiveness of changes.

Individual Counseling and Therapy

The individual counseling and therapy approach to organizational change assumes that through changing a person's basic personality, his role behavior within the organization will be restructured and his interpersonal relationships will be improved and, as a result, the effectiveness of the organization will be improved. The target for change is the individual's personality. There is some empirical evidence that this approach can be effective. For example, Katz, Sarnoff, and McClintock (1956) demonstrated that prejudices toward Negroes could be changed momentarily by information, but that more lasting change resulted from giving people insight into their own motivation about prejudice. They conclude that although information may result in changed cognitions, a deeper process of counseling or therapy is needed where basic change in behavior is required. Katz and Kahn (1966) note, however, that despite such supporting evidence this approach is not as yet a very predictable tool for organizational change as it is difficult to predict at this time whether therapy will be successful or not or what its outcomes will be.

In extreme cases, personality change might help the functioning of the organization, especially if the individual is either the most powerful figure in the organization or close to the top of the authority hierarchy. Here the change achieved through individual therapy may have reverberations in the organization as a whole (Katz and Kahn, 1966). That is, since such a person is in a position to introduce legitimized change in the organization through utilizing its authority structure, any real changes in his personality can have important organizational consequences. Most top officials, however, tend to see therapy as more appropriate for their subordinates than for themselves; they do not have the time and, as they are usually successful, they do not see the need.

The conditions under which this approach will be successful in changing an organization, therefore, are when the superintendent or principal is blocking needed changes because of personal problems, or when the personal problems of the principal cause adaptive behavior on the part of his subordinates which is dysfunctional for the school as a whole. Successful therapy with such a key person may change the school's effectiveness.

Sensitivity-Group Training

Sensitivity-group training is a group experience where such goals can be accomplished as: (1) increasing awareness of and sensitivity to the behavioral and emotional reactions of oneself and others, (2) increasing awareness and understanding of the types of processes that facilitate or inhibit group functioning and interactions between different groups, (3) heightening diagnostic skill in social, interpersonal, and intergroup situations, (4) experimenting with behavioral styles that are not ordinarily a part of one's repertoire, and (5) clarifying personal goals and values concerning interpersonal relationships and developing new values and goals consistent with a democratic approach to individual and group problem solving. It is a group experience designed to provide maximum possible opportunity for the individual to expose his behavior, give and receive feedback, experiment with new behavior, develop an awareness and acceptance of self and others, and learn the nature of effective group functioning (Argyris, 1964b).

To achieve the goals of sensitivity-group training, participants typically meet in a group that has no planned agenda other than a general plan to study itself and the members within it. The participants' learning is a consequence of a self-analytic appraisal of their behavior and their reactions to one another. This appraisal is aided by a professional trainer who, through his own behavior (which is likely to be nondirective and permissive in character), tries to help the participants clarify their feelings and experiences (Deutsch and Hornstein, in preparation).

The use of sensitivity-group training for organizational change has gone through two stages (Leavitt, 1965). Stage one settled for sending individual members of the organization to sensitivity-training group sessions away from the organization to groups composed of personnel from several organizations. These individuals then bore the burden of adapting their experiences to their organization, which often failed. The target for change in this stage was the individual's interpersonal and problem-solving skills and values.

Stage two involved the carrying of the sensitivity-group training to the organization so that members of the organization are trained together, either in groups that cut diagonally across hierarchical levels (that is, all vice-presidents or assistant principals) or in groups which represent direct vertical slices of the organization (that is, administrators, teachers, students). In this stage the sensitivity training is built into the organization, encouraging direct, intimate, and power-free communication across several organizational levels. Sometimes small parts of the organization participate, such as the top decision-making team, and sometimes the majority of the members of the organization participate. In this stage the target for change is, in addition to the individuals involved, the roles and norms of the organization and the ways in which the organization handles its decision making and problem solving.

Argyris (1964b) notes that there are, in his experience, two problems with the use of sensitivity-group training in an organization. First, change is not effective and permanent until the total organization accepts the new values, norms, and role definitions. When sensitivity training is used with only a small number of the members of an organization, therefore, organizational change will not result, even when the individuals trained are the top administrators of the system. Second, effective change does not mean that the members of the organization who receive sensitivity-group training will or even should behave according to their new, democratic values under all conditions. Argyris notes that the old, authoritarian values and behavior are effective for dealing primarily with routine, programmed decisions while the new, democratic values and behavior seem to be best suited for decisions that are unprogrammed, innovative, and require high commitment. Research by Feidler (1964) supports Argyris' notions. Feidler found that situations where groups were very high or very low on (1) task structure, (2) favorableness of leader-member relations, and (3) power invested in the leader position, the groups performed more effectively with a directive, task-oriented leader than with a permissive, person-oriented leader. The latter, in turn, is more effective with groups that have these properties only to a moderate degree.

Sensitivity-group training is a widely used method of organizational change that can have as its target the individual, the work team, or the organization as a whole. It may be useful by itself or as part of a larger laboratory training program, which might include role playing, case studies, theory presentations, skill exercises, and inter-group exercises. There is some evidence that the impact of sensitivity-group training on a work team will increase the more carefully a diagnosis of the prior functioning of the team is conducted and the more elaborate the followup by the change agent to help integrate the results of the training into the ongoing operation of the team (Friedlander, 1968). Finally, sensitivity-group training is one of the most frequently researched methods of organizational change and management training. Two recent reviews of the evidence (Campbell and Dunnette, 1968; House, 1967) indicate that the use of sensitivity training results in changes in behavior of participants in work situations and it frequently results in changes in attitudes and inter-personal styles of behavior.

Survey Feedback

Survey feedback is a method of organizational change where outside staff and members of the organization collaboratively gather, analyze, and interpret data that deal with various aspects of the organization's functioning and its members' work lives (Miles et al., 1966). A typical survey-feedback approach might go through the following stages. First, data on the organization's functioning is gathered by interviews and questionnaires, which the change agents construct with the help of members of the organization. These instruments may deal with such issues as the perception of norms and goals, employee satisfaction, or perceived influence of self and superior in decision making. After gathering the data, analyzing it, and summarizing it in a way that is clear and useful to the particular audience, the data are fed back to the work teams within the organization. A work team is a group who reports to a common superior, with jobs related in some meaningful fashion. In a school, an organizational family would consist of the principal, vice-principals, and other members of the administrative staff, or a department chairman and all the teachers within the department. The data are usually shown first to the "head" of the organizational family highest in the authority hierarchy. For a school system, this would be the superintendent. At this meeting the presentation of the data to the rest of the family is discussed. The data are then presented to the entire family, many of whom are, in fact, heads of other organizational families. Subsequently, they examine the data with their groups. The survey feedback, therefore, takes place through an interlocking set of organizational families until everyone in the organization has discussed the data that are relevant for their family. That is, each organizational family is presented with feedback about its own problems in detail, with comparative information about the organization as a whole and with feedback about the organization's problems and the implications of those problems for the organizational family. Typically, outside staff members are present at each of the data feedback meetings.

As the appropriate data are fed back and discussed by all the organizational families, the data form the base for correctively altering the organizational structure and the members' work relationships. Ordinarily, the examination of the data leads to action planning in response to problems made salient by the data. Consequently, these feedback meetings provide the organizational family with the opportunity to engage in problem-solving activities in the presence of outside staff members, who attempt to use their skills to help members of the groups improve their work relationships.

This approach gives objective, factual bases to the problems of the organization (Katz and Kahn, 1966). The emphasis is upon group discussion of facts and figures in a task-oriented atmosphere where people are seeking to analyze the problem, identify possible causes as objectively as possible, and agree upon possible solutions. The data about the problems has an objectifying quality which makes this possible.

The objective of survey feedback, therefore, is the clarification and improvement of organizational functioning through an objective assessment of problems by the organizational members themselves (Katz and Kahn, 1966). In addition, it facilitates effective working relationships between supervisory levels and two-way communication between levels. The target of survey feedback is the improvement of both personal and role relationships within the organizational family and between organizational families, through their discussion of common problems. In order for it to be effective (1) it must include group discussion and group involvement in gathering, analyzing, and interpreting the data, (2) each organizational family must have the opportunity to consider the implications of the findings at its own level, and (3) the outcome of the meetings at the lower organizational levels must be reported up the line to the higher levels.

The survey feedback approach to organizational change is one of the most promising methods now available; the results of the few research studies conducted on it, however, are only partially supportive. Miles and his associates (1966), for example, asked the teachers and administrators of a school system to respond to several questionnaires dealing with such areas as the actual and desired distributions of influence among different role groups within the school system, the perceived and actual roles, and the perceived norms. The resulting data were summarized and presented to the school administrators, while individual principals and their teachers diagnosed and evaluated their own data at a later date. As the implications of the data became apparent, efforts were started to find solutions to the problems that had been identified, with intermittent conferences with the consultants. The research data gathered to measure the effect of the intervention were inconclusive. The research instruments, which the investigators state were poorly constructed, failed to indicate that any change in practices had taken place. Interview data, however, provided clear evidence that there was improvement in communication, at least among the eleven top administrators. Other research on industrial and research organizations (see Katz and Kahn, 1966; and Friedlander, 1968) provides further evidence that survey feedback can be used effectively in changing the functioning of an organization.

The Clinical-Experimental Method

The clinical-experimental method is an approach to organizational change used by Miles and his associates (Benedict, et al., 1967) and other behavioral scientists (Argyris, 1962, 1965; Greiner, 1967b; Friedlander, 1968) that combines elements of the survey-feedback and sensitivity-group training approaches. This method has both research and change objectives. Similar to survey feedback, the research half of the change-agent team collects data about the functioning of the organization. Part of this data is then given to the action half of the change-agent team, which then makes a clinical diagnosis of the organization. On the basis of their diagnosis the change agents then intervene within the organization to facilitate the organization's defining and solving its problems in a way that improves the organization's future ability to diagnose and solve problems. This may involve feeding back some of the data gathered to the organizational families and providing them with sensitivity-group training or specific skill training to increase their effectiveness. The research half of the change agent team then gathers data about the effectiveness of the intervention to evaluate its success and further behavioral science knowledge about organizational change.

The targets for change using this method are usually organizational or work-team variables, such as problem-solving effectiveness and norms about the openness and authenticity of communication within the organization. Under this method, team teaching would be adopted by a school after a clinical diagnosis of the school revealed that team teaching would improve the quality of the school's functioning. A specific method of instituting team teaching would be devised to fit the special, unique qualities of the school. Before and after team teaching was adopted the research half of the change-agent team would collect data on the school's functioning, which would be used to evaluate the success of team teaching and increase the knowledge about organizational change.

Initiating Change in Teacher Behavior

There are many approaches to initiating change in teacher behavior, most of which have been discussed in this chapter. Brickell (1964), however, in two surveys of the schools in New York State in 1961, made two major conclusions about the successful process of changing teacher behavior. The first was that among all the ways of learning about an innovation, the most persuasive seemed to be that of visiting a successful program and observing it in action. Nothing persuades like a visit. Anything seen, however, as appreciably different from conditions in the visitor's own school can rob the visit of persuasive effect. The surveys gathered overwhelmingly conclusive evidence that administrators and teachers are primarily persuaded to adopt innovations through seeing them succeed in run-of-the-mill situations in schools very similar to their own. They tended to reject any demonstration, however, which was at all artificial or in a situation dissimilar to their own.

The second conclusion was that the most successful innovations are those that are accompanied by the most elaborate help to teachers after they begin to engage in the new behaviors. The amount of help provided teachers seems to be far more critical in determining the success of an innovation than the initial faculty reaction to the proposed change. The surveys indicated that successful inservice help reached all teachers who were using the innovation simultaneously, extended over a long period of time, involved the use of the equipment and materials needed to instruct students, and was interspersed with actual classroom practice.

The Influence of Organizational Leaders upon Planned Change

A major question in the area of organizational change is who decides that (1) a change is needed in the school, (2) what the target for change will be, and (3) what methods will be used to bring about the change. In a school system the superintendent or the school board usually has the most powerful role and the students usually have the least powerful role. Watson (1966) states that the pattern of behavior set at the top of an organization moves down through the whole organization. The chief executive in any organization, therefore, is a key figure for facilitating or blocking organizational change efforts. There is considerable research which indicates that organizational change efforts are more successful if they can begin at the top or if they have the direct support of the top administrators. Trying to change the behavior of organization members who are low on the authority hierarchy is usually unrewarding unless they believe that their bosses will look favorably on the change. The success of an organizational change effort, therefore, depends upon the support of the top administrators in the organization. It should be remembered, however, that the members lower on the organizational authority hierarchy need to be committed to any changes that affect their organizational behavior, and that the primary means for gaining that commitment is through involving them in the planning and implementation of the changes (see Chapter 12).

On the basis of an analysis of 18 studies of organizational change, Greiner (1967a) states that there are two key notions about power redistribution within an organization and successful organizational change. First, successful change depends basically on a redistribution of power within the structure of an organization, toward the greater use of shared power. Second, power redistribution occurs through a developmental process of change. It is the developmental process of change that we will deal with in the next section.

Phases of Planned Organizational Change

There have been a number of models proposed for the phases of planned change in organizations. Perhaps the most influential was that of Lewin (1947b), which basically states that three phases are involved in planned change: the unfreezing of an old pattern, the changing to a new one, and the refreezing of the new pattern. This model assumes that opposing forces create varying amounts of pressure on a situation. When the opposing pressures are equal, the situation does not change, when the pressures are unequal (due to the addition or subtraction of forces) change begins to occur and the equilibria move to another level. The Lewinian model provides a rough picture of the change process and has dominated the applied field of organizational change for the past twenty years. Recently, however, there have been attempts to derive models of the change process that are based upon the experience of those behavioral scientists who have been involved in changing organizations.

In a survey of eighteen studies of planned organizational change, Greiner (1967a) identified a series of phases which, he states, evolved very distinctly when the successful change programs were compared with the unsuccessful. The successful organizational change programs followed a sequence where:

1. The organization is under considerable external and internal pressure for improvement long before an explicit organization

change is contemplated. Performance and or morale are low. The top management is groping for a solution to its problems.

2. A new man, known for his ability to introduce improvement, enters the organization, either as the official head of the organization, or as a consultant who deals directly with the head of the organization.

3. An initial act of the new man is to encourage a re-examination of past practices and current problems within the organization.

4. The head of the organization and his immediate subordinates assume a direct and highly involved role in conducting this re-examination.

5. The new man, with top management support, engages several levels of the organization in collaborative, fact-finding, problem-solving discussions to identify and diagnose current organization problems.

6. The new man provides others with new ideas and methods for developing solutions to problems, again at many levels of the organization.

7. The solutions and decisions are developed, tested, and found creditable for solving problems on a small scale before an attempt is made to widen the scope of change to larger problems and the entire organization.

8. The change effort spreads with each success experience, and as management support grows, it is gradually absorbed permanently into the organization's way of life.

Greiner (1967a) summarizes his organizational change model into six phases, which appear in Table 2. In comparison with the successful organizational change programs, the unsuccessful programs were inconsistent in the places where they began change, in the sequence of the change steps, and in the approach used to introduce change.

In another article, Greiner (1967b) emphasizes that the major impetus to change within an organization is due to marked changes in the environment, which results in the organization suddenly being in severe trouble. He states that it is the relationship between the organization and its environment that is the crucial force for organizational change, especially in that it creates a readiness for change and a strongly perceived need for immediate change within the organization. In other words, in order to obtain organizational readiness for change there needs to be a discrepancy between the environment

TABLE 2

DYNAMICS OF SUCCESSFUL ORGANIZATION CHANGE

	Stimulus on the Power Structure	Reaction of the Power Structure
Phase 1	Pressure on Top Management	Arousal To Take Action
Phase 2	Intervention at the Top	Reorientation to Internal Problems
Phase 3	Diagnosis of Problem Areas	Recognition of Specific Problems
Phase 4	Invention of New Solutions	Commitment to New Courses of Action
Phase 5	Experimentation with New Solutions	Search for Results
Phase 6	Reinforcement from Positive Results	Acceptance of New Practices

Adapted from L. E. Greiner, Patterns of Organization Change. *Harvard Business Review*, 45: 119–131, 1967.

and the organization; for example, a dynamic, changing environment within which a static, rigid, unchanging organization is trying to survive.

It should be noted, however, that in the past educational organizations have rarely faced the type of crises confronted by business and industrial organizations. As is discussed in Chapter 2, a school is usually a static organization that has a monopoly upon the services it offers and, therefore, is not greatly effected by the fluctuations within the environment.

Two Principles of Planned Organizational Change

There are two general principles of planned organizational change that, although they have been discussed elsewhere in this book, should be emphasized. The first is that in order to achieve change within an organization there should be coordinated changes in the organization's norms and role expectations and the values and attitudes of the members. Leavitt (1965) has noted that change attempts which have focused upon the attitudes and values of one role in an organization have failed for the most part due to the organizational pressures to conform to the old norms and role expectations. Correspondingly, directives from high administrators that change the organizational structure without regard to the values and attitudes of the members have been unsuccessful (Greiner, 1967a). When coordinated changes take place in both the organization and the individual, however, change can be successfully introduced.

Second, the successful introduction of change within an organization depends upon the commitment to the change of the organization's members at all levels of the authority structure. Administrators, teachers, students, all must be committed to changes within a school, with the commitment of the administrators being the most important. Commitment is usually built by involvement and participation in the planning for, and decision-making about, the change. People enjoy and affirm changes they make for themselves and they resist changes imposed upon them by others.

Barriers to Planned Change in Educational Organizations

There are a series of barriers to planned change in educational organizations that, in comparison with other organizations, inhibit the rate of educational change under most conditions. The national education system (see Chapter 2) serves as a brake to innovation on a local level (Miles, 1964a; Wayland, 1964). Any change that would require materials not readily available from publishing companies, impair the ability of students or school personnel to move from school to school, or harm performance on the state and national standardized examinations is discouraged. The lack of evaluation of educational practices and the absence of any experimental comparison of different practices makes it impossible to offer rational judgments about the efficacy of proposed innovative changes. The absence of valid knowledge about educational practices inhibits change within the school. The "domestication" of the school (see Chapter 2) restricts the need for change in schools, as the environment is therefore more stable than it is for other types of organiza-

271

tions (Carlson, 1965). When important elements of the environment are stable, the necessity for change is reduced. Finally, as discussed in Chapter 2, the vulnerability of the schools to outside influence, the use of persons rather than physical technology as primary instruments of change, and the lay control of the schools may all inhibit change in educational organizations compared with other types of organizations (Miles, 1964a).

Resistance to Change

There are many pressures for change in any school. Any questions dealing with change, therefore, have to state not why organizations do or do not change, but rather how they select *which* changes to make from the variety of alternatives presented to them. Change agents, however, often complain about and suffer over the resistance to change they face within schools. Actually, every school and every person within the school is eager for some kind of change, such as better health, more pay, more freedom, more student-achievement motivation, and so on. On the other hand, all forces that contribute to stability in personality and in social systems resist change. Most often such resistances are perceived to be obstructing progress and contributing to the ineffectiveness of the organization. There are, however, many functional effects of resisting change.

Resistance to change can serve several functions for the organization (Klein, 1967; Watson, 1967). It protects the organization against random change that may harm the organization; that is, given a good defense, only worthwhile changes will make it through the screening system. People have vested interests in change just as others have vested interests in the status quo. Resistance to change can stop individuals who do not have the organization's good at heart from moving into control. Any change, furthermore, is a mixed blessing in that it will have both functional and dysfunctional effects upon the organization. It will raise the standing of some members and lower the standing of other members. Resistance to change can force a more equitable result of the change by protecting the individuals who may be harmed by the change. Finally, resistance to change may insure that unanticipated consequences of the change which could be a threat to the entire organization may be spelled out and avoided.

Defenders of the status quo who are quick to doubt new values and new ideas are, therefore, important to an organization for several reasons (Klein, 1967). They are the ones most apt to perceive and point out the real threats, if such exist, to the well-being of the organization that may be the unanticipated consequences of projected changes. They are especially apt to react against any change that might reduce the integrity of the organization. Finally, they are sensitive to any indication that those seeking to produce change fail to understand or identify with the core values of the organization they seek to influence.

When analyzing the resistance to change within an organization, a distinction can be drawn between rational and nonrational resistance (Barnes, 1967). Resistance to change can be based either upon rational evidence or upon emotional feelings that lead to a traditional stance toward the organization. The rational resisters to change represent reality-based resistance, either because of the lack of clear evidence concerning the desirability of change or because they represent those elements in the organization who would lose status, prestige, or influence because of the proposed changes. Rational resisters represent potential resources for change agents and are often valuable members of the organization. They are the members of the organization who fulfill the functions of resistance to change.

There are, however, several nonrational ways in which change can be resisted (Barnes, 1967; Watson, 1967). One is a type of conservatism that tends to respond negatively to almost any change other than changes "back" to the old ways. Such traditionalists cling to conventional practice as an end in itself. These individuals do not represent a resource either to the organization or to the change agents. Individuals can also resist change for reasons of inertia and habit; that is, they resist change because of internal pressures to respond to situations in their accustomed way. For example, there is evidence that teachers, despite inservice-training programs and supervisory efforts, continue to teach in much the same way they themselves were taught or in the same way they taught during their first years as teachers (Watson, 1967). Other nonrational resistances to change may be due to overdependence upon authority figures, illusions of impotence with regard to the organization and feelings that one has no power to effect change within the school, and insecurities about the consequences of the change for one's behavior.

Finally, it should be noted that with regard to any organization, a proposed change will receive a great deal of resistance under some conditions and almost no resistance under other conditions. Bennis and Peter (1966) state that resistance to anticipated change will be great where the client system possesses little or incorrect knowledge about the change and the reasons for it, has relatively little trust in those promoting the change, and has comparatively low influence in controlling the nature and direction of the change. The more profound and anxiety-provoking the change, furthermore, the more collaboration and closer relationships between the change agent and the client system are required.

The Initiation of Change

Most organizational change programs in schools appear to be stimulated, triggered, and nurtured by some active person or group, either external to or within the school (Miles, 1964a). Initiation of change in schools appears to come from the outside in most cases. In his study of a successful organizational change program Greiner (1967b) states that such programs begin with an outside change agent intervening at the top of the organization, gathering conflicting information about the effectiveness of the organization, and confronting the top administrators with his findings in a series of problem-solving discussions. Finally, Barnes (1967) states that the initiation of change is often proposed by creative individuals who are marginal or atypical members of the organization and who have no real power within the organization. The members of an organization who are prepared to initiate change within their own groups are often in a very unfavorable position from which to do so. In stable groups especially, it is the marginal or atypical person who is apt to initiate change.

Within an organization there are rational advocates of change who base their position upon rational, objective evidence and nonrational advocates of change who base their position upon subjective feelings (Barnes, 1967). The rational advocates tend to create pressures for change within the organization based upon objective evidence and respond favorably to pressures from change from the outside. Their understanding and advocacy of the proposed change is based upon data. Nonrational advocates, on the other hand, become change advocates primarily in response to emotional influences and nonrational appeals. Their advocacy of change depends upon subjective identification with the change program rather than upon objective analysis of the organization. They support change programs almost regardless of the proposals' real merits. Since most innovations in education are not evaluated and little data exists as to their efficacy, most advocates in educational organizations have to be considered nonrational advocates.

There is some research on the characteristics of individuals who initiate and advocate change within organizations. Miles (1964a) states that the innovator seems to be intelligent with high verbal ability, less bound by local group norms, and more individualistic and creative. Rogers (1965b), in summarizing the research on innovative individuals in such diverse areas as farming, school administration, industry and aboriginal tribes, states that they are young; have relatively high social status in terms of amount of education, prestige ratings, and income; are cosmopolitan in that they travel widely and participate in affairs beyond the limits of their local setting; obtain new ideas from impersonal sources such as the mass media and journals and from outside their organization; are often in a position to influence the adoption decision of their peers as they are often opinion leaders; and are likely to be viewed as deviants by their peers and by themselves. In addition, and perhaps most important of all, innovative individuals have a spirit of risk-taking, of experimentation, which their counterparts do not possess. They are venturesome individuals. Finally, Steiner (1965) has summarized much of the research dealing with creative individuals. The attributes of such persons are very similar to those identified by Rogers, with the addition of such characteristics as the following: the creative individual has conceptual fluency, being able to produce a large number of ideas quickly; he has originality and generates unusual ideas; he is able to separate source from content in evaluating information; he is motivated by an interest in the problem he faces and follows the problem wherever it leads; he suspends judgment and avoids early commitment, spending considerable time in analysis and exploration; he is less authoritarian than most people, and has a relativistic view of life; he accepts his own impulses and is playful and undisciplined in his explorations; he exercises independence of judgment and is not prone to conformity; and, while he has a rich and even "bizarre" fantasy life, he has a superior reality orientation.

The characteristics of innovative individuals are difficult if not impossible to separate from the characteristics of the organizations in which they are members. A rigid, highly controlling organization can take a potentially highly creative individual and stifle him to the extent that he becomes a rather dull, conforming member. A highly innovative organization, on the other hand, may take a rather dull, conforming individual and provide him with a setting in which he develops into a creative, innovative member. The above summarizers of research, however, point out that young, capable, cosmopolitan individuals who are high in risk-taking and autonomy and who engage in divergent thinking and behavior within organizations are potentially great resources for innovation for an organization. Such a person is the antithesis of the so-called "organizational man." It is sad, but rather obvious, that such a person has a great deal of difficulty in adjusting to the demands for conformity that are characteristic of most existing educational organizations. Certainly these are not the type of individuals who have been attracted to teaching in the past (see Chapter 3). It is also sad, but obvious, that most educational organizations are not settings in which such characteristics will be developed in students.

The Development of Cooperation between the Rational Advocate and the Rational Resister

Change is almost inevitably faced with resistance and opposition. The advocates of change, when faced with opposition, have a choice of dealing with the resistance in a productive or an unproductive way. The unproductive use of opposition entails avoiding, destroying, ignoring, or submitting to the opposition. Such approaches either involve capitulation to the resistance or ignorance of the fact that the resisters usually have something of great value to communicate about the nature of the organization. The defenders of the status quo, for example, usually represent value positions that have been important not only to themselves but to larger groups of members and, presumably, to the maintenance of the organization itself. An understanding of those values can facilitate the union between the proposed changes and the present state of the organization. In many cases, furthermore, the participation of the defender in the change process leads to the development of more adequate plans and to the avoidance of unforeseen consequences of the projected change. To ignore what is being defended often means ignoring flaws in the planned change. It may also mean that the process of change becomes transformed from a problem-solving situation to a win-lose conflict between subgroups within the organization, which ties up vital energies in dysfunctional activity.

It may well be that one of the most important skills an administrator can develop is the ability to create conditions under which the interplay between advocates and resisters of change can occur with minimum rancor and maximum mutual respect. They both are valuable to the organization and represent valuable potential resources to each other.

Organizational Influences on Innovation and Change

There are a variety of organizational factors that influence the introduction of change within an organization (Rogers, 1965). A high correlation has often (not always) been found, for example, between the financial resources of a school system and its innovativeness. The community's attitude toward providing financial support for the school, however, is an important intervening variable between community wealth and school innovativeness. Administrators may create an innovative staff by choosing young teachers with breadth of training and cosmopolitan sources of information and travel patterns. The finding that teachers who attend out-of-town educational meetings are more innovative than those who do not suggests that sending teachers to workshops, conferences, and lectures—where they may be exposed to new educational methods—may be a wise investment. If such trips are not possible, the school could bring similar influences into the organization through consultants. The absence of change agents within the school may be a factor in the slowness with which schools adopt innovations. By creating a change-agent staff role related to innovation the amount of innovation within a school system may be increased. Finally, the maintenance of contacts with laboratory or experimental schools and with universities may increase the amount of innovativeness within a school.

Pellegrin (1966) states that generally speaking, the literature emphasizes that innovative organizations are those that create conditions that allow innovative individuals to operate in a facilitating setting. The innovative organization not only tolerates divergent behavior and other forms of originality, but encourages and rewards it. Organizations may encourage or stifle originality, and those that fail to establish institutionalized procedures for rewarding originality have a low rate of innovativeness.

Steiner (1965; see Pellegrin, 1966) has summarized the literature with regard to creative organizations. He finds that such organizations encourage "idea men"; they have open channels of communication and they encourage contact with outside sources. They employ heterogeneous types of personnel, assign nonspecialists as well as experts to problems, and use an objective, fact-founded approach. Such organizations encourage the evaluation of ideas on their merits, rather than according to the status of the persons originating them, and make systematic efforts to select personnel and to reward them solely on the basis of merit. They invest in basic research and are flexible with regard to long-range planning and experiment with new ideas rather than prejudging things on "rational" grounds—that is, everything "gets a chance." They are more decentralized and diversified than less innovative organizations, have "administrative slack," permitting time and resources to be used to absorb errors, have a "risk-taking ethos," tolerating and expecting that chances will be taken, and are not run as a "tight ship," but permit employees to have fun, to have freedom in choosing and pursuing problems, and to discuss ideas. They are organizationally autonomous, and do not try to pattern their interests and activities on other organizations that serve as models, have "separate units or occasions for generating versus evaluating ideas," and separate creative and productive functions.

Evaluation of Organizational Change Programs

The successful introduction of change does not mean per se an improvement in organizational functioning. Whether or not an innovation in a school improves its functioning is an empirical question that can be answered only through rigorous evaluation procedures. As noted in Chapter 2, the goal ambiguity of schools results in a lack of criteria for evaluating educational practices. This lack of criteria makes it difficult to compare or contrast one educational practice against another and thereby contributes to a lack of knowledge about educational methods. It is rare to find an educational innovation that is based upon solid research or that has been fully developed and subjected to careful trial and experimentation (Carlson, 1965). In fact, it is rare to find an education innovation which has been evaluated at all (Miles, 1964a). Selections from Miles' 1964 book, *Innovation In Education*, show that less than one-half of one percent of nationally financed experimental programs in a large state were systematically evaluated; it was never decided whether a multimillion-dollar program of teacher evaluation was worth the money and the effort; and reading instruction has not really been influenced by research findings for the past thirty years. The lack of evaluation of educational methods and of experimental comparison of different teaching practices makes rational judgments about the efficacy of proposed innovations impossible. Educational innovations, therefore, are usually adopted *not* on the basis of empirical evidence, but rather upon the salesmanship of the promoter and the current fads in educational circles.

The findings that teachers use highly subjective and personal criteria to evaluate their success is therefore, not unexpected. Jackson (1968), in a study of fifty suburban Chicago elementary-school teachers who had been labeled as "outstanding" by their principals, notes that the teachers did not use "hard sources of data" such as pupil performance on teacher-made and commercial achievement tests in evaluating the effectiveness of their teaching practices. Instead, they used such highly subjective (and, therefore, susceptible to bias) criteria as apparent interest and enthusiasm on the part of students and the judged quality of the students' contributions to daily sessions.

Since there is no valid or reliable way employed to evaluate its effectiveness, there is probably no teaching practice that can be shown to be ineffective. This means that, by and large, teachers will not be dissatisfied with their present practices sufficiently to be highly motivated to find new ones. Most theories of planned change and psychotherapy are based upon the assumption that the major force for change in an individual's or organization's behavior is the dissatisfaction with or disconfirmation of its present behavior (Watson, 1966; Schein and Bennis, 1965; Ford and Urban, 1965). Since empirical disconfirmation of a teaching practice is rare, one can hypothesize that teachers will rarely be highly motivated to accept or develop new teaching practices.

Other reasons for the infrequency of evaluation of educational innovations are that adequate evaluation of an innovation is expensive in terms of time and money, requires the use of controlled situations and measurable procedures maintained for a significant period of time, and demands careful measurement of effects (Miles, 1964a). These conditions are rarely met in educational practice. Finally, there are a multitude of problems in gathering information about organizational change efforts (Benedict, et al., 1967). Criteria for success are usually multiple and often vague, the change agent's interventions are hard to specify, and dozens of methodological monsters raise their heads when one tries to measure change precisely.

Noting the failures of evaluation in the past should not be a council of despair but rather an incentive to change. The development of more valid instruments for measuring organizational values such as climate and norms within schools and advances in the field of evaluation promise to make the evaluation of educational innovations much simpler than it has been in the past. Hopefully the current training of educators will help them to conceptualize better what they want an innovation to accomplish. Perhaps the surest way for a school to ensure adequate evaluation of its current practices and innovations is to hire a behavioral scientist as a research consultant and cooperate with his attempts to institute innovations in ways that facilitate their being effectively evaluated.

The Value of Divergent Behavior in Organizations

In order to accomplish its objectives and to maintain itself over time, any organization must be in a constant state of innovation, growth, and change in order to cope with a changing environment. As has been discussed in this chapter, an innovative organization is one that creates conditions that allow innovative individuals to operate in a facilitating setting. In every organization there are convergent forces aimed at inducing conformity to the organization's norms and values and at coordinating the role behaviors within the organization. In every organization there are also divergent forces aimed at changing the norms, values, and role requirements of the organization. The choice each organization must make is whether to use the divergent forces to create a facilitating setting for its innovative members, to increase the organization's long-term ability to adapt to its environment, or to stifle the divergent forces in order to increase short-term efficiency. Most schools have chosen the latter course, attempting to enforce rigid role prescriptions for students, faculty, and staff, even for such peripheral behaviors as the clothes and hair styles worn. In doing so they do themselves and the American society a disservice. In order to improve their functioning schools need to become more innovative and creative; in order to produce a functioning member of a pluristic, democratic society the schools need to encourage such divergent skills as personal autonomy, self-reliance, independence, and appreciation for differences in values and behavior.

It is unfortunate that a bureaucracy with tight controls and a high degree of predictability of human action appears to be unable to distinguish between destructive and creative deviations from established values (Scott, 1961). Thus, the only thing which is safeguarded is the status quo. Katz (1964) states that the great paradox of a social organization is that it must not only reduce human variability to ensure reliable role performance, but that it must also allow room for some variability and in fact encourage it. There must always be a certain number of actions of an innovative or relatively spontaneous sort. No organizational planning can foresee all contingencies within its operations, or can anticipate with perfect accuracy all environmental changes, or can control perfectly all human variability. The resources of people in innovation, in spontaneous cooperation, in protective and creative behavior are thus vital to organizational survival and effectiveness. Without norms that legitimize such behaviors schools will not be able to change in appropriate and creative ways.

SUMMARY

The continual effectiveness of a school as an organization not only depends on conformity to its role requirements but on its ability to grow, develop, and change in productive ways over time. Planned organizational change involves a collaborative relationship between the client system and a change agent in which both work together to bring about organizational change in a conscious, deliberate, and intended manner.

There are two separate aspects of organizational change—the methods employed to bring about change and the target at which such methods are directed. The primary targets for organizational change are: (1) the personality traits of individual members, (2) the informal group structure of members, (3) the formal structure of the organization, (4) organizational technology, and (5) the task objectives of the organization.

After the target for change has been specified, the appropriate method or combination of methods should be chosen for enacting the change. Eight commonly used methods for organizational change were mentioned in this chapter. A *decree by a high authority* is a one-way announcement to the lower levels of the organization with the expectation that the members will comply. The *replacement of personnel* assumes that resistance to change resides in a few strategically located individuals and, as such, these people are removed. The *presentation of information* assumes that if a change is shown to be in line with the rational self-interests of organization members, they will adopt it. Information about innovation in itself, however, is not necessarily a source of individual motivation for change and even if it were, it would not necessarily lead to a change in the actual structure or roles of the organization. *Skill training* proposes that once members are given the appropriate skills the organization, as a whole, will be more effective. The *individual counseling and therapy* approach assumes that organization effectiveness can be improved by changing individuals' basic personalities. This technique, however, will probably only be fruitful when the individuals involved are in the top authority positions. One of the most effective methods for changing the informal structure of an organization is *sensitivity-group training*. Through meetings in which direct, intimate, and power-free communication is encouraged, organization members are given an opportunity to experiment with new behavior, develop an awareness of self and others, and learn the nature of effective group functioning. A promising method that is directed at both individual attitudes and organizational structure is the *survey-feedback* approach. Change agents first gather data on the organization's functioning. This data is analyzed, summarized, and then fed back to different groups in the organization. These groups discuss this objective, factual information, analyze the problems it reveals concerning both personal and role relationships within and between organizational groups, and agree upon possible solutions. The final method mentioned was the *clinical-experimental* approach. This method has both research and change objectives. The research half of the change agent collects data about organization functioning. Using this data, the action half of the change agent team makes a clinical diagnosis of the organization and intervenes to assist the organization in defining and solving its problems. The research half then gathers data about the effectiveness of the intervention.

This chapter emphasized two general principles of planned organizational change. First, in order to achieve change there should be coordinated changes in the organization's norms and role expectations and in the values and attitudes of the members. Second, the successful introduction of change within an organization depends upon the commitment to the change of the organization's members at all levels of the authority structure.

Most change programs in schools appear to be triggered and nurtured by some active person or group, either external to or within the school. Within the organization, those individuals who are most likely to be sources of constructive proposals for change typically are intelligent, cosmopolitan, high in risk-taking and autonomy, and base their proposals upon rational, objective evidence as opposed to subjective feelings.

The advocates of change, when faced with rational opposition, have a choice of dealing with the resistance in a productive or unproductive way. The unproductive use of opposition entails either ignoring or submitting to the opposition. A more productive approach involves an awareness and respect for a rational opposition's position, since they have certain legitimate interests which must be taken into account and are frequently more apt to perceive the unanticipated dysfunctional consequences of the proposed changes.

There are also organizational factors that influence the introduction of change. The literature emphasizes that innovative organizations are those that create conditions that allow individuals to operate in a facilitating setting. They not only tolerate divergent behavior and other forms of originality, but encourage and reward it. They promote contact with outsiders, are flexible with regard to long-range planning, and experiment with new ideas.

Whether or not an innovation in a school improves its functioning is an empirical question that can be answered only by rigorous evaluation procedures. It is unfortunate, however, that educational innovations are almost never evaluated systematically and in the absence of evaluatory evidence, educators must use inferior, substitute bases for judgment such as educational ideology, sentiment, or persuasive claims by salesmen.

BIBLIOGRAPHY

Abravanel, E., A psychological analysis of the concept of role. Unpublished master's thesis, Swarthmore College, 1962.

Allen, V. L., Situational factors in conformity. *In* L. Berkowitz (Ed.), *Advances In Experimental Social Psychology*, Vol. 2. New York: Academic Press, 1965, pp. 133–175.

Allinsmith, F., Directness with which anger is expressed. *In* D. R. Miller and G. E. Swanson (Eds.), *Inner Conflict and Defense.* New York: Holt, Rinehart and Winston, Inc., 1960.

Allport, G. W., and L. J. Postman, The basic psychology of rumor. *Transactions of New York Academy of Sciences, Series II*, 1945, *8:* 61–81.

Altman, E. R., The effect of rank in class and size of high school on academic achievement of Central Michigan College, class of 1957, *Journal of Educational Research*, 1959, *52:* 307–309.

American Friends Service Committee, *Peace in Vietnam.* New York: Hill & Wang, Inc., 1966.

Amidon, E. J., and N. A. Flanders, *The Role of the Teacher in the Classroom.* Minneapolis: Paul Amidon and Associates, 1963.

Amidon, E. J., and J. B. Hough, *Interaction Analysis: Theory, Research and Application.* Reading, Mass.: Addison-Wesley Publishing Company, Inc., 1967.

Amidon, E. J., and E. Hunter, *Improving Teaching.* New York: Holt, Rinehart and Winston, Inc., 1966.

Anderson, K. E., A frontal attack on the basic problem in evaluation: The achievement of the objectives of instruction in specific areas. *Journal of Experimental Education,* 1950, *18:* 163–174.

Anderson, R. H., *Teaching in a World of Change.* New York: Harcourt, Brace & World, Inc., 1966.

Anderson, T. B., and L. C. Olson, In consequence of self and ideal self and occupational choices. *Personnel and Guidance Journal,* 1965, *44:* 171–176.

Angyal, A., *Foundations for a Science of Personality.* New York: Commonwealth Fund, 1941.

Argyris, C., *Personality and Organization.* New York: Harper & Row, Publishers, 1957.

Argyris, C., *Interpersonal Competence and Organizational Effectiveness.* Homewood, Ill.: Dorsey Press, 1962.

Argyris, C., *Integrating the Individual and the Organization.* New York: John Wiley & Sons, Inc., 1964.(a)

Argyris, C., T-groups for organizational effectiveness. *Harvard Business Review,* 1964, *42:* 60–75.(b)

Argyris, C., *Organization and Innovation.* Homewood, Ill.: Dorsey Press, 1965.

Aronson, E., and M. Carlsmith, Performance expectancy as a determinant of actual performance. *Journal of Abnormal and Social Psychology,* 1962, *68:* 178–182.

Asch, S. E., *Social Psychology.* Englewood Cliffs, N.J.: Prentice-Hall, Inc., 1952.

Astin, A. W., Productivity of undergraduate institutions. *Science,* 1962, *136:* 129–135.

Astin, A. W., and J. L. Holland, The environmental assessment technique: A way to measure college environments. *Journal of Educational Psychology,* 1961, *52:* 308–316.

Atkinson, J. W., The mainsprings of achievement-oriented activity. *In* J. D. Krumboltz (Ed.), *Learning and the Educational Process.* Skokie, Ill.: Rand McNally & Company, 1965, pp. 25–66.

Atkinson, J. W., and N. T. Feather (Eds.), *A Theory of Achievement Motivation.* New York: John Wiley & Sons, Inc., 1966.

Ayllon, T., The application of reinforcement theory toward behavior problems: The psychiatric nurse as a behavioral engineer. *Dissertation Abstracts,* 1960, *20:* 3372.

Ayllon, T., and J. Michael, The psychiatric nurse as a behavioral engineer. *Journal of Experimental Analysis of Behavior,* 1959, *2:* 323, 334.

Backman, C. W., and P. F. Secord, The self and role selection. *In* C. Gordon and K. J. Gergen (Eds.), *The Self in Social Interaction*. New York: John Wiley & Sons, Inc., 1967.

Backman, C. W., and P. F. Secord, *A Social Psychological View of Education*. New York: Harcourt, Brace & World, Inc., 1968.

Bales, R. F., Task roles and social roles in problem solving groups. *In* E. E. Maccoby, T. M. Newcomb, and E. L. Hartley (Eds.), *Readings in Social Psychology* (3rd ed.). New York: Holt, Rinehart and Winston, Inc., 1958, pp. 396–413.

Bandura, A., Punishment revisited. *Journal of Consulting Psychology*, 1962, *26:* 298–301.

Bandura, A., and A. C. Huston, Identification as a process of incidental learning. *Journal of Abnormal and Social Psychology*, 1961, *63:* 311–318.

Bandura, A., and R. H. Walters, *Social Learning and Personality Development*. New York: Holt, Rinehart and Winston, Inc., 1963.

Barker, R. G., and P. V. Gump, *Big School, Small School: High School Size and Student Behavior*. Stanford, Calif.: Stanford University Press, 1964.

Barnes, L. B., Organizational change and field experiment methods. *In* V. H. Vroom (Ed.), *Methods of Organizational Research*. Pittsburgh: University of Pittsburgh Press, 1967, pp. 57–113.

Barton, A. H., *Organizational Measurement and its Bearing on the Study of College Environments*. New York: College Entrance Examination Board, 1961.

Battle, E. S., and J. B. Rotter, Children's feelings of personal control as related to social class and ethnic group. *Journal of Personality*, 1963, *31:* 482–490.

Bavelas, A., A. H. Hastorf, A. E. Gross, and W. R. Kite, Experiments on the alteration of group structure. *Journal of Experimental Social Psychology*, 1965, *1:* 55–70.

Baxter, M. G., R. H. Ferrell, and J. E. Wiltz, *The Teaching of American History in High Schools*. Bloomington, Ind.: Indiana University Press, 1964.

Beck, C. E., N. R. Bernier, J. B. MacDonald, T. W. Walton, and J. C. Willers, *Education for Relevance: The Schools and Social Change*. Boston: Houghton Mifflin Company, 1968.

Becker, W. C., C. H. Madsen, Jr., C. R. Arnold, and D. R. Thomas, The contingent use of teacher attention and praise in reducing classroom behavior problems. Mimeographed report, 1967.

Beez, W. V., Influence of biased psychological reports on teacher behavior. Unpublished manuscript, Indiana University, 1967.

Benedict, B. A., P. H. Calder, D. M. Callahan, H. A. Hornstein, and M. B. Miles, The clinical-experimental approach to assessing organizational change efforts. *Journal of Applied Behavioral Science*, 1967, *3:* 347–381.

Bennett, E. B., Discussion, decision, commitment, and consensus in group decision. *Human Relations*, 1955, *8:* 251–273.

Bennis, W. G. *Changing Organizations.* New York: McGraw-Hill, Inc., 1966.

Bennis, W. G., and H. W. Peter, Applying behavioral science for organizational change. *In* H. W. Peter and W. G. Bennis (Eds.), *Comparative Theories of Social Change.* Ann Arbor, Mich.: Foundation for Research on Human Behavior, Agency for International Development, 1966.

Berelson, B., and G. A. Steiner, *Human Behavior: An Inventory of Scientific Findings.* New York: Harcourt, Brace & World, Inc., 1964.

Bhalnogtar, K. P., Academic achievement as a function of one's self-concept and ego functions. *Educational Psychology Review*, 1966, *6:* 178–182.

Biddle, B. J., and E. J. Thomas, *Role Theory: Concepts and Research.* New York: John Wiley & Sons, Inc., 1966.

Bidwell, C. E., The school as a formal organization. *In* J. G. March (Ed.), *Handbook of Organizations.* Skokie, Ill.: Rand McNally & Company, 1965, pp. 972–1023.

Blake, R. R., and J. S. Mouton, The intergroup dynamics of win-lose conflict and problem-solving collaboration in union-management relations. *In* Muzafer Sherif (Ed.), *Intergroup relations and leadership.* New York: John Wiley & Sons, Inc., 1962.

Blake, R. R., and J. S. Mouton, *The Managerial Grid.* Houston, Tex.: The Gulf Publishing Company, 1964.

Blau, P. M., *Bureaucracy in Modern Society.* New York: Random House, Inc., 1956.

Bledsoe, J. C., Self-concepts of children and their intelligence, achievement, interests, and anxiety. *Journal of Individual Psychology*, 1964, *20:* 55–58.

Bodwin, F. B., The relationship between immature self-concept and certain educational disabilities. Doctoral thesis, Michigan State University, 1957.

Borg, W. R., *Ability Grouping in the Public Schools.* Madison, Wis.: Dembar Educational Research Services, 1966.

Borg, W. R., *An Evaluation of Ability Grouping.* Coop. Res. Proj. No. 577. Salt Lake City: Utah State University, 1964.

Borislow, B., Self evaluation and academic achievement. *Journal of Counseling Psychology*, 1962, *9:* 246–253.

Borland, M., and D. E. Yett, The cash value of college—for Negroes and for whites. *Trans-Action*, 1967, *5:* 44–50.

Boye, R. P., The effect of the high school on students' aspirations. *American Journal of Sociology*, 1965, *71:* 628–639.

Brickell, H. M., State organization for educational change: A case study and a proposal. *In* M. B. Miles (Ed.), *Innovation in Education.* New York: Teachers College Press, Columbia University, 1964, pp. 493–533.

Broadbeck, M., Logic and scientific method in research on teaching. *In* N. L. Gage (Ed.), *Handbook of Research on Teaching.* Skokie, Ill.: Rand McNally & Company, 1963, 44–94.

Broedal, J., M. Ohlsen, F. Proff, and C. Southard, The effects of group counseling on gifted underachieving adolescents. *Journal of Counseling Psychology*, 1960, *7:* 163–170.

Bronfenbrenner, U., The mirror image in Soviet-American relations: A social psychologist's report. *Journal of Social Issues*, 1961, *17:* 45–47.

Bronfenbrenner, U., Soviet methods of character education. Some implications for research. *Religious Education,* 1962, *57:* (4, Res. Suppl.) S45–S61.

Brookover, W. B., et al., The relationship of self-image to achievement in junior high school subjects. Final Report of Cooperative Research Project #845, Michigan State University, Office of Education, U.S. Dept. of Health, Education and Welfare, 1962.

Brookover, W. B., and S. Thomas, Self-concept of ability and school achievement. *Sociology of Education*, 1964, *37:* 271–278.

Brown, R., *Social Psychology.* New York: The Free Press, 1965.

Bruner, J. S., and A. L. Miturn, Perceptual indentification and perceptual organization. *Journal of Genetic Psychology.* 1955, *53:* 21–28.

Burchard, W., Role conflicts of military chaplains. *American Sociological Review*, 1954, *19:* 528–535.

Burris, R. W., The effect of counseling on achievement motivation. Doctoral dissertation, University of Indiana, 1958.

Cairns, R. B., Antecedents of social reinforcer effectiveness. Paper read at the Biennial Meeting of the Social Research Child Development, Berkeley, California, 1963.

Campbell, J. P., and M. D. Dunnette, Effectiveness of T-group experiences in managerial training and development. *Psychological Bulletin*, 1968, *70:* 73–105.

Campbell, P. B., Self-concept and academic achievement in middle grade public school children. *Dissertation Abstracts*, 1966, *27:* 1535–1536.

Campbell, P. B., School and self-concept. *Educational Leadership*, 1967, *29:* 510–515.

Canavan, D., Development of individual differences in the perception of value and risk-taking styles. Ph.D. dissertation, Teachers College, Columbia University, 1968.

Carlson, R. O., Barriers to change in public schools. *In* R. O. Carlson, et al., *Change Processes in the Public Schools.* Eugene, Oregon: Center for the Advanced Study of Educational Administration, 1965, pp. 3–11.

Cartwright, D., and A. Zander (Eds.), *Group Dynamics*. New York: Harper & Row, Publishers, 1968.

Charters, W. W., Jr., The social background of teaching. *In* N. L. Gage (Ed.), *Handbook of Research on Teaching*. Chicago: Rand McNally & Company, 1963, pp. 715–814.

Charters, W. W., Jr., and T. M. Newcomb, Some attitudinal effects of experimentally increased salience of a membership group. *In* G. E. Swanson, T. M. Newcomb, and E. L. Hartley (Eds.), *Readings in Social Psychology* (2nd ed.). New York: Holt, Rinehart and Winston, Inc., 1952.

Chesler, M., and J. Franklin, Interracial and intergenerational conflict in secondary schools. Paper presented at the Annual Meeting of the American Sociological Association, Boston, Massachusetts, August, 1968.

Chesler, M., R. Schmuck, and R. Lippitt, The principal's role in facilitating innovation. *Theory into Practice*, 1963, *2:* 269–277.

Child, I. L., *Italian or American? The Second Generation in Conflict*. New Haven, Conn.: Yale University Press, 1943.

Child, I. L., T. Storm, and J. Veroff, Achievement themes in folk tales related to socialization practice. *In* J. W. Atkinson (Ed.), *Motives in Fantasy, Action, and Society*. Princeton, N.J.: D. Van Nostrand Company, Inc., 1958.

Chin, R., and K. D. Benne, General strategies for effecting changes in human systems. *In* W. G. Bennis, K. D. Benne, and R. Chin, *The Planning of Change* (2nd ed.). New York: Holt, Rinehart and Winston, Inc., 1969, pp. 170–174.

Clark, H. F., The return on educational investment. *In* R. K. Hall and J. A. Lauwergys (Eds.), *Education and Economics: The Year Book of Education, 1956*. London: Evans Brothers Limited, 1956, pp. 495–506.

Clark, K. B., *Dark Ghetto: Dilemmas of Social Power*. New York: Harper & Row, Publishers, 1965.

Clarke, W. E., The Relationship between College Academic Performance and Expectancies. Doctoral thesis, Michigan State University, 1960.

Coch, L., and J. R. P. French, Jr., Overcoming resistance to change. *Human Relations*, 1948, *1:* 512–533.

Cohen, J., Technique of role-reversal. The study of international conferences, World Federation for Mental Health (Paris Meeting), August-September 1950.

Cohen, J., The technique of role-reversal: A preliminary note. *Occupational Psychology*, 1951, *25:* 64–66.

Coleman, J. S., *The Adolescent Society*. New York: Crowell-Collier and Macmillan, Inc., 1961.

Coleman, J. S., E. Q. Campbell, C. J. Hobson, J. McPartland, A. M. Mood, F. D. Weinfeld, and R. L. York, *Equality of Educational Op-*

portunity. Washington, D.C.: U.S. Office of Health, Education, and Welfare, 1966.

Combs, C. F., Perception of self and scholastic underachievement in the academically capable. *Personnel and Guidance Journal*, 1964, *43:* 47–51.

Cooley, C. H., *Human Nature and the Social Order*. New York: Charles Scribner's Sons, 1902.

Corwin, R. G., *A Sociology of Education*. New York: Appleton-Century-Crofts, 1965.

Cousins, A. N., Social Equilibrium and the psycho-dynamic mechanisms. *Social Forces*, 1951, *30:* 202–209.

Crow, L., Public attitudes and expectations as a disturbing variable in experimentation and therapy. Unpublished paper, Harvard University, 1964.

Crutchfield, R. S., Conformity and character. *American Psychologist*, 1955, *10:* 191–198.

Davidson, H. H., and G. Lang, Children's perceptions of their teachers' feelings toward them related to self-perception, school achievement, and behavior. *Journal of Experimental Education*, 1960, *29:* 107–118.

Davis, J. A., Intellectual climates in 135 American colleges and universities: A study in "social psycho-physics." *Sociology of Education*, 1963, *37:* 110–128.

Davis, J. A., *Great Aspirations*. London: Aldine Publishing Co., 1964.

Dearborn, D. C., and H. A. Simon, Selective perception: A note on the departmental identification of executives. *Sociometry*, 1958, *23:* 667–673.

Deutsch, M. An experimental study of the effects of cooperation and competition upon group process. *Human Relations*, 1949, *2:* 199–231.

Deutsch, M., Cooperation and trust: Some theoretical notes. *Nebraska Symposium on Motivation*, 1962, Lincoln, Neb.: University of Nebraska Press, 1962, pp. 275–320.(a)

Deutsch, M., Psychological alternatives to war. *Journal of Social Issues*, 1962, *18:* 97–119.(b)

Deutsch, M., Conflict and its resolution. Presidential Address, Division of Personality and Social Psychology, American Psychological Association, 1966.

Deutsch, M., Conflicts: Productive and destructive. *Journal of Social Issues*, 1969, *25:* 7–43.

Deutsch, M., Group behavior. *Encyclopedia of the Social Sciences*, revised edition. New York: Crowell-Collier and Macmillan, Inc., 1968, pp. 265–276.

Deutsch, M., and H. Hornstein, The social psychology of education. *In* J. Davitz and S. Ball (Eds.), *Handbook Of Educational Psychology*. In preparation.

Deutsch, M., and R. M. Krauss, Studies of interpersonal bargaining. *Journal of Conflict Resolutions*, 1962, *6:* 52–76.

Deutsch, M., and R. M. Krauss, *Theories in Social Psychology*. New York: Basic Books, Inc., 1965.

Deutsch, M., and L. Solomon, Reactions to evaluations by others as influenced by self-evaluations. *Sociometry*, 1959, *22:* 93–112.

Dewey, J., The relation of theory to practice in education. *National Society for the Scientific Study of Education, 3rd Yearbook*, 1904. Reprinted by the Association for Student Teaching, Bulletin 17, Cedar Falls, Iowa: State College of Iowa, 1962.

Dickenson, W., and C. Traux, Group counseling with college underachievers. *Personnel and Guidance Journal*, 1966, *45:* 243–247.

Dolan, K. G., Effects of individual counseling on selected test scores for reading delayed readers. *Personnel and Guidance Journal*, 1964, *42:* 914–917.

Douglas, A., Peaceful settlement of industrial and intergroup disputes. *Journal of Conflict Resolution*, 1957, *1:* 69–81.

Douglas, J. W. B., *The Home and the School*. London: MacGibbon & Kee, 1964.

Douvan, E., Social status and success strivings. *Journal of Abnormal and Social Psychology*, 1956, *52:* 219–223.

Dreeben, R., *On What Is Learned in School*. Reading, Mass: Addison-Wesley Publishing Company, 1968.

Eash, M. J., Grouping: What have we learned? *Education Leadership*, April 1961, *18:* 429–434.

Emerson, R., Deviation and rejection: An experimental replication. *American Sociological Review*, 1954, *19:* 688–693.

Emerson, R. M., Power-dependence relations. *American Sociological Review*, 1962, *27:* 31–40.

Empey, L. T., and J. Rabow, The Provo experiment in delinquency rehabilitation. *American Sociological Review*, 1961, *26:* 679–695.

Engle, K. B., D. A. Davis, and G. E. Meyer, Interpersonal effects on underachievers. *Journal of Educational Research*, 1968, *61:* 208–210.

Etzioni, A., *Modern Organizations*. Englewood Cliffs, N.J.: Prentice-Hall, Inc., 1964.

Farguhar, W., and D. A. Payne, A classification and comparison of the techniques used in the selecting of under and over achieving groups. *Personnel and Guidance Journal*, 1964, *42:* 874–878.

Farwell, E. D., J. R. Warren, and T. R. McConnell, Student personality characteristics associated with groups of colleges and fields of study. *College and University*, 1962, *37:* 229–241.

Festinger, L. Informal social communication. *Psychological Review*, 1950, *57:* 271–282.

Festinger, L., S. Schachter, and K. Back, The operation of group standards.

In D. Cartwright and A. Zander (Eds.), *Group Dynamics*, (2nd ed.). New York: Harper & Row, Publishers, 1962, pp. 241–260.

Fiedler, F. E., *Leader Attitudes and Group Effectiveness*. Urbana, Ill.: University of Illinois Press, 1958.

Fiedler, F. E., A contingency model of leadership effectiveness. *In* L. Berkowitz (Ed.), *Advances in Experimental Social Psychology*. New York: Academic Press, Inc., 1964, pp. 150–192.

Fiedler, F. E., Personality and situational determinants of leadership effectiveness. *In* D. Cartwright and A. Zander (Eds.), *Group Dynamics* (3rd ed.). New York: Harper & Row, Publishers, 1968, pp. 362–381.

Fink, M. B., Self-concept as it is related to academic achievement. *California Journal of Educational Research*, 1962, *13:* 57–62.

Fleishman, E., E. Harris, and H. Burtt, *Leadership and Supervision in Industry: An Evaluation of a Supervisory Training Program*. Columbus: Ohio State Bureau of Educational Research, 1955.

Foley, J. P., Jr., and F. L. Macmillan, Mediated generalization and the interpretation of verbal behavior: V. Free association as related to differences in professional training. *Journal of Experimental Psychology*, 1943, *33:* 299–310.

Ford, D. J., and J. B. Urban, *Systems of Psychotherapy*. New York: John Wiley & Sons, Inc., 1965.

Fox, D. J., and P. M. Schwarz, Effective interaction between older and younger pupils in an elementary school "Peace Corps" project. Final Report, City University of New York, City College, School of Education, 1967.

Frank, J. D., *Persuasion and Healing*. New York: Schocken Books, 1963.

Freedman, M. B., *The Student and Campus Climates of Learning*. Washington, D.C.: U.S. Department of Health, Education and Welfare, 1967.

French, J. R. P., Field studies of power in organizations. *In* R. L. Kahn and E. Boulding (Eds.), *Power and Conflict in Organizations*. New York: Basic Books, Inc., 1964, pp. 52–67.

French, J. R. P., and B. H. Raven, The bases of social power. *In* D. Cartwright (Ed.), *Studies in Social Power*. Ann Arbor, Mich.: University of Michigan Press, 1959, pp. 118–149.

French, J. R. P., W. W. Morrison, and G. Levinger, Coercive power and forces affecting conformity. *Journal of Abnormal and Social Psychology*, 1960, *61:* 93–101.

Friedenberg, E. Z., *The Vanishing Adolescent*. New York: Dell Publishing Company, 1962.

Friedlander, F., A comparative study of consulting processes and group development. *Journal of Applied Behavioral Science*, 1968, *4:* 377–401.

Getzels, J. W., and E. G. Guba, Role, role conflict, and effectiveness. *American Sociological Review*, 1954, *19:* 164–175.

Gillham, H. L., *Helping Children Accept Themselves and Others*. New York: Teachers College Press, Columbia University, 1959.

Gillham, I., Self-concept and reading. *Reading Teacher*, 1967, *21:* 270–273.

Glass, D. C., Changes in liking as a means of reducing cognitive discrepancies between self-esteem and aggression. *Journal of Personality*, 1964, *32:* 531–549.

Goldberg, M. L., A. H. Passow, and J. Justman, *The Effects of Ability Grouping*. New York: Teachers College Press, Columbia University, 1966.

Goodson, M. R., Models for effecting planned educational change. *In* H. J. Klausmeier, W. L. Goodwin, J. Prasch, and M. R. Goodson, Project Models: *Maximizing Opportunities for Development and Experimentation in Learning in the Schools*. Madison, Wis.: Research and Development Center for Learning and Re-Education, 1966, pp. 16–29.

Gordon, C. W., *The Social System of the High School*. New York: The Free Press, 1957.

Gordon, L. V., and M. A. Durea, The effect of discouragement on the revised Stanford Binet Scale. *Journal of Genetic Psychology*, 1948, *73:* 201–207.

Gowan, J. C., Relation of the "K" scale of the MMPI to the teaching personality. *California Journal of Educational Psychology*, 1955, *6:* 208–212.

Greiner, L. E., Patterns of organizational change. *Harvard Business Review*, 1967, *45:* 119–131.(a)

Greiner, L. E., Antecedents of planned organizational change. *Journal of Applied Behavioral Science,* 1967, *3:* 51–86.(b)

Griffiths, D. E., System theory and school districts. *Ontario Journal of Educational Research*, 1965, *8:* 175–183.

Gross, N., W. S. Mason, and A. W. McEachern, *Explorations in Role Analysis*. New York: John Wiley & Sons, Inc., 1958.

Gumpert, P., and C. Gumpert, On the psychology of expectation in the classroom. *The Urban Review*, 1968, *3:* 21–26.

Gurnee, H., Learning under competitive and collaborative sets. *Journal of Experimental Social Psychology*, 1968, *4:* 26–34.

Guthrie, E. R., *The Psychology of Human Conflict*. New York: Harper & Row, Publishers, 1938.

Haggstrom, W. C., The power of the poor. *In* F. Riesman, J. Cohen, and A. Pearl (Eds.), *Mental Health of the Poor*. New York: Crowell-Collier and Macmillan, Inc., 1964, pp. 205–223.

Haines, D. B., and W. J. McKeachie, Cooperative versus competitive discussion methods in teaching introductory psychology. *Journal of Educational Psychology*, 1967, *58:* 386–390.

Halpin, A., and B. Winer, *The Leadership Behavior of the Airplane Commander*. Columbus: Ohio State University Research Foundation, 1952.

Halpin, A. W., and D. B. Croft., *The Organizational Climate of Schools*. Chicago: University of Chicago, Midwest Administration Center, 1963.

Hare, A. P., *Handbook of Small Group Research*. New York: The Free Press, 1962.

Heider, F., *The Psychology of Interpersonal Relations*. New York: John Wiley & Sons, Inc., 1958.

Heist, P., T. R. McConnell, F. Matsler, and P. Williams, Personality and scholarship. *Science*, 1961, *133:* 362–367.

Helper, M. M., Parental evaluations of children and children's self-evaluations. *Journal of Abnormal and Social Psychology*, 1960, *56:* 190–194.

Hemphill, J. K., Leadership behavior associated with the administrative reputation of college students. *Journal of Educational Psychology*, 1955, *46:* 385–401.

Himmelweit, H., and J. Wright, The school system, social class, and attainment after school. Paper presented to the Annual Conference of the British Psychological Society, 1967.

Hoffman, M. L., Power assertion by the parent and its impact on the child. *Child Development*, 1960, *31:* 129–143.

Holland, J. L., and J. M. Richards, Jr., Academic and non-academic accomplishment: Correlated or uncorrelated? *Journal of Educational Psychology*, 1965, *56:* 165–174.

Hollander, E. P., and J. W. Julian, Contemporary trends in the analysis of leadership processes. *Psychological Bulletin*, 1969, *71:* 387–397.

Hollander, E. P., and R. H. Willis, Some current issues in the psychology of conformity and nonconformity. *Psychological Bulletin*, 1967, *68:* 62–76.

Homans, G. C., *Social Behavior: Its Elementary Forms*. New York: Harcourt, Brace & World, Inc., 1961.

Hornstein, M., Accuracy of emotional communication and interpersonal compatibility. *Journal of Personality*, 1967, *35:* 20–30.

House, R. J., T-group education and leadership effectiveness: A review of the empiric literature and a critical evaluation. *Personnel Psychology*, 1967, *20:* 1–32.

Hovland, C. I., I. L. Janis, and H. H. Kelley, *Communication and Persuasion*. New Haven, Conn.: Yale University Press, 1953.

Hughes, E., H. Becker, and B. Geer, Student culture and academic effort. *In* N. Sanford (Ed.), *The American College*. New York: John Wiley & Sons, Inc., 1962.

Hummel, R. A., and N. W. Sprinthall, Underachievement related to interest, attitudes, and values. *Personnel and Guidance Journal*, 1965, *44:* 388–395.

Husen, T., and N. Svensson, Pedagogic milieu and development of intellectual skills. *School Review*, 1960, *68:* 36–51.

Icheiser, G., Misunderstandings in human relations. *American Journal of Sociology*, 1949, *55:* 1–70.

Inkeles, A., Social structure and the socialization of competence. *Harvard Educational Review*, 1966, *36:* 279–295.

Jackson, B., *Streaming: An Education System in Miniature.* London: Routledge & Kegan Paul Ltd., 1964.

Jackson, P. W., *Life in Classrooms.* New York: Holt, Rinehart and Winston, Inc., 1968.

Jacob, P., *Changing Values in College.* New York: Harper & Row, Publishers, 1957.

Jenkins, D. H., and R. Lippitt, Interpersonal perceptions of teachers, students, and parents. Washington, D.C.: Division of Adult Education Services, National Education Association, 1951.

Johnson, D. W., The use of role reversal in intergroup competition. *Journal of Personality and Social Psychology*, 1967, *7:* 135–142.

Johnson, D. W., and R. J. Lewicki, The initiation of superordinate goals. *Journal of Applied Behavioral Science*, 1969, *5:* 9–24.

Julian, J. W., and F. A. Perry, Cooperation contrasted with intra-group and inter-group competition. *Sociometry*, 1967, *30:* 79–90.

Kahn, R., and D. Katz, Leadership practices in relation to productivity and morale. *In* D. Cartwright and A. Zander (Eds.), *Group Dynamics: Research and Theory.* New York: Harper & Row, Publishers, 1960.

Katz, D., The motivational basis of organizational behavior. *Behavioral Science,* 1964, *9:* 131–146.

Katz, D., and R. L. Kahn, *The Social Psychology of Organizations.* New York: John Wiley & Sons, Inc., 1966.

Katz, D., I. Sarnoff, and C. McClintock, Ego defense and attitude change. *Human Relations*, 1956, *9:* 27–45.

Kausler, D. H., Aspiration level as a determinant of performance. *Journal of Personality*, 1959, *27:* 346–351.

Kelley, H. H., Two functions of reference groups. *In* G. E. Swanson, T. M. Newcomb, and E. L. Hartley (Eds.), *Readings in Social Psychology.* New York: Holt, Rinehart and Winston, Inc., 1952, pp. 410–414.

Kelley, H. H., Salience of membership and resistance to change of group anchored attitudes. *Human Relations*, 1955, *8:* 275–289.

Killian, L. M., The significance of multiple-group membership in disaster. *American Journal of Sociology*, 1952, *57:* 309–314.

Kinch, J. W., A formalized theory of the self-concept. *The American Journal of Sociology*, 1963, *68:* 481–486.

Klapper, J. T., *The Effects of Mass Communication.* New York: The Free Press, 1960.

Klein, D., Some notes on the dynamics of resistance to change: The defender role. *In* G. Watson (Ed.), *Concepts for Social Change.* Washington, D.C.: National Training Laboratories, 1967, pp. 26–37.

Knapp, R. H., and J. J. Greenbaum, *The Younger American Scholar.* Chicago: University of Chicago Press, 1953.

Komarovsky, M., Cultural contradictions and sex roles. *American Journal of Sociology,* 1946, *52:* 184–189.

Kostick, M. M., An experiment in group decision. *Journal of Teacher Education,* 1957, *8:* 67–72.

Kounin, J. S., and P. V. Gump, The ripple effect in discipline. *Elementary School Journal,* 1958, *59:* 158–162.

Kounin, J. S., and P. V. Gump, The comparative influence of punitive and nonpunitive teachers upon children's concepts of school misconduct. *Journal of Educational Psychology,* 1961, *52:* 44–49.

Krech, D., and R. S. Crutchfield, *Elements of Psychology.* New York: Alfred A. Knopf, 1962.

Krech, D., R. S. Crutchfield, and E. L. Ballachey, *Individual in Society.* New York: McGraw-Hill, Inc., 1962.

Kvaraceus, W., Negro youth and school adaptation. *In* W. Kvaraceus et al., *Negro Self Concept.* New York: McGraw-Hill, Inc., 1965.

Learned, W. S., and B. D. Wood, *The Student and His Knowledge.* New York: Carnegie Foundation for the Advancement of Teaching, 1938.

Leavitt, H. J., Applied organizational change in industry: Structural, technological, and humanistic approaches. *In* J. G. March, *Handbook of Organizations.* Chicago: Rand McNally & Company, 1965, pp. 1144–1171.

Lee, E. C., Career development of science teachers. *Journal of Research in Science Teaching,* 1963, *1:* 54–63.

Levine, J., and J. Butler, Lecture vs. group decision in changing behavior. *Journal of Applied Psychology,* 1952, *36:* 29–33.

Levine, J. M., and G. Murphy, The learning and forgetting of controversial material. *Journal of Abnormal and Social Psychology,* 1943, *38:* 507–517.

Lewin, K., Frontiers in group dynamics: I. Concept, method, and reality in social science: Social equilibra and social change. II. Channels of group life: Social planning and action research. *Human Relations,* 1947, *1:* 5–40, 143–153.(a)

Lewin, K., Group decision and social change. *In* T. M. Newcomb and E. L. Hartley (Eds.), *Readings in Social Psychology.* New York: Holt, Rinehart and Winston, Inc., 1947, pp. 340–344.(b)

Lewin, K., T. Dembo, L. Festinger, and P. Sears, Level of aspiration. *In* J. M. V. Hunt (Ed.), *Personality and the Behavior Disorders.* New York: The Ronald Press Company, 1944, pp. 333–378.

Lewin, K., R. Lippitt, and R. K. White, Patterns of aggressive behavior in experimentally created "social climates." *Journal of Social Psychology*, 1939, *10:* 271–299.

Likert, R., *New Patterns of Management*. New York: McGraw-Hill, Inc., 1961.

Likert, R., Trends toward a worldwide theory of management. *Newsletter of Institute of Social Research*. Ann Arbor, Mich.: University of Michigan, October 1963.

Lindesmith, A. R., and A. L. Strauss, *Social Psychology* (3rd ed.). New York: Holt, Rinehart and Winston, Inc., 1968.

Lippitt, R., The effects of authoritarian and external controls on the development of mental health. *In* R. H. Ojemann (Ed.), *Recent Research on Creative Approaches to Environmental Stress*, Iowa City, Iowa: University of Iowa Press, 1964.

Loomis, J. L., Communication, the development of trust, and cooperative behavior. *Human Relations*, 1959, *12:* 305–315.

Lorenz, K., *On Aggression*. New York: Harcourt, Brace & World, Inc., 1963.

Lowe, C. M., A multi-dimensional approach to self-concept in three patient groups. *Journal of Counseling Psychology*, 1964, *11:* 251–261.

McClelland, D. C., *The Achieving Society*. Princeton, N.J.: D. Van Nostrand Company, Inc., 1961.

McClelland, D. C., Toward a theory of motive acquisition. *American Psychologist*, 1965, *20:* 321–334.(a)

McClelland, D. C., Achievement motivation can be developed. *Harvard Business Review*, 1965, November–December.(b)

McClelland, D. C., and G. A. Friedman, A cross-cultural study of the relationship between child-training practices and achievement motivation appearing in folk tales. *In* G. E. Swanson, T. M. Newcomb, and E. L. Hartley (Eds.), *Readings in Social Psychology*. New York: Holt, Rinehart and Winston, Inc., 1952.

McCorkle, L. W., A. Elias, and F. L. Bixby, *The Highfields Story: A Unique Experiment in the Treatment of Juvenile Delinquency*. New York: Holt, Rinehart and Winston, Inc., 1958.

McGregor, D., *The Human Side of Enterprise*. New York: McGraw-Hill, Inc., 1960.

McGregor, D., *Leadership and Motivation*. Cambridge, Mass: The M.I.T. Press, 1966.

McKeachie, W. J., Individual conformity to attitudes of classroom groups. *Journal of Abnormal and Social Psychology*, 1954, *49:* 282–289.

McKenzie, J. D., The dynamics of deviant achievement. *Personnel and Guidance Journal*, 1964, *42:* 683–686.

McLean, M. S., M. S. Gowan, and J. C. Gowan, A teacher selection and counseling service. *Journal of Educational Research*, 1955, *48:* 669–677.

Marx, M. H., The general nature of theory construction, *In* M. H. Marx

(Ed.), *Theories in Contemporary Psychology.* New York: Crowell-Collier and Macmillan, Inc., 1963, pp. 4–47.

Maslow, A. H., *Motivation and Personality.* New York: Harper & Row, Publishers, 1954.

Mead, G. H., *Mind, Self, and Society.* Chicago: University of Chicago Press, 1934.

Merei, F., Group leadership and institutionalization. *Human Relations,* 1949, *2:* 23–39.

Merton, R. K., Bureaucratic structure and personality. *Social Forces,* 1940, *57:* 560–568.

Merton, R. K., *Social Theory and Social Structure.* New York: The Free Press, 1957.

Michael, J. A., High school climates and plans for entering college. *The Public Opinion Quarterly,* 1961, *25:* 585–595.

Mierke, K., *Wille und Leistung.* Gottingen: Verlag Fur Psychologie, 1955.

Miles, M. B., Innovation in education: Some generalizations. *In* M. B. Miles (Ed.), *Innovation in Education.* New York: Teachers College Press, Columbia University, 1964, pp. 631–663.(a)

Miles, M. B., Educational innovation: The nature of the problem. *In* M. B. Miles (Ed.), *Innovation in Education.* New York: Teachers College Press, Columbia University, 1964, pp. 1–49.(b)

Miles, M. B., Planned change and organizational health: Figure and ground. *In* R. O. Carlson, A. Gallaher, Jr., M. B. Miles, R. J. Pellegrin, and E. M. Robers, *Change Processes in the Public Schools.* Eugene, Ore.: The Center for the Advanced Study of Educational Administration, 1965, pp. 11–37.

Miles, M. B., P. H. Calder, H. A. Hornstein, D. M. Callahan, and R. S. Schiavo, Data feedback and organizational change in a school system. Paper read at the American Sociological Association Annual Meeting, Miami, Florida, August 29, 1966.

Milgram, S., Some conditions of obedience and disobedience to authority. *Human Relations,* 1965, *18:* 243–263.

Miller, S. M., The credentials trap. Speech to National Meeting of Neighborhood Youth Corps, St. Louis, 1966.

Millman, J., and M. Johnson, Jr., Relation of section variance to achievement gains in English and mathematics in grades 7 and 8. *American Educational Research Journal,* 1964, *1:* 47–51.

Minturn, L., A test for sign-Gestalt expectancies under conditions of negative motivation. *Journal of Experimental Psychology,* 1954, *48:* 98–100.

Misumi, J., and T. Tasaki, A study on the effectiveness of supervisory patterns in a Japanese hierarchical organization. *Japanese Psychological Reseach,* 1965, *7:* 151–162.

Mitchell, J. V., Jr., An analysis of the factorial dimensions of the achievement motivational construct. *Journal of Educational Psychology*, 1961, *52:* 179–187.

Mitchell, J. V., Jr., Dimensionality and differences in the environmental press of high schools. *American Educational Research Journal*, 1968, *5:* 513–531.

Moeller, G. H., and W. W. Charters, Relation of bureaucratization to sense of power among teachers. *Administrative Science Quarterly*, 1966, *10:* 444–465.

Moore, G. A., Jr., *Urban School Days.* New York: Hunter College (Project True), 1964.

Myrdal, G., *An American Dilemma.* New York: Harper & Row, Publishers, 1944.

Murray, H. A., *Explorations in Personality.* New York: Oxford University Press, 1938.

Naught, G. M., and S. E. Newman, The effect of anxiety on motor steadiness in competitive and non-competitive conditions. *Psychonomic Science*, 1966, *6:* 519–520.

Neisser, U., On experimental distinction between perceptual process and verbal response. *Journal of Experimental Psychology*, 1954, *47:* 399–402.

Newcomb, T. M., *The Acquaintance Process.* New York: Holt, Rinehart and Winston, Inc., 1961.

Newcomb, T. M., Attitude development as a function of reference groups: The Bennington study. *In* G. E. Swanson, T. M. Newcomb, and E. L. Hartley (Eds.), *Readings in Social Psychology* (rev. ed.). New York: Holt, Rinehart and Winston, Inc., 1952.

O'Connell, E. J., Jr., The effect of cooperative and competitive set on the learning of imitation and nonimitation. *Journal of Experimental Social Psychology*, 1965, *1:* 172–183.

Orne, M. T., On the social psychological experiment: With particular reference to the demand characteristics and their implications. *American Psychologist*, 1962, *17:* 776–783.

Orth, C. D., *Social Structure and Learning Climate: The First Year at the Harvard Business School.* Boston: Harvard Business School, 1963.

Oskamp, S., Attitudes toward U.S. and Russian actions—a double standard. *Psychological Reports*, 1965, *16:* 43–46.

Otto, H. J., Elementary education—II. Organization and administration. *In* W. S. Monroe (Ed.), *Encyclopedia of Educational Research.* New York: Crowell-Collier and Macmillan, Inc., 1941, pp. 439–440.

Pace, C. R., Differences in campus atmosphere. *In* W. W. Charters, Jr. and N. L. Gage (Eds.), *Readings in the Social Psychology of Education.* Boston: Allyn and Bacon, Inc., 1963.

Pace, C. R., and G. G. Stern, An approach to the measurement of psychological characteristics of college environments. *Journal of Educational Psychology*, 1958, *49:* 269–277.

Parsons, T., A sociological approach to the theory of organizations. *Administrative Science Quarterly*, 1955, *1:* 63–85, 225–239.

Parsons, T., The school class as a social system: Some of its functions in American society. *Harvard Educational Review*, 1959, *29:* 297–318.

Passow, H., and M. Goldberg, The talented youth project: A progress report, 1962. *Exceptional Children*, 1962, *28:* 228–229.

Peabody, R. L., *Organizational Authority*. New York: Atherton Press, 1965, pp. 74–76.

Pellegrin, R. J., An analysis of sources and processes of innovation in education. A paper presented at the Conference on Educational Change sponsored by the Demonstration Project for Gifted Youth and the U.S. Office of Education, February 1966.

Pelz, E. B., Some factors in group decision. *In* E. E. Maccoby, T. M. Newcomb, and E. L. Hartley (Eds.), *Readings in Social Psychology*. New York: Holt, Rinehart and Winston, Inc., 1958, pp. 212–219.

Pennington, D. F., F. Hararey, and B. M. Bass, Some effects of decision and discussion on coalescence, change, and effectiveness. *Journal of Applied Psychology*, 1958, *42:* 404–408.

Pepinsky, P. N., J. K. Hemphill, and R. N. Shevitz, Attempts to lead, group productivity, and morale under conditions of acceptance and rejection. *Journal of Abnormal and Social Psychology*, 1958, *57:* 47–54.

Pilnick, S., A. Elias, and N. W. Clapp, The Essexfields concept: A new approach to the social treatment of juvenile delinquents. *Journal of Applied Behavioral Science*, 1966, *2:* 109–130.

Polansky, L., Group social climate and teacher's supportiveness of group status systems. *Journal of Educational Sociology*, 1954, *26:* 116–123.

Postman, L., and D. R. Brown, The perceptual consequences of success and failure. *Journal of Abnormal and Social Psychology*, 1952, *47:* 213–221.

Quimby, V., Differences in self-ideal relationships of an achiever group and an underachiever group. *California Journal of Educational Research*, 1967, *18:* 23–31.

Ramsy, N. R., *American High Schools at Mid-Century*. New York: Bureau of Applied Social Research, Columbia University, 1961.

Rapoport, A., *Fights, Games, and Debates*. Ann Arbor, Mich.: University of Michigan Press, 1960.

Rapoport, A., Aggressiveness, gamesmanship, and persuasion. *In* A. Wright, W. Evan, and M. Deutsch (Eds.), *Preventing World War III*. New York: Simon and Shuster, Inc., 1962.

Raven, B. H., and J. R. P. French, Group support, legitimate power and social influence. *Journal of Personality*, 1958, *26:* 400–409.(a)

Raven, B. H., and J. R. P. French, Legitimate power, coercive power and observability in social influence. *Sociometry*, 1958, *21:* 83–97.(b)

Raven, B. H., and J. Rietsema, The effects of varied clarity of group goal and group path upon the individual and his relation to his group. *Human Relations*, 1957, *10:* 29–45.

Rice, J. G., The campus climate: A reminder. *In* S. Basking (Ed.), *Higher Education: Some Newer Developments.* New York: McGraw-Hill, Inc., 1965.

Rock, R. T., Jr., A critical study of current practices in ability grouping. *Educational Research Bulletin*, Catholic University of America, Nos. 5 and 6, 1929.

Roethlisberger, F. J., and W. J. Dickson, *Management and the Worker.* Cambridge, Mass.: Harvard University Press, 1939.

Rogers, C. R., *Client-centered Therapy.* Boston: Houghton Mifflin Company, 1951.

Rogers, C. R., Communication: Its blocking and its facilitation. *Etc., A Review of General Semantics*, 1952, *9:* 83–88.

Rogers, C. R., Dealing with psychological tensions. *Journal of Applied Behavioral Science*, 1965, *1:* 6–25.

Rogers, E. M., What are innovators like? *In* R. O. Carlson, A. Gallaher, M. B. Miles, R. J. Pellegrin, and E. M. Rogers, *Change Processes in the Public Schools.* Eugene, Ore.: Center for the Advanced Study of Educational Administration, The University of Oregon, 1965, pp. 55–65.

Rosen, B. C., and R. D'Andrade, The psychosocial origins of achievement motivation. *Sociometry*, 1959, *22:* 185–195; 215–218.

Rosen, S., G. Levinger, and R. Lippitt, Desired change in self and others as a function of resource ownership. *Human Relations*, 1960, *8:* 187–192.

Rosenberg, M., *Occupations and Values.* New York: The Free Press, 1957.

Rosenberg, M., Parental interest and children's self-conceptions. *Sociometry*, 1963, *26:* 35–49.

Rosenberg, M. A., *Society and the Adolescent Self Image.* Princeton, N.J.: Princeton University Press, 1965.

Rosenhan, D., and G. M. White, Observation and rehearsal as determinants of prosocial behavior. *Journal of Personality and Social Psychology*, 1967, *5:* 424–432.

Rosenthal, R., *Experimenter Effects in Behavioral Research.* New York: Appleton-Century-Crofts, 1966.

Rosenthal, R., The social psychology of the behavioral scientist: On self-fulfilling prophecies in behavioral research and everyday life. Paper presented at the 4th Annual Research Conference of the New Directions in Social Science Research, North Dakota State University, November 11, 1967.

Rosenthal, R., and L. Jacobson, *Pygmalion in the Classroom*. New York: Holt, Rinehart and Winston, Inc., 1968.

Roth, R. M., Role of self-concept in achievement. *Journal of Experimental Education*, 1959, *28:* 265–281.

Sacks, E. L., Intelligence scores as a function of experimentally established social relationships between child and examiner. *Journal of Abnormal and Social Psychology*, 1952, *47:* 354–358.

Samuels, J. J., Bureaucratization of school districts and teacher autonomy. Paper presented at the Annual Meeting of the American Educational Research Association, New York City, February 1967.

Sanford, N., *Where Colleges Fail*. San Francisco: Jossey-Bass, Inc., 1967.

Schein, E. H., and W. G. Bennis, *Personal and Organizational Change through Group Methods*. New York: John Wiley & Sons, Inc., 1965.

Schmuck, R., Some aspects of classroom social climate. *Psychology in the School*, 1966, *3:* 59–65.

Scott, W. G., Organizational theory: An overview and an appraisal. *Journal of Academy of Management*, 1961, *4:* 7–27.

Scott, W., *The Management of Conflict: Appeal Systems in Organizations*. Homewood, Ill.: Dorsey Press, 1965.

Schachter, S., Deviation, rejection, and communication. *Journal of Abnormal and Social Psychology*, 1951, *46:* 190–207.

Schachter, S., et. al., Cross-cultural experiments on threat and rejection. *Human Relations*, 1954, *7:* 403–439.

Seashore, C., What is sensitivity training? *NTL Institute: News and Reports*, 1968, *2:* 1–3.

Seashore, S. E., *Group Cohesiveness in the Industrial Work Group*. Ann Arbor, Mich.: University of Michigan, Survey Research Center, 1954.

Secord, P. F., and C. W. Backman, *Social Psychology*. McGraw-Hill, Inc., 1964.

Seigel, A. E., and S. Seigel, Reference groups, membership groups, and attitude change. *Journal of Abnormal and Social Psychology*, 1957, *55:* 360–364.

Sexton, P., *Education and Income*, New York: The Viking Press, Inc., 1961.

Sgan, Mabel L., Social reinforcement, socioeconomic status, and susceptibility to experimenter influence. *Journal of Personality and Social Psychology*, 1967, *5:* 202–210.

Shartle, C., *Executive Performance and Leadership*. Englewood Cliffs, N.J.: Prentice-Hall, Inc., 1956.

Shaw, M. C., Definition and identification of academic under-achievers. *Guidance for the Underachiever with Superior Ability*, 1961, *8:* 15–30.

Shaw, M. C., and Alves, G. J., The self-concept of bright academic under-achievers. *Personnel and Guidance Journal*, 1963, *42:* 401–403.

Sherif, M., *The Psychology of Group Norms.* New York: Harper & Row, Publishers, 1936.

Sherif, M., *In Common Predicament.* Boston: Houghton Mifflin Company, 1966.

Short, J. F., Jr., Aggressive behavior in response to status threats. Paper read at the American Sociological Association, New York, August 1960.

Singer, D., The influence of intelligence and an interracial classroom on social attitudes. *In* R. A. Dentler, B. Mackler, and M. E. Warshauer (Eds.), *The Urban R's: Race Relations as the Problem in Urban Education.* New York: Frederick A. Praeger, Inc., 1967.

Smith, L. M., and W. Geoffrey, *The Complexities of an Urban Classroom.* New York: Holt, Rinehart and Winston, Inc., 1968.

Snyder, C., Comment. *Journal Of Counseling Psychology,* 1964, *11:* 261–262.

Snyder, C., General and specific role expectations for teachers. Unpublished manuscript, Michigan State University. Cited in W. B. Brookover and D. Gottlieb, *A Sociology of Education.* New York: American Book Company, 1964.

Staines, J. W., Self-picture as a factor in the classroom. *British Journal of Educational Psychology,* 1956, *28:* 97–111.

Steiner, G. A. (Ed.), *The Creative Organization.* Chicago: University of Chicago Press, 1965.

Stern, G. G., Characteristics of the intellectual climate in college environments. *Harvard Educational Review,* 1963, *23:* 5–41.

Stinchcombe, A., *Rebellion in a High School.* Chicago: Quadrangle Books, 1964.

Street, P., J. H. Powell, and J. W. Hamblem, Achievement of students and size of school. *Journal of Educational Research,* 1962, *55:* 261–265.

Strong, E. K., Jr., *Vocational Interests of Men and Women.* Stanford, Calif.: Stanford University Press, 1943.

Svensson, N., *Ability Grouping and Scholastic Achievement.* Stockholm: Almqvist and Wiksell, 1962.

Thibaut, J. W., and H. H. Kelley, *The Social Psychology of Groups.* New York: John Wiley & Sons, Inc., 1959.

Thistlethwaite, D. L., College press and student achievement. *Journal of Educational Psychology,* 1959, *50:* 183–191.

Thistlethwaite, D. L., College press and changes in study plans of talented students. *Journal of Educational Psychology,* 1960, *51:* 222–234.

Thistlethwaite, D. L., and N. Wheeler, Effects of teacher and peer subcultures upon student aspirations. *Journal of Educational Psychology,* 1966, *57:* 35–47.

Thomas, E. J., Effects of facilitative role interdependence on group functioning. *Human Relations,* 1957, *10:* 347–366.

Tillman, R., and J. H. Hull, Is ability grouping taking schools in the wrong direction? *Nation's Schools*, 1964, *73:* 70–71; 128–129.

Triplett, N., The dynamogenic factors in pacemaking and competition. *American Journal of Psychology*, 1897, *9:* 507–533.

Trow, M., Student cultures and administrative action. *In* R. L. Sutherland, W. H. Holtzman, E. A. Koile, and B. K. Smith (Eds.), *Personality Factors on the College Campus*. Austin, Tex.: University of Texas Press, 1962, pp. 203–226.

Truax, C. B., and D. G. Wargo, Psychotherapeutic encounters that change behavior: For better or for worse. *American Journal of Psychotherapy*, 1966, *22:* 499–520.

Turner, R. H., *The Social Context of Ambition*. San Francisco: Chandler Publishing Company, 1964.

Videbeck, R., Self-conception and the reaction of others. *Sociometry*, 1960, *23:* 351–359.

Walberg, H. J., and G. J. Anderson, Classroom climate and individual learning. *Journal of Educational Psychology*, 1968, *59:* 414–420.

Waller, W., *The Sociology of Teaching*. New York: John Wiley & Sons, Inc., 1932.

Wallin, P., Cultural contradictions and sex roles: a repeat study. *American Sociological Review*, 1950, *15:* 288–293.

Walters, R. H., and R. D. Parke, Social motivation, dependency, and susceptibility to social influence. *In* L. Berkowitz (Ed.), *Advances in Experimental Social Psychology*. New York: Academic Press, Inc., 1964, pp. 232–278.

Walters, R. H., and R. D. Parke, The influence of punishment and related disciplinary techniques on the social behavior of children: Theory and empirical findings. *In* B. A. Maher (Ed.), *Progress in Experimental Personality Research*, Vol. 3. New York: Academic Press, Inc., 1966.

Walton, R. E., and R. B. McKersie, *A Behavioral Theory of Labor Negotiations*. New York: McGraw-Hill, Inc., 1965.

Ware, J. R., B. Kowal, and R. A. Baker, Jr., The role of experimenter attitude and contingent reinforcement in a vigilance task. Unpublished paper. Fort Knox, Ky.: U.S. Army Armor Human Research Unit, 1963.

Wattenberg, W., and C. Clifford, Relation of self-concept to beginning achievement in reading. *Child Development*, 1964, *35:* 461–467.

Watson, G., *Social Psychology: Issues and Insights*. Philadelphia: J. B. Lippincott Company, 1966.

Watson, G., Resistance to change. *In* G. Watson (Ed.), *Concepts for Social Change*. Washington, D.C.: National Training Laboratories, 1967, pp. 10–26.

Watson, W. S., and G. W. Hartmann, The rigidity of a basic attitudinal frame. *Journal of Abnormal and Social Psychology*, 1939, *34:* 314–335.

Wayland, S. R., Structural features of American education as basic factors in innovation. *In* M. B. Miles (Ed.), *Innovation in Education.* New York: Teachers College Press, Columbia University, 1964, pp. 587–615.

Weber, M., *The Protestant Ethic and the Spirit of Capitalism.* New York: Charles Scribner's Sons, 1930. Originally published 1904.

Webster, H., M. Freedman, and P. Heist, Personality changes in college students. *In* N. Sanford (Ed.), The American College: *A Psychological and Social Interpretation of Higher Learning.* New York: John Wiley & Sons, Inc., 1962, pp. 811–847.

Williams, C. D., The elimination of tantrum behavior by extinction procedures. *Journal of Abnormal and Social Psychology,* 1959, *59:* 269.

Williams, R. L., and S. Cole., Self concept and school adjustment. *Personnel and Guidance Journal,* 1968, *46:* 478–481.

Willis, R. H., Two dimensions of conformity-nonconformity. *Sociometry,* 1963, *26:* 499–513.

Wilson, A. B., Residential segregation of social classes and aspirations of high school boys. *American Sociological Review,* 1959, *14:* 836–845.

Wilson, A. B., Social stratification and academic achievement. *In* A. H. Passow (Ed.), *Education in Depressed Areas.* New York: Teachers College Press, Columbia University, 1963, pp. 217–235.

Winborn, B., and L. G. Schmidt, The effectiveness of short-term group counseling upon the academic achievement of potentially superior but underachieving college freshmen. *Journal of Educational Research,* 1962, *55:* 169–173.

Winterbottom, M. R., The relation of childhood training in independence to achievement motivation. University of Michigan. Abstract on University Microfilms, Publication No. 5113. Cited by D. C. McClelland et al., *The Achievement Motive.* New York: Appleton-Century-Crofts, 1953.

Woodhall, M., and M. Blaug, Productivity trends in British secondary education, 1950–63. *Sociology of Education,* 1968, *41:* 1–36.

Yablonsky, L. The anticriminal society: Synanon. *Federal Probation,* 1962, *26:* 50–57.

Yates, A. (Ed.), *Grouping in Education.* New York: John Wiley & Sons, Inc., 1966.

Younge, G. D., Students: Higher education. *Review of Educational Research,* 1965, *35:* 253–261.

Zdep, S. M., and W. I. Oakes, Reinforcement of leadership behavior in group discussion. *Journal of Experimental Social Psychology,* 1967, *3:* 310–320.

Zeigler, H., *The Political Life of American Teachers.* Englewood Cliffs, N.J.: Prentice-Hall, Inc., 1967.

AUTHOR INDEX

SUBJECT INDEX